GN298 .C85 2004

0134106639831

Cultural bodies :
  ethnography and theory /
      2004.

2004 04 16

Cultur

D0887045

GEORGIAN COLLEGE LIBRARY 2501 $102.95
250101 (00)

Cultural Bodies

Ethnography and Theory

Edited by

Helen Thomas and Jamilah Ahmed

Learning Resource Centre
Georgian College
One Georgian Drive
Barrie, ON
L4M 3X9

Blackwell
Publishing

© 2004 by Blackwell Publishing Ltd

350 Main Street, Malden, MA 02148-5020, USA
108 Cowley Road, Oxford OX4 1JF, UK
550 Swanston Street, Carlton, Victoria 3053, Australia

The right of Helen Thomas and Jamilah Ahmed to be identified as the Authors of the Editorial Material in this Work has been asserted in accordance with the UK Copyright, Designs, and Patents Act 1988.

All rights reserved. No part of this publication may be reproduced, stored in a retrieval system, or transmitted, in any form or by any means, electronic, mechanical, photocopying, recording or otherwise, except as permitted by the UK Copyright, Designs, and Patents Act 1988, without the prior permission of the publisher.

First published 2004 by Blackwell Publishing Ltd

Library of Congress Cataloging-in-Publication Data

Cultural bodies : ethnography and theory / edited by Helen Thomas and Jamilah Ahmed.
    p. cm.
Includes bibliographical references and index.
    ISBN 0–631–22584–6 (alk. paper) — ISBN 0–631–22585–4 (pbk. : alk. paper)
    1. Body, Human—Social aspects.   2. Ethnology.   I. Thomas, Helen, 1947–   II. Ahmed, Jamilah.

    GN298. C85 2004
    306.4—dc22

                                                                2003014909

A catalogue record for this title is available from the British Library.

Set in 10/12^{1}/$_{2}$pt Meridian
by Graphicraft Limited, Hong Kong
Printed and bound in the United Kingdom
by T.J. International, Padstow, Cornwall

For further information on
Blackwell Publishing, visit our website:
http://www.blackwellpublishing.com

Contents

Acknowledgments

We would like to thank the authors in this collection for contributing such stimulating papers, which we think will make an outstanding contribution to contemporary debates on the body. We also wish to thank Jayne Fargnoli, our editor at Blackwell, for her enthusiasm and guidance, and Annie Lenth, the editorial assistant. Karen Wong, a PhD student at Goldsmiths, did a brilliant job of formatting and processing five of the chapters and compiled the comprehensive indexes. Parts of Chapter 10, by Thomas J. Csordas, were originally published as "Health and the Holy in African and Afro-American Spirit Possession," in *Social Science and Medicine* 24:1 (1987), pp. 1–11, and are reprinted with permission from Elsevier Science.

Jamilah Ahmed and Helen Thomas
September 2002

Notes on Contributors

Jamilah Ahmed has a PhD from Goldsmiths College, where she was research assistant to Helen Thomas, and she has also worked as a freelance editor. She is currently assistant editor at Sage Publications.

Suki Ali is Lecturer in Sociology at the London School of Economics. Her current research interests continue to explore gender, class, and ethnicity in feminist cultural theory and how they are experienced in everyday contexts. Her monograph *Mixed Race, Post Race: New Ethnicities and Cultural Practices* will be published shortly.

Les Back is Professor of Sociology at Goldsmiths College where he teaches sociology and urban studies. His recent books include *Out of Whiteness: Colour, Politics and Culture* (2002) and *The Changing Face of Football: Racism and Multiculture in the English Game* (2001). His contribution to this book is part of a new project with Paul Halliday that attempts to combine photography with sociological, autobiographical, and documentary writing.

Simon Carter teaches sociology at the London School of Hygiene and Tropical Medicine. His research interests are currently centered on science and technology studies as applied to health systems and services. He has previously carried out research on tourism and health, and edited a collection (with Stephen Clift), *Tourism and Sex: Culture,*

Commerce and Coercion (2000). He is currently preparing a book on a sociology of the sun that will examine how symbolization around the sun is intimately tied to body techniques and a range of sociotechnical artifacts.

Thomas J. Csordas is Armington Professor of Anthropology and Religion, and Chair of the Department of Anthropology at Case Western Reserve University. He is author of *The Sacred Self: A Cultural Phenomenology of Charismatic Healing* (1994), *Language, Charisma, and Creativity: The Ritual Life of the Catholic Charismatic Renewal* (2001), and *Body/Meaning/Healing* (2002).

Joanne Entwistle is Lecturer in Sociology at the University of Essex, UK. She was awarded her doctorate in Sociology from Goldsmiths College in 1997 and since then has published widely on fashion, the body, and gender. She is author of *The Fashioned Body: Fashion, Dress and Modern Social Theory* (2000) and co-editor (with Professor Elizabeth Wilson) of *Body Dressing* (2001).

Paul Halliday is a photographer and filmmaker currently based at the Centre for Urban and Community Research, Goldsmiths College, London, where he teaches a postgraduate degree in Photography and Urban Cultures. He is particularly interested in the visual representation of urban spaces, communities, and cultures. He is currently completing a 12-year photographic and film project focusing on street cultures in London. His contribution to this book is part of a collaboration with Les Back on London's hinterlands.

Emily Martin is Professor of Anthropology at New York University. Author of *The Woman in the Body: A Cultural Analysis of Reproduction* (1987) and *Flexible Bodies: Tracking Immunity in America from the Days of Polio to the Age of AIDS* (1994), her present work is on concepts of rationality and the evolving constitution of selfhood in contemporary US society.

Mike Michael is Professor of Sociology of Science and Technology and Head of the Sociology Department, Goldsmiths College. His interests lie in the sociology of science and technology. Currently his research addresses the cultural dimensions of xenotransplantation and the role of mundane technologies in everyday life. He is author of *Reconnecting Culture, Technology and Nature* (2000).

Sally Ann Allen Ness received her doctorate in Anthropology from the University of Washington, Seattle, in 1987. She is currently an

Associate Professor of Anthropology at the University of California, Riverside. She is author of *Body, Movement, and Culture: Kinesthetic and Visual Symbolism in a Philippine Community* (1992) and *Where Asia Smiles: An Ethnography of Philippine Tourism* (2002).

Elspeth Probyn is Professor of Gender and Cultural Studies at the University of Sydney. Her books include *Carnal Appetites: FoodSexIdentities* (2000), *Blush: Essays in Shame* (forthcoming), and *Remote Control: New Media, New Ethics* (co-edited with Catharine Lumby, 2003). She is currently working on a book about the food media.

Simon Shepherd has been Director of Programmes at Central School, London, since April 2001. Prior to that he was Professor of Drama at Goldsmiths, from 1996, and before that Professor of Drama at Nottingham University. His most recent publications include: *English Drama: A Cultural History*, with Peter Womack (1996) and *Studying Plays*, with Mick Wallis (1998, second enlarged edition 2001). New work on the staged body has led to an essay on *The Tempest*, "Revels End, and the Gentle Body Starts," in *Shakespeare Survey* 55 (2002); an essay on vocal production, "Voice, Script, Noise," in *Performance Research* (forthcoming spring 2003), and a book for Routledge, *Gut Reactions: Body and Stage from Herod to Cyborg* (forthcoming).

Helen Thomas is Professor of Sociology of Dance and Culture at Goldsmiths College. Her books include *Dance, Modernity and Culture* (1995), *Dance and the City* (editor, 1997), and *The Body, Dance and Cultural Theory* (2003). Her recent research project on aging and social dance, which was funded by the Arts and Humanities Research Board, can be viewed at http://dance.gold.ac.uk

Nigel Thrift's research interests include nonrepresentational theory, management knowledges, the new economy, international finance, and the history of clock time. He is currently working on the history of the address. His recent books include *Spatial Formations* (1996) and *Cities* (with Ash Amin) (2002).

Bryan S. Turner is Professor of Sociology at the University of Cambridge and (with Mike Featherstone) is the founding editor of the journal *Body & Society*.

Steven P. Wainwright is a Research Fellow at the Florence Nightingale School of Nursing, King's College, and has conducted research in medical sociology.

Introduction

Helen Thomas and
Jamilah Ahmed

This volume was conceived as a means of interweaving three strands of social and cultural research: developments in epistemological theories, an evolving ethnographic movement, and, importantly, the ongoing tensions that surround the body. These three themes constitute specific fields in their own right, but it seemed to us that there was a real need to bring them into direct dialog with each other.

"The body" is a well-established component of social and cultural research. To a greater or lesser degree, it is an ever-present part of all interaction and indeed it is perhaps all that we can be sure of when there is no interaction and we are completely on our own. It is also the focus of many taboos, prejudices, and judgments. How we move, dress, maintain, discipline, and interact with our bodies determines our place in society. As postmodernism, poststructuralism, and postcolonialism have introduced profound changes to perspectives on reading and understanding the western cultural landscape, so the volume of writing on the body has exploded in a bid to keep pace with these changes.

As the subject of much debate, the body has been central to work on varied subjects including gender, race, identity, science and technology, and so on. However, the literature has developed in a largely theoretical vein, and has neglected the experiential and the empirical. Although this is frequently noted, it has not been sufficiently addressed and Shilling's (1993) reference to the elusive and disappearing body remains relevant today. From Douglas's theory of the "two bodies" (1973), the typologies began to grow in number and breadth. These included models of discursive and material bodies (Turner 1984), physical, communicative, consumer and medical bodies, individual, and social bodies (O'Neill 1985; Turner 1991), and medicalized, sexualized, disciplined, and talking bodies (Frank 1990). Although this proliferation of the functions and roles possible for the body might be seen as indicating an increasing engagement with the body, Shilling argues that in fact the number of thematized models show "the difficulties sociologists have had in pinning down precisely what is meant by the body" (1993: 39). Similarly, Frank argues that such categories for the body are used to serve academic agendas and do not necessarily take us any closer to understanding the materialities of the body: "In all of this the body itself slips away, lost in the social practices which constitute our dispositions and understandings of it" (1990: 160).

As we head toward an era when discussions of the cyborg and virtual bodies will become an increasing part of our "everyday life," it is particularly important that the significance and the problematic of the embodied self be examined in an empirically grounded fashion. A concern with the body must also take into account the concerns of the late twentieth century that have given rise to these different voices. Along with the changing politics of identity and difference have come the growth of mass culture, the aestheticization of the body in consumer culture, the rapid growth of technology, the "moral panics" associated with the advent of HIV and AIDS, and a concern with the environment and pollution, or biopolitics.

Sociology has developed many theories of the body, and anthropology has provided many case studies of the body in different societies: this volume seeks to synthesize both these approaches. In this way the volume addresses, and contributes to, the recent work in cultural studies, which has shifted away from a concentration on theory, and toward an empirical focus on the body in a cultural context. The focus on method ensures that the body is engaged with, and maintained as very present, throughout the discussions. This approach has previously been sorely lacking in much of the available literature, but is now growing across a number of academic fields which engage with key issues of the body, and ethnography.

Much early work on ethnography has been done by anthropologists, who are traditionally "in the field" far more than sociologists have been. It is this organic involvement in the spaces in which other bodies move and create their environments that suggests ethnography as a logical source to mine when researching the body. The researcher's body is immersed in the field and is simultaneously outside the research (by means of its strangeness and lack of knowledge) and in the research (by the fact of its physical presence). If this juxtaposition can be recognized and examined reflexively, it can bring many more issues to the surface than a more controlled method, such as the static interview, might generate.

Similarly, a motivation for developing this volume was to recognize and engage with the various uses of the ethnographic method across a range of disciplines and research concerns. Contributors to the volume bring a range of disciplinary perspectives and concerns to the problems and advantages of the ethnographic method. In doing so, valuable empirical work on the body is collected here, along with insightful and innovative perspectives on the potential that ethnography can offer.

Anthropological accounts of ethnography can be overly concerned with the details of the culture involved, and thus do not always develop the methodological implications of their work. On the other hand, theoretical explorations of method are an ever-present concern for sociologists, who sometimes neglect empirical studies of the body. In bringing these different approaches into conjuncture with each other, it is perhaps helpful to first loosely trace the theoretical and cultural ground that has been covered and acknowledged across the disciplinary boundaries.[1]

Bodily Matters

The body has traditionally been a marginal presence in sociology, owing to the Cartesian binaries that became entrenched in the early development of the discipline. The core dichotomies of man/woman, public/private, and nature/culture all combine to place the body in opposition to the rational mind. Turner (1991) has demonstrated that the classical theorists such as Marx, Weber, Durkheim, and Simmel, who established the early canon of sociology, were concerned to understand the industrial public face of society, in order to analyze and critique systems of social order. Consequently, the opposite elements of those categories were neglected throughout the development of social theory. The body was paid considerable attention by Darwinists and neo-Darwinists, who combined evolutionary theory with developing biological trends; but they nevertheless continued to position the body as "outside" culture.

The nature/culture debate[2] began to be seriously challenged in the radical social and cultural climate of the latter years of the twentieth century. Mary Douglas (1970; 1973; 1975) developed an analysis that sought to escape the body's connotations with "dirt" and "the animal." She argued that these kinds of associations were not based on actual conditions, but on the social meaning imposed by the dominant discourse. Douglas suggested that the issue was not actual dirt, but a "matter of disorder" attached to the body that pushed it beyond the cultural boundaries. She posited an alternative theory of the "two bodies" (a physical and a social body) as a means of assessing the symbolism of the body as a physical and social carrier of meaning in all cultures. Although Douglas starts from an epistemological belief in the "natural body," her work signified a breakthrough in understanding that the body holds great import in any society. Thus the nature/culture debate was moved closer to home and was no longer used to distance the analysis of the body only, as represented in other cultures.

In the same climate of change, the feminist movement was beginning to generate new theories on the body, which also challenged the unequal position that both "the body" and "the female" suffered from. Feminists began to challenge the social meanings that had been pinned on to the biology of bodies and that had resulted in a common acceptance of the female body as a weaker, unpredictable entity, in comparison to the male body, which was strong and allowed unhindered social interaction in any situation (best exemplified by Germaine Greer's highly influential work *The Female Eunuch*, 1970). Once this hierarchical foundation began to be undermined, the "facts" began to lose value. Thus, the issues of gender and sex began to blur their former tight boundaries and instead came to be recognized as constructed "truths." Theories of the body that had developed out of social constructionist (Marxist or socialist feminists) or essentialist (radical feminists who argued that biology was destiny) approaches had to recognize that the body was a key site of political struggle. Bordo (1993) writes that this was an important turning point and that the legacy of the social movements of the sixties (both black power and women's liberation) represented the "awakening consciousness of the body as 'an instrument of power'" (ibid.: 16).

Foucault's works on discourse analysis and the body as a construct of power relations in society also contributed to and influenced the growing anti-foundationalist and anti-essentialist approaches to the body. His explication of the relations of power that regulate the body led to many feminist engagements with the political implications of his theory. His politicization of public institutions demonstrated how social inequalities are constructed and maintained and how they are therefore not innate. Foucault also developed Sartre's work on the gaze and argued that the possibility of being observed by an unknown and omnipresent "eye" renders the actual presence of this power almost superfluous to the process of discipline. Thus he argued that the gaze was constitutive of the individual and that:

> the sexed body is to be understood not only as a primary target of the techniques of disciplinary power, but also as the point where those techniques are resisted and thwarted. (McNay 1992: 39)

However his discussion of resistance, as deployed by "technologies of the self," maintains a duality between the body and the self, and posits the body as the manifestation or outcome of the self's position within the dominant discourse. Foucault's unified concept of the "socially constructed body" does not enable a consideration of the embodied subjects that constitute such an environment and that are nonunified (differently raced/sexed/classed etc). Turner (1984) states that a significant limitation in Foucault's analysis is the denial of "the immediacy of personal sensuous experience of embodiment which is involved in the notion of my body" (ibid.: 245). It might come as no surprise, then, that when work did finally come to focus on the material and experienced body, it was largely generated by those whose bodies were marked by difference.

The discussions surrounding "the other" and "difference" have been enabled by the contemporary academic culture of postmodernism and poststructuralism. Such a culture questions the legitimacy of knowledge claims and, in doing so, collapses the notion of the "grand narrative" that has characterized many previous knowledge claims. An important outcome of postmodernism is the concept of "situated knowledges" whereby statements can no longer assume a generalized frame of reference but must be explicitly located as specific, owned perspectives (Haraway 1991). Jay (1986) points out that this has implications for identity politics: the ideological "I" – capable of rational thought, responsible for enlightenment – was a concept dependent on the totalizing gaze. More recent knowledge claims are characterized by an openness, as fewer absolute statements can be made. In the contemporary intellectual climate (whose counterpart in popular culture is characterized by political correctness), it is becoming difficult to claim knowledge of "the truth." This has begun to create opportunities for those previous subjects of "the gaze" to begin to speak.

Many postcolonial and feminist theories of difference agree that the nexus between power and knowledge works to reproduce the dominant discourse within the social sciences (for further examples, see Lennon and Whitford 1994). Yeatman argues that we can only ever reach representations of realities in order to compare and understand "the differences in the positioning of knowing subjects in relation to the historicity of interconnected relationships of domination and contestation" (1994: 190). This position not only acknowledges multiple experiences and representations of realities, it also recognizes that although these versions may conflict with each other, their validity is not diminished. Instead an epistemological and methodological framework must be able to accommodate and make sense of those different voices.

The discourses of postmodernism, poststructuralism, and postcolonialism have unavoidably raised questions across the social sciences, and in particular have forced an interrogation of qualitative research: how you "tell the tale" is now given as much attention as the tale itself. This has brought together common issues across the disciplines and generated a form of dialog that previously was lacking between, for example, sociology and anthropology. The questioning of textual supremacy and a shift toward more empirical work has raised the profile and uses of ethnography, which was previously the central method of anthropology. The combination of the blurring of boundaries between disciplines, and the "cultural turn" that has colored contemporary social research agendas, has resulted in a developing trend in favor of qualitative ethnographic research both in sociology (Denzin 1997; Seale 1999) and in cultural studies (McGuigan 1997; McRobbie 1997).

However, there have been challenges to this epistemological development. Some have argued that while the universal "view from nowhere" has been displaced, the "view from everywhere" may in fact substitute objectivism with an equally unsatisfactory subjectivism (Bordo 1990; Haraway 1988). The key is to situate the research and the researcher and thus to avoid the distanced representation of "the other." This is particularly true when examining the body. In order to engage with the body, researchers must be seen to recognize that they are involved in a process of sense-making, and that the process will only generate one version of many possible senses.

Cultural Bodies

The papers in this volume have all developed in the wake of these cultural and academic shifts; however, the strength and insight of the volume is that the papers make this explicit. The themes of ethnography, the body, and theory are combined in a deliberate effort to connect and reconnect these elements. In this way, new directions and possibilities are evoked and engaged with. These interconnections are not fixed, and indeed the intention is to avoid their meaning becoming ossified in a discourse or a discipline. Thus the papers should be read as continuous readings around the key themes, and are intended to speak to and across each other.

This collection is divided into three separate parts: Ethnography, Theory, and Theory and Ethnography. This division was not an entirely arbitrary construction. It seemed to us that some papers were orientated toward "doing" research on the body, while others were focusing more on theoretical issues or were giving equal weighting to theory and doing research. However, as will become clear in the reading of the chapters, there are overlaps between papers in different sections and the individual papers within a section are also marked by differences. This should not be entirely surprising, given the range of topics covered in the collection and the variety of disciplinary bases from which the authors begin, if not always remain within. This introduction to Part I and those that follow for Parts II and III are not intended to provide a detailed summary of the papers that follow. Our aim is to map out certain common themes and concerns within a section as well as differences between the papers. In a sense we are trying to provide a pathway through the book and to make connections between the papers, which would clearly be impossible for the individual authors. We would like to stress that our introductory discussion is no substitute for reading "the real thing." We cannot hope to convey the subtleties of the arguments and depth of insight that the individual papers in this collection contain. Our reading of these papers is just that, "an interpretation," which may or may not be as good as that of any other informed reader.

Part I

The papers in Part I use a "case study" approach to show how the body is both marked by culture and "speaks" of and to cultural practice, the self, and history. They bring an empirical focus to bear on the various aspects of cultural bodies under discussion. The authors are engaged in "doing" ethnographic or qualitative research. The "body stories" told here invoke concerns around identity and difference, touching on the thorny issues of race, class, masculinity and sexuality, and age and aging. The narratives are not linear (they do not necessarily have a beginning or end) and they contain contradictions. The authors are concerned to pay attention to the voices of those individuals or groups who are not generally given space in research: the white working class in the inner city in Back's study; male fashion models in Entwistle's project; children in Ali's research; aging dancers in Wainwright and Turner's case study. This is not to imply that the authors dismiss theoretical considerations. Rather, as will become clear in the reading of the chapters, the case studies in this section draw on a range of contemporary theoretical approaches. The authors variously cite social and cultural theorists whose work has had an impact on the rise of the body as a topic and resource of study in recent years, particularly Michel Foucault (Back; Entwistle; Ali; Wainwright and Turner), Judith Butler (Entwistle; Ali), Pierre Bourdieu (Turner and Wainwright), and Merleau-Ponty (Back).

This first section begins with a paper by Les Back, entitled "Inscriptions of Love," which draws attention to bodily inscriptions in the form of tattoos and the "stories" they tell. The act of tattooing, for Back, is a corporeal experience. Back does not focus on the spectacular neoprimitive tattooing revival within consumer culture, which became a fashion statement and the subject of much academic attention in recent years. Rather, his chapter addresses a more ignored tradition of tattooing in western culture, which, as its history shows, bears the marks of class and difference and which can be seen to both "attract and repel attention."

The chapter begins by exploring a variety of ways in which the tattoo has been deployed to inscribe the body in western culture: from an old sailor whose tattoos relate a life of travel, to the penal colonists who bodies were branded as means of punishment and as a visible sign of their wrongdoing, to contemporary prisoners who brand themselves and mark their identities and differences in the face of the prison authorities who prohibit tattooing. The paper focuses on individuals from white working-class communities in southeast London whose bodies are inscribed with tattoos. Expression takes many forms apart from words and in this case it is manifested through the markings of the body made by tattooing. Thus, it is not through their voices that these individuals' stories may be heard. Rather, it is through the stories told by their tattoos, which constitute inscriptions of "Love." This love, according to Back, is "illocutionary," that is, it is a love that does not shout out its name from the rooftops, but is written on and in the body by tattooing: the expression of love by a fan for a football team and a locality, a father for his children, a granddaughter for the parents and her familial past, an older son for his father. These stories are told through a set of photographs of these individuals displaying their bodily etchings, taken by photographer Paul Halliday, which are realist in a matter-of-fact, unspectacular sort of way, but also aesthetically evocative. This chapter could perhaps be best described as operating within the framework of a visual ethnography. Back's photographic study shows how tattoos not only mark the individual body in a way that expresses the self, but also "speak" in a metaphorical sense of "past, present, and place." There is an attempt, here, to wrestle vision from the colonizing gaze, which traditionally commodified and objectified its subject, and restore it to the photographed individual.

In Chapter 2, Joanne Entwistle addresses "shifting, contemporary masculinities" through an ethnographic study of male fashion models. Entwistle shows how, in this growing occupational area for young men, the male body becomes an object "to be looked at" and desired. The male model's body is not the traditionally perceived masculine "doing" body, but is increasingly an "appearing" body to be surveyed and desired, which in turn creates a series of tensions and contradictions concerning how these models perform or "do" masculinity. Entwistle seeks to extend Judith Butler's (1990) theoretical insights on gender as performance into a consideration of the ways in which gender is reproduced and negotiated in the context of the everyday embodied practices of the male models in her study. Entwistle's study included participant observation in a model agency and in-depth interviews with male fashion models and "bookers."

Entwistle considers the bodily requirements that the male model in the UK must have in order to be successful: like his female counterpart, he must be taller and slimmer and lower in body fat than the vast majority of "ordinary" people. At the same time, she shows how models undermine their (masculine) heterosexuality in the work place, which appears to be dominated by gay or bisexual men and in which they become objectified by the "gay gaze," through a range of performances and strategies. By examining the "narrative strategies of embodiment," Entwistle argues that male models have to negotiate a bodily habitus that has traditionally lain within the province of the feminine and the "queer." This is not without its problems and contradictions. Male fashion modeling, according to Entwistle, can be seen to undermine and at the same time shore up the masculine heterosexual economy.

In Chapter 3, the focus shifts from masculinity and heterosexuality to children and their perceptions of "race" and "raciality." Suki Ali's paper draws on a larger ethnographic project that investigated "the formation of mixed-race identities in children." She begins from the premise that "race" is necessarily "lived and experienced through the body." Here, she explores the methods young children between the ages of eight and 11, in both multiethnic and mostly white areas, used to navigate their own and other people's "racialization" through the ways in which they "read" bodies. That is, she is concerned with the children's sense-making processes and practices of negotiating their everyday world. While children have constituted a major topic of educational research, their "voices" have not constituted a significant resource in the field. In effect, children have been seen but not heard. The children in this chapter, however, are treated as agents of knowledge.

The discussion is set against a background of recent theoretical approaches to race, which have predominated in the "microenvironment of schools" in the British context. Although the children in the study were learning to "read" race inside and outside of the school environment, Ali found that the educators had little knowledge of the children's perceptions of racial matters. Ali's research revealed that the children's understandings of race and racism were influenced by their location and, thus, "locatedness" became a key focus of attention. Bodies, too, were important to the children's understanding of "race," which they associated with "skin color." Despite recent attempts within the academy to deconstruct the construct of "race," the children's talk demonstrated that "race" still matters. Although the skin was a marker of identity and difference, the children perceived this difference to be only "skin deep." Ali argues that while "race" is important, it is also "unremarkable." Drawing on Butler's insights, Ali shows that the children did not necessarily "fix" people racially in terms of skin color and often needed to have additional biographical details to make sense of "race." As with the previous two chapters, Ali's research questions and casts doubt on the dominant narratives associated with the topic.

The final paper in this section sets out to carve out a space for developing a sociological approach to the study of classical ballet by placing the sociology of the body and the "centrality of embodiment" in dance in a "productive" relation to each other. Steven Wainwright and Bryan Turner's paper is based on interview material from their recent study of the Royal Ballet in London, which involved particip- ant observation and ethnographic interviews. Like Back, Entwistle, and Ali, Wainwright and Turner pay close attention to the voices of the agents in their study, who were former dancers in the Royal Ballet and are now "teachers, administrators, and 'character' dancers" in the company. Dancers, it has to be said, like children, are more often seen than heard. The chapter focuses on the "ex-dancers' per- ceptions of their bodies," their experiences and understandings of injury, aging, and retirement. Professional dancers, like athletes (and male fashion models), have a relatively short career span. At a time when most other professionals are still climbing the career ladder, ballet dancers are forced to think about hanging up their shoes because they may not be able to perform to the required and ever-increasing technical demands of the form.

Wainwright and Turner draw on Pierre Bourdieu's constructs of bodily "habitus," "capital," and "field" to examine both the dancers' narrative experiences of "embodiment" in their work place and the ways in which the social world of ballet shapes the bodies of dancers. The professional dancer's sense of identity is rooted in his or her body, which has to be worked on to an extraordinary degree, day in and day out. However, ballet dancers, as the study shows, do not routinely think about "how" to perform in a ballet, rather the technique has so deeply marked their bodies over the years that it is treated as "natural." This "taken for granted" attitude is disrupted or brought to the surface of consciousness through injury or aging. The dancers' experiences of coming up against the limits of the physical body through injury or aging, as Wainwright and Turner argue, pose a challenge to "radical social constructionist" approaches to the body by showing that the world, far from being a social construction, "acts back on our claims about it." That is, the physical body does age and there comes a point when individuals cannot accomplish the physical tasks that once came "naturally" to them. For professional dancers, particularly, this means that their career is over earlier and they have to renegotiate their relation to their bodies and make decisions about reinventing them- selves within or outside of the "family" of the company.

Part II

If the papers in Part I are overwhelmingly concerned with "doing" research on the body, the four chapters in Part II direct attention toward theoretical issues surrounding bodies in culture. The authors in this section explore different subject matter and begin from different disciplinary bases and yet there are thematic overlaps. All the papers (Ness, Thrift, Shepherd, and Martin) draw critical attention to new developments in the academy and/or new technologies that have impacted on the ways in which we perceive and make sense of "the body." In order to explain or advance their argument, the authors use a variety of examples. Three of the papers address recent shifts in cultural thought regarding the relation of "culture" and "nature" (Thrift, Shepherd, Martin). The notion of performance practice as it relates to the body is topicalized in three chapters (Ness, Thrift, Shepherd). As indicated before, our introductory text cannot hope to reveal the theoretical sources, nuances, insights, and explanatory depth to be found in the papers that follow. The "proof of the pudding," as the saying goes, "is in the eating."

Wainwright and Turner's paper on the sociology of dance and the body in the previous section contained an implicit critique of contemporary, postmodernist approaches in dance studies, which view dance as a "text" at the expense of overlooking or displacing the corporeal. In the first chapter of Part II, "Being a Body in a Cultural Way," Sally Ness develops that critique of dance studies in a fuller theoretical voice. Ness situates her argument in relation to cultural and cross-cultural approaches to dance ethnography.

The study of dance offers the student of human body movement an important site for generating cultural meanings and understandings. The past ten years or so have witnessed, or so some scholars believe, a paradigmatic shift in cultural approaches to dance. Ness's paper, in effect, sets out to examine this contention. She indicates the import of philosophical phenomenological theory, which stresses "experience" and "embodiment," to this paradigmatic shift. It will be recalled that several of the case studies in Part I also referred to these two concepts. Ness notes that philosophical phenomenology excludes the realm of the cultural from its analysis in order to "reflect on the lived body in an untainted manner." Because the phenomenological method seeks to "bracket" out the cultural from the analysis, Ness suggests that proponents of embodied research in dance may encounter some problems regarding the "cultural" if they characterize the shift toward a participatory model in terms of a turn to phenomenology.

With these issues in mind, Ness examines examples of cultural approaches to dance from either end of the "observation–participation" spectrum: from "extreme" (disembodied) observation to "total" (embodied) participation. She also compares and contrasts these with "mid-spectrum" examples.

From an analysis of the descriptions of movement given in the examples, Ness argues that a paradigmatic shift from an observational-based model of analysis to a participatory-based embodied approach does not "necessarily" generate new knowledge or understanding. Indeed, as Ness shows, participatory research can lead to more observation (through detailed movement analysis, for example), not less. Nevertheless, she points to examples of participatory, embodied research that do generate new insights into the cultural aspects of human movement in dance and which challenge the notion that "culture" and dance are "fixed" in time and space. These participatory approaches stress the "how" of movement, rather than the "what" and "where" of movement, which is evidenced in observational approaches. That is, participatory approaches do not indicate "that a foot moved" but "how the movement is experienced." They are more fluid, plastic, and contingent. Ness concludes that such studies do not represent a shift to phenomenology but perhaps may be "post" or even "anti" phenomenology.

The focus of Nigel Thrift's paper, "Bare Life," moves away from the construct of "cultural bodies" discussed in Ness's paper toward a consideration of the ways in which a renewed interest in "the natural," along with an attention to minute detail, is refiguring and manipulating the "the body" in culture. The chapter seeks to explore some of the ways that "very small spaces and times" are being utilized by "key institutions" as the basis for "increasingly large projects of domination." The paper is divided into two main sections. The first part is largely theoretical and the second part is orientated toward exemplifying and showing how the theory is being put into practice by the business economy.

In the first part, Thrift explores the trope of "bare life," which he develops to understand the cultural shift of interest toward "new human natures." The construct of "bare life" is borrowed from the Classical Greek philosopher Aristotle, for whom it meant "simple natural sweetness," that is, the "simple fact of living itself." This is rather a complex and illusive notion. It does not simply refer to survival, so it is not purely biological. At the same time, as Thrift notes, the "simple fact of living itself" in Aristotle's formulation stands outside politics because it is not a product of the society. Despite this, Thrift argues, following Foucault, that this "simple natural life" has become a motivating "target" for contemporary biopolitics. Words such as "experience," "sense," and "embodiment," all of which have been mobilized in the pages of this collection in an attempt to escape the "zone" of politics, have ended up generating their own politics, according to Thrift.

"Bare life," he argues, exists in the almost simultaneous "timespace" between "consciousness" and "action." Through advancing technology's achievements in capturing smaller and smaller segments of movement, this brief, imperceptible, in-between instant has become increasingly available to us. Thus, Thrift argues, that task of understanding what "bare life" might be is made easier in "modern civilization."

In the second part of the chapter he explores how "capitalist business" has built up a presence in "bare life" and in "biopolitical" culture by operationalizing practical and theoretical knowledges derived from developments in the "new human natures." Thrift uses three examples to explore the ways in which business is increasingly encroaching on the domain of "bare life": "the brand," "the experience economy," and "the conduct of business." He notes, for example, the importance of the arts, and particularly the performing arts, which crucially implicate the body, movement, gesture, improvisation, etc. to developments in "business management" and "commodity education," which seek to mobilize creativity in business. Whereas dancing, for instance, used to be a means of civilizing the body in leisure, employers are having their management teams take up dancing in order to give them self-confidence and a sense of (business) community. Following Foucault, Thrift argues that "it is through the production and ordering of bodies that power is experienced." Our every move and perception is being habitually captured, revealed, and anticipated. "Bare life," concludes Thrift, "must be retaken" from the instrumentality of consumer capitalism.

Simon Shepherd's paper has the intriguing title, "Lolo's Breasts, Cyborgism and a Wooden Christ." He also is concerned with artistic performance practices and knowledge bases, but from a more theatrical standpoint than Thrift or indeed Ness. Shepherd's paper critically addresses performance practices that attempt to transport the body away from the everyday, routine world into the "de-natured," the "cyborged," the "posthuman." The performance practices that Shepherd discusses attempt to take the performer beyond what is human, perhaps beyond the simple fact of living or the "bare life" discussed by Thrift.

Shepherd's paper begins by offering specific examples of performance practice that attempt to go beyond the mundane. These practices endeavor to negotiate the relation between the body and the non-body, which operate on different levels. The first example refers to the exercise regime for training performers, which was forged through the influential work of Tadashi Suzuki. This training system is designed to develop actors' "physical concentration" by imposing difficult physical tasks, which place the performers in a battle to control their unruly bodies. The body on the stage becomes part of the world, not separate from it, as it is in everyday life. Shepherd points out that in Suzuki's philosophical framework, the object world is animated. Through their physical concentration on their own bodies, performers summon up the energy or spirits contained within the object world and take them into themselves. In Suzuki's system this mingling of "body to non-body" celebrates a "loss of individuality" through a "loss of physical integrity." This celebration of "pure form," as Shepherd argues, is underpinned by a critique of the modernity project with its emphases on individuality and difference. However, he also points out that the above losses are not always treated as "pure," which leads him on to his second performance example, Lolo Farrari, a former soft-porn star who became a performer on the television program *Eurotrash*.

Lolo's performed body was presented as embodying the "trash of *Eurotrash*." Shepherd compares the valorized purity of Suzuki's exercise regime with Lola's transformed body, with its larger-than-life silicone breast implants and surgically refigured face, which produced her as an object of heterosexual desire; however, the men performers in the show showed no desire for her, and her performed body showed only bodily ineptitude. The most significant difference between the two is that Suzuki is viewed as "serious," whereas Lola is treated as "trash." The distinction, however, as Shepherd argues, is locatable in a "set of value judgments" concerning the two projects, which he explores in some detail.

The third example of the melding of the human body and the nonhuman is the performance artist Stelarc, the driving force of whose work has been an attempt to produce and inhabit a "posthuman body." In Stelarc's experiments, the relationship between the exterior body and the interior body is reversed. In his experimental "performances" his inner body is exteriorized by inserting a camera into it. He does not control the movement of his muscles. His body is electronically wired up to external ports where controllers activate the performer's muscles electronically. Stelarc's experiments "set up a performance" that "concretizes" and images "neurophysical processes," which are usually hidden from spectatorship. Thinking back to Thrift's discussion, we can see that Stelarc's experimental performances also make use of those previously unseen and unseeable very small spaces of the body, which have been made available through new technologies, although perhaps for different ends.

In contemporary popular culture the merging of the human body with the nonhuman is associated with the cyborg. The rhetoric of the cyborg, as Shepherd demonstrates, is associated with an epochal shift from the modern to the postmodern. Shepherd develops his argument to show that the cyborg is not a melding of the human and the nonhuman into the posthuman body. Rather, he maintains the "assimilation of the body and machine remains merely human." The cyborg, he argues, "is firmly situated in the histories of performed practices. These histories, as the paper goes on to exemplify, via a discussion of puppetry and religious idolatry, are not fixed. Rather, they delineate shifting relations between body and non-body at a level of physical contact and conceptualization. As such, Shepherd suggests, they may provide an inroad into gaining insights into a given culture.

Much of the recent work on the body has sought to overcome the mind/body dichotomy, which has constituted the backbone of the western humanist tradition of thought. Within this tradition, the mind is accorded an elevated status over and above the (mechanistic) body. In "Talking Back to Neuro-reductionism," Emily Martin proposes that a range of current "modes of thought" are in fact performing a reduction of "mind" to "body." This, she argues, is a consequence of explanations of "psychological processes" now being viewed in terms of "neuronal" processes. This suggests that there has been a paradigmatic or epistemological shift underway in certain areas of scientific discourse, although Martin does not use this term. Martin examines two examples of neuro-reductionism: the first in "biological psychiatry" and the second in "cognitive science." She compares and contrasts the differences between these two case studies in order to explore the consequences of these "accounts" for "cultural concepts of mind" in key associated areas of social life, such as "mental illness and health and the self." She is also concerned to explore the reception of these neuro-reductionist discourses in other "social contexts."

Drawing on the work of Nikolas Rose, Martin explains that biological psychiatry sets up a causal connection between "genes" and "brains" and the resulting behaviors that emerge from the appearance of "genes" in "brains." Within this framework, the causes of depression can be explained in terms of a chemical malfunctioning of the brain, as opposed to biographical or environmental conditions. Making reference to her recent fieldwork at several points in the paper, Martin shows how the reasoning of biological psychiatry has found its way into a range of areas in contemporary culture, including advertisements for drugs. Through a brief excursion into the history of psychiatry, she argues that this shift toward the brain in biological psychiatry represents a significant "turning point."

Martin's second case study, neuro-reductionism in cognitive science, refers to new modes of thought called "computational neuroscience." Research in this field is directed toward making computer models which are modeled on "what neurons in the brain do." The "logic" of computational neuroscience, as Martin shows, goes as follows: if a computer model can perform (brain) tasks such as "remembering" or decision making, then this is because the brain functions like a computer. This means that all kinds of learning within culture "can be reduced to neural nets."

The combination of biological psychiatry and computational neuroscience is formidable, Martin argues. All manner of things which might be the product of history, culture, and identity, as well as "nature," get reduced to the workings of the brain. Hence, "culture" gets reduced to "nature." Martin, like Thrift, points to the "business interests" affiliated to these discourses. The supremacy of the "brain" in neuro-reductionism, as Martin's detailed analysis shows, covers over the fact that the "brain is a product of the relation to culture."

Part III

The chapters in Part III combine theory and ethnography in ways that raise challenges for the development of "ethnographies of the body" at a theoretical and methodological level. The authors write from the perspectives of sociology, cultural studies, and anthropology and to a certain extent speak to debates within the subdisciplines within which they work. Although the disciplinary boundaries of the social sciences and cultural studies have become increasingly blurred since the mid-1980s, particularly at the level of theory, many of the debates within the disciplines remain context-bound – that is, they are situated within the current concerns and past debates in a particular area of inquiry. For example, Simon Carter and Mike Michael's chapter, which focuses on the social aspects of the sun on cultural bodies, is situated within the context of current debates in social studies of science. Thomas Csordas's paper, which highlights the importance of embodiment and experience to understanding aspects of health-related or religious phenomena, speaks to debates within the anthropology of medicine and comparative religion. These and other papers in this volume, particularly those in Part II, highlight the fact that interdisciplinarity is not a *fait accompli*. At the same time, they also show that the body has indeed become an important topic and resource, which has helped to break down traditional barriers between disciplines.

Elspeth Probyn's paper, "Eating for a Living," takes us away from the mind and the brain and back into the body. Probyn notes that every time we begin to speak about the body, we always end up discussing something else, such as gender, sexuality, difference, etc. One of her key questions is: What is it to speak of the flesh and blood of the body? The object of Probyn's chapter is twofold. To begin with, the intention is to think through a current three-year research project, examining the "role of food writing in mediating taste," which sets out to explore "not only what food writers do," but also their impact on the "eating public." This comparative project involves interviews and ethnographic data. Secondly, the aim is to use the occasion to refigure "traditional notions of ethnography." Ethnography maps the structures of meaning within a culture through a detailed descriptive account of "people's interactions." Probyn seeks to replace this normative version of ethnography with a different kind of "mapping" of meaning, which, following the work of Giles Deleuze and Felix Guattari, she terms a "rhizomatic" approach. She offers a clear and concise discussion of key concepts within Deleuze and Guattari's framework, which at first appear difficult to understand, such as: "rhizome," "BwO" (body without organs), "deterritorialization," "assemblages," and "ethology."

"The body" in this Deleuzian framework is not treated as a "thing-like" entity, as it is in many approaches to the sociology of the body. Rather, is viewed as both multiple (made up of many bodies) and fluid. Bodies from this perspective are not fixed, bounded entities. They exist only in connection with other bodies and "entities." "Movement," as Probyn notes, is a principle of "connection and contact" between bodies. She grounds her Deleuzian theory of body into her ethnographic analysis of "bodies in action."

The ethnographies Probyn describes to begin with are somewhat unorthodox: a chef's "tell all" auto-ethnography about the workings in a professional kitchen, and her own recollections of waiting at tables between the ages of 16 and 25. In both these culinary ethnographic accounts, from behind and in front of the restaurant, the importance of movement and the engagement of bodies with other bodies is highlighted. Probyn indicates, for example, that the impact of the economy of movement of bodies on other bodies, the feel of bodies in action, stayed with her long after she had ceased to work in a restaurant. These memories, she suggests, echoing Bourdieu's notion of habitus, "marked" her body.

From these personalized ethnographic accounts of working with bodies and food, Probyn moves on to examine the "reification of food" in the "celebratory mode of food writing," which is part of the above-mentioned research project. The research reveals how talk about food quickly opens up into areas of the personal, such as past memories, which may have painful as well as happy connotations. However, the relation between the body and food is more difficult to tie down. Discussants hardly ever respond directly to questions about the body and food. Just as discussions of the body in the sociology of the body seem always to end up talking about something else, such as gender, identity, etc., so discussions of food and the body lead to talk of "health, taste, or habits." The body, in everyday life, then, is already connected to other bodies and entities (assemblages).

Bodily connections are also a central focus of Thomas Csordas's paper, "Health and the Holy in the Afro-Brazilian *Candomblé*." The theoretical framework of the chapter, however, is somewhat different from the Deleuze-meets-Bourdieu approach that is evident in Probyn's paper. Csordas takes up the notion of experience and embodiment, which is central to phenomenology, particularly that branch stemming from the work of Merleau-Ponty. Csordas begins from two basic premises: the first is that "the body" lies at the intersection between "medical and religious understanding of human experience"; second, in "cross-cultural" analysis of illness and healing, "the medical and religious" are a central issue. These two subdisciplines, medical anthropology and the study of comparative religions, may analyze the same phenomenon and offer accounts which have nothing whatsoever to do with each other, or make no sense to each other. Csordas's task in this essay is to explore a way out of this dilemma.

Csordas considers that "spirit possession and possession trance" is a clear instance where the relation between the religious and the medical gets played out in the field of embodiment. The empirical focus of the chapter centers on the African–Brazilian possession cult, *candomblé*. The *candomblé* is derived from the Yoruba of West Africa and was transported to Brazil in the nineteenth century. The congregation of the *candomblé* was made up of ex-slaves but the Catholic authorities in Brazil often suppressed the cult. It is only in recent years, as Csordas notes, that the *candomblé* has gained some acceptance in Brazil. They appear at the Bahian carnival and members include those of European descent as well as those of African descent.

Csordas's discussion is based on a series of in-depth interviews with a Brazilian psychiatrist. This psychiatrist had "a unique role" in that he was a prominent academic and an elder in a key *candomblé* congregation. Csordas sets out the hierarchical structure of the congregation, which is organized around a female "mother of saints," who is of African descent. Through a discussion of three case studies, in which individuals of European descent sought help from *candomblé* congregations or wanted to go through the initiation process, it emerges that "illness" is not a primary concern of participants of the cult or of those who consult the *candomblé*. Despite this, the case studies reveal how, in each case, the "mother of saints" was able to distinguish between religious spirit possession, simulated possession, and hysteria. In one case, for example, "the mother of saints" would not proceed further with the initiation of a young woman because she attributed the initiate's agitated behavior to a medical cause (mental illness), not a religious cause (spirit possession). Csordas concludes from this that individuals are not necessarily initiated into possession cults to assist them to overcome psychic dispositions, as some writers have suggested. He proposes that in certain instances, greater cultural knowledge of "religious and health-related phenomena" may be gained by examining both the religious and medical aspects involved, as opposed to viewing them as mutually exclusive.

Simon Carter and Mike Michael's chapter, "Here Comes the Sun," takes its point of departure from the concern with material culture and "relationalities" in social studies of science and culture. As with a number of other papers in this volume, the authors seek to shed light on the notion of the cultural body in contemporary culture. They align their approach to sociology with the current turn toward "materiality and objects" (material culture), which is underpinned by "heterogeneous relationalities," and which gives rise to realities such as "the body and technology and the sun." Thus, like Probyn, they are not concerned with the "thingness" of the body but with the shifting, varied relations of the body and the world. Like Thrift, they seek to locate the spirit of an era "in the smallest and least noticeable." Although they acknowledge that "the sun" is not small, they note that it has been substantially neglected from a sociological point of view, much as the body had been prior to the mid-1980s. Although the title of the paper may at first seem frivolous, it is worth noting that little work has been conducted on the "social aspects of the sun on people's bodies." This is surprising, given the importance of the sun in many aspects of our cultural life.

The sun, as their study shows, is indeed a material culture, or perhaps more precisely "culturalized materiality." That is, it is through the processes of culture that the sun is brought into being as an object and is given meaning. Moreover, Carter and Michael argue that the "cultural and technological artifacts of the sun" are not mutually exclusive. They do not intend to offer a blanket "sociology of the sun," rather they direct their attention to two interrelated aspects. First they examine how the "material impact of the sun on bodies" is mediated through what they term "sociotechnical artifacts," such as therapeutic remedies involving the sun and suntanning lotions. In other words, they are concerned to show how we might go about researching "a sociology of the sun." For example, they offer a brief history of tanning the skin by exposing it to the sun. A suntan was viewed as a sign of low status (a peasant) in the nineteenth century and women, in particular, were warned of the dangers of the sun on their skins. In the twentieth century, a tanned skin became a marker of high status (evidence that you could afford to go on holiday abroad) and an indicator of good health. Despite recent medical warnings regarding the health dangers associated with tanning the skin, the desire for "sun-seeking" and a tanned (heightened aesthetic) body remains high on the agenda of a large majority of the population in our consumerist-orientated "tourist" culture. Carter and Michael show how "historical shifts" in the meanings of the sun on "cultural bodies" were accompanied by and mediated through "technological" innovations like suntan lotions and heliotherapy, and social movements such as scouting and the Garden City. As such, they argue that the sociology of the sun could shed light on a range of important "social and cultural trajectories."

Secondly, Carter and Michael explore the epistemological implications that arise from this configuration of body, sun, and technology through a consideration of the "materiality and corporeality of vision"; by for example, using "sunglasses" as a case study. Sunglasses are a technological stylistic object which both screen out the sun and the eyes of the wearer but at the same time enable him/her to see other people and objects. Several other papers in this volume have also addressed the relation of "vision" to the body and embodiment (Back, Ali, Shepherd). Here, Carter and Michael use their case study of sunglasses to show how the "visual screening of sunlight" can cast light on issues such as "identity, consumption, material culture, corporeality, and so on." In so doing, they point to the corporeality of vision and suggest a revisioning or repositioning of the disembodied sense of "vision" that has dominated sociology, and much of western social thought. The disembodied sense of vision in sociology may be seen in the relationship between the researcher (observer) and the researched (observed) which, traditionally, has been viewed in terms of distance. The authors, like Thrift, point to the increased surveillance of bodies through the development of new technologies. They argue that these technologies are not disinterested or disembodied, any more than the sociological researcher is when s/he is observing the actions of those under study. At the same time they argue against an overhumanizing of the gazes made available through the relations with technologies. Rather, they perceive that the gazes are enacted through a combination of "human and nonhuman" and in so doing both are changed. It is the specific enactments of these relationalities of "body-sociotechnical artifact that should become the object of a 'hybridized' sociological gaze."

The final chapter in this volume, "Reaching the Body: Future Directions," draws together these themes and methodologies as a means of exploring how ethnography can be used to develop research on the body.

Notes

1 This introduction does not aim to rehearse the debates but rather to point to the context and climate that has generated the pieces in this volume. However, the references should be used as suggestions for further reading since they will expound the directions alluded to here.

2 This debate is extensive and not the focus of this chapter, but for further detail readers should turn to Bateson and Mead (1942), Hall (1969), Efron (1972), and Birdwhistell (1973).

References

Bateson, G. and Mead, M. (1942) *Balinese Character: A Photographic Analysis*, vol. 2. New York: Special Publications of the New York Academy of Sciences.

Birdwhistell, R. (1973) *Kinesics in Context: Essays in Body-Motion Communication*. Harmondsworth: Penguin.

Bordo, S. (1990) "Feminism, Postmodernism and Gender-Scepticism," in L. Nicholson (ed.), *Feminism/Postmodernism*. London: Routledge.

Bordo, S. (1993) *Unbearable Weight: Feminism, Western Culture and the Body*. Berkeley, CA: University of California Press.

Butler, J. (1990) *Gender Trouble: Feminism and the Subversion of Identity*. London: Routledge.

Denzin, N.K. (1997) *Interpretive Ethnography*. London: Sage.

Douglas, M. (1970) *Purity and Danger: An Analysis of Concepts of Pollution and Taboo*. Harmondsworth: Penguin.

Douglas, M. (1973) *Natural Symbols*. Harmondsworth: Penguin.

Douglas, M. (1975) "Do Dogs Laugh? A Cross-Cultural Approach to Body Symbolism," in *Implicit Meanings: Essays in Anthropology*. London: Routledge.

Efron, D. (1972) *Gesture, Race and Culture*. The Hague: Mouton.

Frank, A.W. (1990) "Bringing Bodies Back In: A Decade Review," *Theory, Culture and Society* 7: 131–62.

Greer, G. (1970) *The Female Eunuch*. London: Granada Publishing.

Hall, E.T. (1969) *The Hidden Dimension*. Garden City, NY: Anchor Books.

Haraway, D. (1988) "Situated Knowledges: The Science Question in Feminism and the Privilege of Partial Perspective," *Feminist Studies* 14 (3): 575–99.

Haraway, D. (1991) *Simians, Cyborgs and Women: The Reinvention of Nature*. London: Free Association Books.

Jay, M. (1986) "In the Empire of the Gaze," in L. Appiganesi (ed.), *Postmodernism*. London: ICA Documents.

Lennon, K. and Whitford, M. (eds.) (1994) *Knowing the Difference: Feminist Perspectives in Epistemology*. London: Routledge.

McGuigan, J. (ed.) (1997) *Cultural Methodologies*. London: Sage.

McNay, L. (1992) *Foucault and Feminism*. Cambridge: Polity Press.

McRobbie, A. (ed.) (1997) *Back to Reality? Social Experience and Cultural Studies*. Manchester: Manchester University Press.

O'Neill, J. (1985) *Five Bodies: The Human Shape of Modern Society*. Ithaca, NY: Cornell University Press.

Seale, C. (1999) *The Quality of Qualitative Research*. London: Sage.

Shilling, C. (1993) *The Body and Social Theory*. London: Sage.

Turner, B. (1984) *The Body and Society*. Oxford: Blackwell.

Turner, B. (1991) "Recent Developments in the Theory of the Body," in M. Featherstone, M. Hepworth, and B.S. Turner (eds.), *The Body, Social Processes and Cultural Theory*. London: Sage.

Yeatman, A. (1994) "Postmodern Epistemological Politics and Social Science," in K. Lennon and M. Whitford (eds.), *Knowing the Difference: Feminist Perspectives in Epistemology*. London: Routledge, pp. 187–202.

Part I
Ethnography

Chapter 1

Inscriptions of Love

Les Back

Photography by Paul Halliday

Introduction

The routes of a life spent in transit are inscribed on his skin. At rest now, he lies motionless, voiceless, in a hospital bed. The nurse interprets the "vital signs" transmitted from his body. An internal struggle is encoded in these readings like a Morse code message from a vessel in peril at sea. There is no external trace of the great effort going on inside him and the elderly man cannot speak of what brought him to this point. As he lies there his body represents something close to an illustrated map of his life.

The tattoos that covered his arms and chest each bore the name of a place – Burma, Singapore, and Malaysia. Each of them had a record of the year the inscription was made. He had been a merchant seaman and had traveled the world. On his right arm was the figure of an Indian woman dancing with her hands clasped together above her head, her skin darkened by the tattooist's ink. In the sailor's autumn years the figure etched on this pale canvass had turned a deep shade of blue. On the left forearm was an inscription that marked his journey's end: a tattoo of Tower Bridge, London and beneath it the dedication – "HOME." It read like an anchor.[1] The voiceless patient spoke beyond sound. These tattoos told a story of the places he had visited, the voyages in between, and contained allusions to intimacies shared in tattoo parlors around the world. Here the sailor trusted local artists enough – in India and Burma – to spill blood and mark his flesh indelibly. On the surfaces of this failing body was a history of the relationship between the sailor's metropolitan home and the hinterlands of trade and Empire. The permeability of that relationship – between imperial center and colonial periphery – was marked on the porous membranes of his dying body.

The most familiar account of the history of the tattoo in Britain and the west is that this practice was brought back to Europe in the eighteenth century when European explorers encountered the tattooing cultures of the south Pacific and Polynesia. Captain James Cook's voyages gave the English language the word "tattoo." He observed the practice on Tahiti in July 1769 (Jones 2000: 1). It is a variation of the Polynesian term *tatu* or *tatau* meaning to mark or strike (Caplan 2000). On Cook's second circumnavigation of the globe he transported *Omai* to London. This man, from Raiatea Island close to Tahiti, became an exotic curiosity in London (Guest 2000), in part because he bore the marks of Polynesian tattooing that Cook had described earlier. Cook's ships and the "specimens" contained within them were unloaded on the south bank of the River Thames just a few miles away from where the sailor lay in his hospital bed.

The emphasis placed on the encounter with Polynesian tattooing cultures has occluded histories of earlier bodily inscription in Britain and Europe. In particular, various historians have shown the connection between tattooing and penal and property rights amongst the Greeks, Romans, and Celts (Gustafson 2000). Also, early Christians in Roman territories inscribed their bodies as an expression of the devotee's servitude to Christ (MacQuarrie 2000). More than this, there is a connection between pilgrimage and tattooing. Early modern pilgrims to Palestine were tattooed with Christian symbols available in Jerusalem and brought their marked bodies home as evidence of their sacred travels. This practice also occurred amongst pilgrims to the Shrine of Lorento in Italy in the sixteenth century (Caplan 2000). There is, then, a strong connection between travel and tattooing.

Alfred Gell (1993: 10) has concluded that the stigma associated with tattooing in the west results from a double association of the "ethnic Other" and the "class Other." But tattooing was drawn into the culture and vernacular of the sailors themselves and the cultural world they created. Historian Marcus Rediker has shown that a life on the sea left its mark on the bodies of working-class seamen:

The tattoo, then and now, often adorned his forearm. "The Jerusalem Cross" and other popular designs were made by "pricking the Skin, and rubbing in a Pigment," either ink, or, more often, gunpowder. Seafaring left other, unwanted distinguishing marks. Prolonged exposure to the sun and its intensified reflection off the water gave him a tanned or reddened – "metal coloured" – and prematurely wrinkled look . . . thus in many ways the seaman was a marked man, much to the delight of the press gangs that combed the port towns in search of seamen to serve the crown.   (Rediker 1987: 12)

Rediker identifies a key paradox. In working-class life, tattooing has provided a way of reclaiming and aestheticizing the body. At the same time, these marks sketch the outline of a "class Other," a target for respectable society to recognize and stigmatize, be it in the form of a press gang, officers of the law, or today's bourgeois moralists.

The painted sailor is gone now; his life has ebbed away. His passing was noted by the registrar of the void, who recorded his lapsed life and issued a flimsy certificate. The inscription of his body was an attempt to make an enduring mark, yet he belonged to a class of people for whom there is little place in the official record. "They are the sort of people," noted Patrick Modiano, "who leave few traces" (2000: 23). Gruesome exceptions are held in the specimen laboratory at Guy's Hospital, London. Here, pieces of marked skin are preserved in the acrid smelling jars of Formalin. The peeled skins are the only traces of nameless men from whose arms they were taken. They show the images of "Hope and Anchor" and of "Christ crucified" (Maxwell-Stewart and Duffield 2000: 133), grafts that were taken, or filched, for medical research. This is still happening, although in today's National Heath Service "progress" demands some payment upfront. Jock Browning, for example, out of Waterloo, London has left his almost completely tattooed body "to science." In return he received the meager sum of £3000.

Having a tattoo, or being pierced, is a moment when boundaries are breached, involving hurt and healing. It is profoundly a corporeal experience – the piercing of the skin, the flow of blood, pain, the forming of a scab, the healing of the wound and the visible trace of this process of incision and closure. This involves perforating the boundary between the internal and external so that the external becomes internal and the internal becomes external. The tattoo itself can be read through a range of metaphors: for example, the relationships between agency and control, permanence and ephemerality, trauma and healing. Such associations are never straightforward and are rarely just a matter of individual choice. As Alfred Gell pointed out: "The apparently self-willed tattoo always turns out to have been elicited by others" (Gell 1993: 37).

The Body as a Political Field

Michel Foucault is perhaps the most eloquent analyst of the ways in which the body acts as a site of cultural and political manipulation. He writes in *Discipline and Punish*:

> The body is also directly involved in a political field; power relations have an immediate hold upon it; they invest it, mark it, train it, torture it, force it to carry out tasks, to perform ceremonies, to emit signs.   (Foucault 1977: 25)

Elsewhere he concludes that "the body is the surface of the inscription of events" (Foucault 1994: 375). For Foucault, this is both a process whereby the "Me" of identity is constituted by history and power, but also a site of perpetual disintegration. In this sense the body is "totally imprinted by history" (ibid.: 376).

Franz Kafka provides a chilling illustration of a Foucauldian sense of discipline through inscription in his short story called the *Penal Colony*. In the story, the law of the prison is enforced through a novel tattooing machine composed of a bed, with cotton wool, and, above the bed, held in place with metal rods, a Designer. Each machine resembles a dark wooden chest. Between the Designer and the Bed shuttles a skin-writing device on a ribbon of steel called the Harrow. The Officer of the Colony explains this method of punishment:

> Whatever commandment the prisoner has disobeyed is written upon his body by the Harrow. "This prisoner for instance" – the officer indicated to the man – "will have written on his body: HONOR THY SUPERIORS!"   (Glatzer 1988: 144)

Prisoners are not informed of their sentence. The Officer in the story explains why: "There would be no point in telling him. He'll learn it on his body" (ibid.: 145).

This chilling tale is not so far from the truth of the ways in which tattooing has been used as a tool for punishment. Think of the numbers tattooed on the Jewish and other prisoners of the Nazi concentration camps. Here the tattoo was a means of regulation, control, and baptism into the world of the camp. In the aftermath of liberation, the survivors have had to carry with them these marks as a permanent reminder. Primo Levi documents his return from Auschwitz in his extraordinary book *The Truce*, writing, as he passed through Germany, "I felt the tattooed number on my arm burning like a sore" (Levi 1987: 76).

Tattooing continues today inside prisons but now it is the prisoners who tattoo themselves. Susan Phillips illustrates this point in her excellent study of gangland tattooing:

> No longer tattooed or branded by those who incarcerate them, prisoners now mark themselves forever into the stigmatized world of the prison. Tattooing creates permanent representations of identity that cannot be taken away by the authorities; they represent positive affirmations of self in an environment full of negatives. Even if the prisoners are stripped of clothes, have their heads shaven, are forced into tiny cells, are bloodied by each other or prison guards, tattoos speak of their pasts and carry the strength of their affiliations. (Phillips 2001: 369–70)

Tattooing, prohibited in US prisons, has become a means to wrest control over the prisoner's body from the gray concrete institutions. Phillips tells the story of one tattoo artist called Gallo. He was in prison for eight years and during this time he earned money as a tattooist. Caught by the guards, he consequently had to serve an extra six months. Gallo's body was marked with gangland tattoos, through which he visibly brought his neighborhood affiliations into the prison. As a result he received protection and support. Outside, his tattoos and his physical appearance had a paradoxical allure. On the one hand, it meant that he was offered parts in hard-core pornography films: for pornographic filmmakers, tattooed gang members apparently provide a means to titillate the viewer with images of dangerous exoticism. But, at the same time, his tattoos also marked Gallo out as a target for the police. Phillips lost contact with Gallo when he was arrested again for possession of soft drugs, and was on the verge of another prison sentence (ibid.: 384). So Gallo's tattoos are about both affirmation and damnation, arousing both desire and disgust.

There are connections between Gallo's experience and tattooing in the United Kingdom. In media representations images of tattooed men are associated with violence and football hooliganism. Similarly, tattooed working-class women have been associated, up until quite recently, with sexual deviance, prostitution, and criminality. In one recent press report a working-class community in southern England was characterized as a place of "cigarettes, hamburgers and tattoos."[2] All of these attributes were connected in one form or another with abuses of the body.

Walter Benjamin commented that historical reconstruction and cultural criticism should aspire to honor the "memory of the nameless" (cited in Berman 1999: 241). More than this, I want to use this impulse to raise a series of questions about the relationship between the body, language, and memory. How does the body become a medium and a fleshy canvass through and on which belonging and structures of feeling are expressed? In what sense does the reliance on elaborated forms of language obscure the modes of expression held within white working-class contexts with regard to emotional life, attachment, love, and loss? It is not only that "the nameless" live and die without trace, but also that the complexity of their emotional lives is lost, ignored, or disparaged.

So the project that is contained here is a reckoning with memory, culture, and history, particularly white working-class communities that traverse inner and outer London south of the river. It is an attempt to approach the biography of "the nameless" through the medium of the tattoo. Photographer Paul Halliday and I have worked closely together on the portraits that form the basis of this chapter. We worked jointly in the production of these images. We approached people who, for one reason or another, had decided to have tattoos inscribed. The participants were all familiar to us, some were friends and others family members. From the outset we wanted this project to be about an exchange that was both palpable – of giving photographs once they were made – but also a dialog of sentiments and recollections that were shown as well as written. It is in the showing that the largest part of the story is told.

Listening with Our Eyes

An implicit impulse in some strains of radical sociology – particularly those inspired by the political projects of feminism and anti-racism – is the desire and expectation that the disenfranchised should speak for themselves. This is a compelling challenge for sociology but ultimately it is a deceptive hope. The idea itself presupposes the form of interaction in which the voice is rendered. The sociological interview, for example, privileges the idioms of elaborated communication, so is often infused with class bias. As the late Basil Bernstein pointed out, class divisions are echoed in language use. On occasions where faithfully, and idiomatically, transcribed working-class speech makes it onto the page it jars the eye; the results can read like a Dick Van Dyke caricature of chirpy Cockney brogue. Bernstein argued that restricted language codes amongst working-class people result in distinctions that are tattooed metaphorically on their tongues (Bernstein 1979, 1990). Within such contexts working-class people articulate themselves through other means.

The prophetic philosopher Simone Weil once commented that "affliction" – a notion that she held to be both material and spiritual – is by its nature inarticulate. She writes:

> the afflicted are not listened to. They are like someone whose tongue has been cut out and who occasionally forgets the fact. When they move their lips no ear perceives any sound. And they themselves soon sink into impotence in the use of language, because of the certainty of not being heard.
>
> That is why there is no hope for the vagrant as he stands before the magistrate. Even if, through his stammerings, he should utter a cry to pierce the soul, neither the magistrate not the public will hear it. His cry is mute.   (Weil 1977: 332–3)

In order to avoid replicating the plight of the magistrate, we need to recognize that people express themselves through a wider range of cultural modalities that operate beyond "The Word."

Paul and I have tried to use photography to access the registers of embodied forms of communication. This involves listening within a wider range of senses. Much has been written about the way the photographic lens operates to survey and govern the definition of what is "real" (Tagg 1987). But it is a mistake, I think, to see the lens as only looking one way. This raises the question posed by John Berger, namely "Who is looking at Who?" (Berger and McBurney 1999). An answer is provided in the philosophical writings of Maurice Merleau-Ponty, who argues against the legacy of Cartesian dualism that separates mind from body, subject from object. He makes a case for the importance of developing a sensuous understanding and stresses that "we are in the world through our body" (Merleau-Ponty 1962: 206). Instead of dividing between subject and object, he stressed an intertwining, or a Chiasm. For him "the look" doesn't produce distance between the viewer and the looked-upon. Rather, the look produces a connection. It involves an openness to being that is potentially two-way, or "reversible" in Merleau-Ponty's language. "It is the coiling of the visible upon the seeing body," he writes:

> I lend them my body in order that they inscribe upon it and give me their resemblance, this fold, this central cavity of the visible which is my vision, these two mirror arrangements of the seeing and the visible, the touching and the touched . . . (Merleau-Ponty 1968: 146)

This process of intertwining occurs at the moment when the seer and the visible are connected. It is made on the stage of everyday life but it also possesses a specific relationship to time. In that fraction of a second when the aperture of the camera opens, a tiny slice of time is preserved in which the relationship between the viewer and the looked-upon is caught, and held, in place.

The Lion's Face

Mick looks back at us from the other side of the lens (figure 1.1). Through his look he addresses us but we have to listen with our eyes as well as our ears. He was born in Lewisham in 1951 and lived as a child in Perry Vale, Forest Hill, South London. Mick shows the two lions inscribed on his chest. They are the totem of his football team, Millwall Football Club, known to friend and foe alike as The Lions. In the public imagination Millwall signifies everything that is deplorable in English football culture – violence, bigotry, and hatred. In his fascinating study of the club and its history, Garry Robson writes:

> The word Millwall, I would suggest, is one of the most evocative in contemporary English. It functions as a condensed symbol, widely and indiscriminately used to express ideas and feelings about an entire sphere of activity and experience well beyond the compass of its original meaning. It has become a byword for, amongst other things, violent mob thuggery, unreconstructed masculinity, dark and impenetrable urban culture and working-class "fascism." (Robson 2000: 19)

This caricature holds little resemblance for the devoted fans for whom the club provides a sense of belonging and affiliation, passion

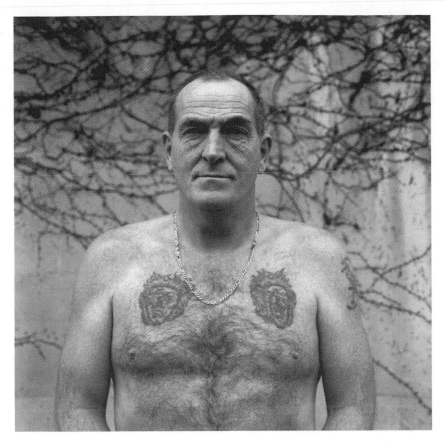

Figure 1.1   Mick and the lion's face

and love. For within this "condensed symbol" are the vestiges of an urban history that is largely ignored by journalists and politicians, who are quick to condemn Millwall's fans as proto-fascist football hooligans. Mick's grandmother was from Donegal in Ireland and his aunts live in various parts of Ireland. He started following Millwall when he was nine years old. He speaks of the fun and the intoxicating atmosphere of football culture of that time:

> The best times – going to watch Millwall play away was special because the excitement, the adrenaline was there from the Friday evening. Going in the old pubs and having a drink, you know, don't matter what age it was . . . we always sneaked you in or they sneaked me in or whatever, but no it was . . . it was, the adrenaline was there on a Friday

evening, or especially if you was travelling on a Friday evening because in them days you had no motorways and you went overnight, places like Carlisle and Barrow and Workington. . . . We went up overnight and it was, it was you know, just brilliant, you know, just travelling and letting other people see that you're arriving. You're there like, and you've come all this way like to see Millwall play and then . . . the, the high point was at the end of the game, you know. . . . If we'd won like, you know what I mean, you was over the moon like, you know. Or very disappointed if you lose because the long dreary drive back like, you know. . . . Well as I say, we've had some brilliant times.   (Interview: 11.4.96)

In 1977 Mick was filmed for a notorious documentary made by the BBC's "Panorama" team. The program was an exposé on football hooliganism, focusing on Millwall as an exemplary case. As a result, his face was plastered up unfairly in football grounds with "mug shots" of the most wanted "Millwall hooligans." The Millwall fraternity was populated by legendary figures like Ginger Bob, Ray Treatment, Harry the Dog, Tiny – who was a black Millwall fan and one of the most respected – and Sid the "Umbrella Man." Mick explains:

Well, we used to go to football matches and when the trouble was on, Sid just walked, [he] always had an umbrella with him as though he weren't causing no trouble. Then when you get the supporters running by like, the opposition he'd chchsh [pull them around the neck], that with the umbrella like and chhh – it was comical. I mean we know it was wrong but in them days it was comical because you was there, you was a part of it.   (Interview: 11.4.96)

This world constituted a public sphere of life for these men between home and work: a place that was controlled by them, enjoyed by them, and which possessed a unique electricity.

Mick had the lions written on his chest when he was 17 in Ringo's tattoo parlor in Woolwich. It was the ultimate gesture of commitment. "I think it just got it in your blood – obviously in them days you were tattooed up and you had sort of lions put on you, and like 'Millwall Forever'" (interview: 11.4.96).

Mick collects statues of lions, which decorate his home. At one point he even owned a tame lion called Sheba, which he kept in Bexleyheath, brought on several match days to The Den, Millwall's ground. These affinities are about much more than a sporting pastime. They are about a sense of place and of being in the world. They are a form of identification that is acted out, performed, and felt both in and through the body. It is something that Mick and others like him struggle to put into words:

> I've . . . been supporting Millwall and um – I don't know, I think it's just territory . . . just, they own it, it's Millwall and that's it, and it's, and it stays [coughs], as I say that, that, that's what it is about Millwall, it's just – Millwall is . . . it's they're in lights, Les, do you know what I mean, it's, it's there, it's there in lights, I mean everybody sees Millwall, everybody sees Millwall, everybody dreams Millwall. (Interview: 11.4.96)

Ultimately, words are not necessary. This passion and commitment is shown on his body. Yet, Mick didn't want the word "Millwall" as part of his tattoo. For him the lions carry a symbolic weight which makes the affiliation to Millwall and south London clear, while remaining partially hidden from the disapproving eyes of the uninitiated.

Darren is a porter at Goldsmiths College who, like Mick, grew up in south London and is a life-long Millwall fan. Like many, he has moved out of the capital, in large part as a response to the inflation in house prices. He lives with his family in Walderslade, Kent. He commutes to his job in New Cross, a return trip of 70 miles a day. Written on Darren's forearm is the fighting lion, above which is the club's name and beneath it the football club's initials (see figure 1.2). This is the most beloved of all Millwall symbols. It was the club's trademark emblem up until 1999, when the club decided to ditch the symbol in an attempt to distance itself from associations within the media with violence and hooliganism. This hasn't dented the popularity of this sign in the tattoo parlors of south London. Darren wears the tattoo proudly on his forearm, alongside others that draw on styles currently sweeping Europe and America as part of what has been referred to as the "tattoo renaissance" (Caplan 2000). The two styles sit together.

Football tattoos attest to the wearer's commitment to their beloved club but are also a mark of rootedness in a particular place. Many have talked about the ways in which football grounds become "sacred turf" (Bale 1994). Some football fans take this "geopiety" (Tuan 1976) further: literally, they ask to be married on the pitch, or request that upon their death their ashes be scattered in the goal-mouth. Many a nighttime guerrilla raid has been performed on stadia in south London

Figure 1.2 Darren's Millwall lion

and elsewhere to honor promises – often illegally – and administer unofficial funeral rites. Tattoos work in the opposite direction. What they do is incarnate a sense of place, community, and history on the skin of the individual. Steve Scholes, a 34-year-old Manchester United fanatic, has had the entire Old Trafford stadium tattooed on his back. The portraits show an aerial view of the ground in detail, along with the words "Old Trafford Theatre of Dreams." He told the *Sun* newspaper: "I just hope they don't do anymore building work" (*Sun*, November 8, 2001: 27). This sense of place, with all its associated affiliations, is deposited on the body like a bearing from which orientations to life are taken as the person moves physically through different localities and over time.

It is not just that collective loyalties are written on the body through the tattoo. One of the characteristics of working-class tattoos is that names of beloved family members and lovers are often written on the skin. This is particular to working-class tattooing. Rarely in the contemporary "modern primitive" European tattooing subcultures – which are largely middle-class – are family names inscribed (Caplan 2000; Randall and Polhemus 1996). There is something telling in this which points to the class-specific nature of such practices. In white working-class culture, the tattooed names are often the embodiment of filial love and kinship.

In her book *All About Loving* bell hooks writes that:

> The men in my life have always been the folks who are wary of using the word "love" lightly . . . They are wary because they believe women make too much of love.   (hooks 2000: 3)

This is a much-needed book. She concluded that the lack of clarity over the meaning of love lay at the heart of the difficulty of loving. Love for her is a matter of will, action, and choice. It is a matter of education:

> To truly love we must learn to mix various ingredients – care, affection, recognition, respect, commitment and trust as well as honest open communication.   (hooks 2000: 5)

But what mode of communication is being insinuated here? Much has been made of the emotional inarticulacy of men in general and working-class men in particular. Gary Oldman's film *Nil by Mouth* is, in my view, the best and most intense example.[3] In the film the main protagonist describes his father's internment in a hospital. Above his bed are the words "Nil by Mouth." This sums up the son's relationship to his father.

Speaking casually of love can debase its currency. Julie Burchill has written that there is a class dimension to the language of emotions (Burchill 2001). Burchill, an acerbic and controversial journalist, has argued that middle-class families profess love easily, leading to a jejune superficiality in emotional matters. There is something in this reproach. We live in the age of the talkshow exposé, in which emotions have been spectacularized. Emotion talk and disclosure is now a big industry. The ratings for the "shocking truth" television shows and the circulation of glossy magazines attest to this fact. The lack of emotional

Figure 1.3 Darren's twins

garrulousness in working-class culture points to alternative modalities in loving.

On the inside of Darren's forearm, distinct from the fierce Millwall Lion, is another tattoo (figure 1.3). It consists of two names – Molly and Charley – that are linked together with a heart, and beneath is a date, April 26, 1999. This marks the birthday of his beloved twin daughters. There is something beautiful and moving in the illustration of parental devotion. Love is given a name, it is incarnate. But this commitment is not made in elaborate speeches. It is performed rather than described. I want to refer to this kind of affinity as illocutionary love: a love that is brought into being without painstaking announcement.

The Name of the Father

In her study *Formations of Class and Gender*, Beverley Skeggs demonstrates the ways in which the body and bodily dispositions carry the markers of social class. The young women in her study concentrate on their bodies as a means of self-improvement. As Julie, one of the respondents, says: "Your body's the only thing you've got that's really yours" (Skeggs 1997: 83). For these women "letting yourself go" is a shorthand way of referring to a surrender to the strictures of class, immobility, and confinement. Another, Therese, observes: "You know you see them walking round town, dead fat, greasy hair, smelly clothes, dirty kids, you know the type, crimpilene [*sic*] trousers and all, they just don't care no more, I'd never be like that" (ibid.). Holding onto the hollow promises of class mobility is reduced to a matter of working on a healthy diet, keeping slim, and working out. Skeggs concludes; "The working-class body which is signalled through fat is the one that has given up the hope of ever 'improving'..." (Skeggs 1997: 83).

Beverley Skeggs doesn't mention the place of tattooing in her discussion of the complexities of working-class femininity. But I would guess that the tattoo would have been added to the attributes connected with the ignominy of the working-class female body. Up until relatively recently, for young women being tattooed would have engendered accusations of involvement in sexual promiscuity or prostitution and being a "slag" or "sluttish." The tattoo renaissance of the last ten years has changed this situation to some degree, as more and more women have worn tattoos and the stigma associated with them has lessened.

On Vicki's shoulder is a tattoo of an angel (see figure 1.4). She did not want her face shown. On her left shoulder, opposite this tattoo, is a "little devil." Her family think these sentinels of the divine and the wicked compete for influence over her personality. She is my niece and lives in New Addington, a large council estate on the outskirts of south London. It is a place where the city and the country cut into each other like the teeth of a saw. In 1956 Sir Hugh Casson, architectural director of the Festival of Britain, said of this estate that it was "cut off, not only from Croydon and London, but even from life itself."[4] Early residents called it "Little Siberia" because it is high up on a hill and exposed to the elements. Today, the skyline is dominated by the three skyscrapers that make up Canary Wharf Tower. They

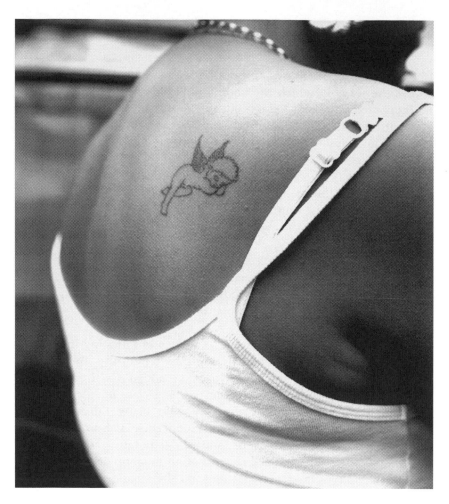

Figure 1.4 Vicki's angel

resemble a giant inverted three-pin plug. Through these towers London
is connected to the financial electricity of globalization. In the digital
age a "Cockney" is defined not by being born within the sound of
Bow Bells, but rather within sight of Canary Wharf.

Vicki is 20 years old and at the time this photograph was taken she
had just come home from her job in a supermarket. I asked her if
there was any stigma involved in girls having tattoos these days.
"No," she replied. "Everyone has got tattoos now. All kinds of things.
Dolphins, things like that. They are cheap, too." I asked her how

Figure 1.5 Vicki's "Mum and Dad"

much. "Depends where you go but you can get a small one done
for £20–£30" (July 22, 2001). She showed the tattoo on her heel
(figure 1.5). She was wearing her work shoes. On her ankle is a small
red rose with "Mum" and "Dad" inked on either side of it. Illocutionary
love.

Vicki shows her hands (figure 1.6). Behind every piece of her gold
jewelry lies a story. The third finger of her left hand warms the ring
once worn by her maternal grandmother, who passed away ten years
ago. Next to the gold rose, on her middle finger is a "keeper ring" like
the one her paternal grandfather wore, this one in fact given to her
by her grandparents for her thirteenth birthday. The rings on her
right hand all carry similar associations and attachments. She bought
the diamond lattice ring on her index finger with the money that her

Figure 1.6 A life in her hands

maternal grandfather gave her the year that he died. The gold ring on the third finger was given to her by her paternal grandparents for her sixteenth birthday. On the middle finger of her right hand is the large gold sovereign ring given to her on her eighteenth birthday by her paternal grandmother alone. Just two months prior to Vicki's coming of age her grandfather died of cancer.

Her nails are done, professionally manicured. The extravagant artificial fingernails contain a jewel in the center of each individual nail, a style currently popular amongst black and white girls in London. The phrase "dripping in gold" is used as a means to pour scorn on working-class women. It is meant to fix young women and the nouveau riche as brash or gaudy, and mark them as inferior within the hierarchies of taste and class distinction (Bourdieu 1986). It is a stock phrase in the lexicon of class conceit. Each of the items that Vicki wears carries a meaning and association that escapes the strictures of bourgeois ignorance and prejudice. Each symbolizes a moment passed in living, a register of love or kinship to those near to her, or to the memory of the lost. The story of her young life is in her hands.

There is a tattoo above the gold bracelet on Vicki's left wrist. It is a simple one in a contemporary style. Its presence beneath the gold jewelry signals a cultural trace from the past alive in the present. In the early period of the Industrial Revolution workers had ornaments written on their skin. They had few possessions but "free labor" meant they held sovereign power over their bodies. James Bradley concluded, in his study of class and Victorian tattooing:

> Tattoos provided a substitute for jewellery, or other material possessions: a means of articulating emotion to, and forging attachments between the body, the self and others.   (Bradley 2000: 151)

The gold jewelry and Vicki's tattoo produce a continuity in which elements oscillate between past and present. They fit together within what Williams (1977) calls a "structure of feeling" that furnishes working-class taste and experience.

Vicki's grandfather, my father, died in 1999 after a long and brutal dance with cancer. After he had his initial surgery I visited him in Mayday Hospital, Croydon. The ward was full of men of his age and background, all smokers, all blighted by the same affliction. Fifty years of factory work had left a lattice of cracks on his hands that were hardened with calluses. Standing at a machine for ten hours a day had thickened his ankles and weakened his knees. The regimes of factory work left traces on the worker's body not always amenable to the naked eye but all too plain in the failing bodies of this room. Like Engels's famous invocation of social murder, the illnesses found on this ward were the work of similar perpetrators – bad working conditions, poor diet, and an industry that profits from the sale of what my father called "cancer sticks."

As a young man things had been so very different. He had fancied himself as a bit of a "spiv," inured with the world and style of the south London gangsters. There are pictures of him posing with his great friend Johnny Graham in the back garden of his mother's ter-raced house. They are dressed in double-breasted suits, silk ties, and long collared shirts. Dad, with Johnny, used to get on the train at East Croydon and head for the jazz clubs of Soho, or the boxing gyms, often over pubs, on the Old Kent Road, or go dog racing at Catford. He carried with him always the humor and love of life that he found in those places.

He served in the Navy but he did not plot his travels in his skin. He forbade my brother and me to have tattoos even though we both wanted them. He "laid down the law" in a Lacanian sense of a symbolic order (Lacan 1977), but specifically for him tattoos signified self-damnation and class stigma and undermined his aspirations for postwar social improvement. Like many, his image of a "step up" was to move to the edge of the city, to the large council estates which offered the promise of better conditions and amenities. In such concrete citadels working-class culture was deracinated and displaced. Yet, even in such "new worlds," the legacy of the past was registered on the working-class body in code (Back 2001). Memories do not have to be consciously held in order for them to be socially alive (Connerton 1989). Rather, they can furnish a structure of feeling, while remaining elusive, even to those who inhabit it. Our father would not tolerate any carping about progress. For him it was simple: he wanted for his family better than he had known. Toward the end of his life he looked on in bewilderment as his granddaughter Vicki presented a new tattoo on a more or less monthly basis.

The overwhelming sense of loss following his death consumed us all in different ways. For my brother Ken – Vicki's father – the particular nature of his death cast a shadow over his own future. He is a sheet-metal worker and for many years he worked in a factory next door to his father. Now he travels all over the capital repairing the steel structures of the metropolis. Even in the "weightless economy" (see Pratt 2000; Tonkiss 2002) dot.com business needs office space to put its computers and pot plants in. While the industrial order of Fordist production has disappeared, cities and citizens still need their buildings repaired and new structures made.

Following our father's death, Ken went through a period of wearing his clothes, even his glasses. He inhabited his father's absence, in a literal way. He filled out his father's clothes with his own body and carried his garb with an almost identical language of movement and social orientation. Father and son possessed what Bourdieu calls a shared "bodily hexis" (Bourdieu 1986: 474).

Like many families in London, we have a small caravan on the south coast, a place we have returned to for summer holidays since 1957. In the 1980s my parents bought a second-hand van at Norman's Bay and in the months after our father's death we continued to

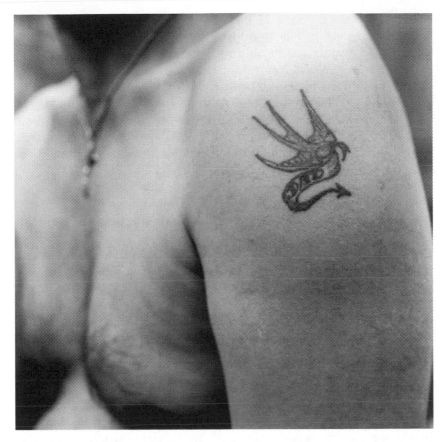

Figure 1.7 Ken's memorial

visit. It was almost impossible to be there. Every place resonated with his absent presence – the beach, the sea, and the sea wall where he stood to smoke a cigarette and look out onto the waves with the wind pushing back his mane of silver hair. Then, one warm summer afternoon, Ken said he had something to show me. He rolled up his shirtsleeve and there on the top of his shoulder was a tattoo, a graphic imago, consisting of a swallow in flight, holding a scroll in its beak, and on that fleshy parchment was inscribed three letters – DAD (see figure 1.7).

The tattoo names the object of an illocutionary love. As Alfred Gell (1993) points out, this apparently individual choice is in fact elicited by others. In Ken's case they are his family, those closest to him, and the specter of his father. It symbolizes a love that was rarely, if ever, brought to speech, yet it is named. It *is* the name. Psychoanalyst Jacques Lacan claims that from the very beginning of their lives children have a distinct relationship to fathers. This stands in contrast to the immediate physical connection to their mothers that is fashioned at birth and through nursing (Lacan 1977). Children develop a corporeal relation to their mother, while they learn of their relationship to their fathers through language and the Word. The veracity of these claims is not the issue here, for what Lacan alerts us to is the symbolic weight contained in the name of the father. The father stands not only for paternity and love but also for a social or moral order.

The inscription of "Dad" on Ken's shoulder points to the complexities of that moral order. Remember, his father had prohibited him from having such inscriptions. Yet, it is precisely through this debarred line that Ken memorializes his father. Ken's tattoo both carries his father's memory and defies parental authority. In the end our father lives in part through the breaching of the law that he "laid down to us" as children. Our father could on occasion be fierce and harsh and inevitably as a young man Ken had fallen foul of his discipline. His tattoo thus contains both sweetness and pepper.

Two years on from our father's death, Ken has become like him, not in terms of physical characteristics, or in the superficial surfaces of appearance. The invisible tattoos that form what Raymond Williams calls a structure of feeling have been imprinted on his thought, action, and conduct. This, to me, is something of a miracle and a comfort. We had not spoken of this – not, that is, until I brought my day job home and turned myself into a putative family ethnographer. All the emotions, palpable support, and love that was demonstrated through the bereavement was never named. I want to suggest that this is much more than a family matter. It can be read as an example of the complexity of plebeian emotional lives which have so often been viewed as indifferent, expressionless, and lacking compassion.

Within white working-class contexts, men, and, to a lesser degree, women possess a kind of laconic halter when it comes to overfamiliarity. This is certainly the case in south London and its hinterlands, and may be specific to the history of this region and the class cultures that have taken hold. This is not quite the process of "making the self smooth," or leveling out the internal and external fluctuations of emotion that Clifford Geertz described so vividly in the context of Java (Geertz 1979: 231). Rather, it is an imperturbable mask that holds still in the face of loquaciousness of any kind. Displays of overfamiliarity and easy affection are met with chilled skepticism. This in part has acted as a defense against external approaches, be it in the form of opportunistic politicians – on the left or the right – or the moral scrutiny of social workers and bourgeois professionals.

The language of love is articulated through acts and gestures within an embodied realm. Here the commonsense maxim, "actions that speak louder than words," takes on a literal significance. The danger inherent in this unspoken love is that its communication might be distorted and not received clearly. These embedded emotional affinities can be misinterpreted, assumed, looked past, or taken for granted. My essential point is that the lack of speech is not necessarily an indicator of an absence of love. More than this, the expression and communication of love needs to be understood through the range of verbal and nonverbal modalities.

The Color in the Portrait

In this essay I have tried to explicate that which is not easily accessible to the written word. The key argument has been that within white working-class contexts the body becomes a figure through which emotions, affinities, and devotions are inscribed. I have tried to show through examining the photographs contained here that the tattooed marks on these bodies contain complex metonymic interconnections, meanings, and symbolism. The coloring of these portraits – which is what I have tried to do through writing – is partial because each contains an enigma. Trying to find meaning in them is like grasping a handful of sand: most of the grains of truth slip through the fingers.

For Lacan, the act of signification, or any form of representation, is inherently unstable. It is what Kirsten Campbell has termed "the slide in the sign," or *glissement* in Lacanian language, i.e. "the process in which the signified constantly slides beneath the signifier" (Campbell 1999: 135). As Lacan argues, it is impossible to "say it all" because ultimately "words fail." Part of this deficit is identified by Raymond Williams, in what he calls the slide toward the past tense in cultural analysis and what he refers to as "fixed forms of understanding." The complexities of the present resist the categories we use to understand them; something always escapes and remains opaque:

> Perhaps the dead can be reduced to fixed forms, though their surviving records are against it. But the living will not be reduced, at least in the first person; living third persons may be different. All the known

complexities, the experienced tensions, shifts, and uncertainties, the intricate forms of unevenness and confusion, are against the terms of the reduction and soon, by extension, against social analysis itself. (Williams 1977: 129–30)

This inadequacy in the act of representation is made all the more apparent here given that the people contained in this study are my immediate family and close friends. What I have offered is very much a first-person narrative in the way Raymond Williams characterizes it. The portraits are inherently incomplete. They are sketches rather than vivid portrayals in which all the shades of experience are detailed. But it is more difficult to indulge in quick judgments and crass sociological objectification when the subjects are your loved ones. This has been a lesson in itself. But the inevitable failure in the act of representation is not necessarily defeat. Ethnographic representation should aspire to better kinds of failure, to paraphrase Samuel Beckett's evocative phrase. This involves being open to the complexities and incomplete nature of present-tense experience, while at the same time avoiding reduction, fixing, and closure.

Perhaps this draws attention to the ethics of thinking itself. If thinking is a moral act, what kind of moral act is it (Geertz 2001), specifically when it involves intimate dialog of the kind described here? Pierre Bourdieu has written that listening involves an intimacy that is both intellectual and emotional:

> Thus, at the risk of shocking both the rigorous methodologist and the inspired hermeneutic scholar, I would say that the interview can be considered a sort of *spiritual exercise* that, through forgetfulness of self, aims at a true *conversion of the way we look at* other people in the ordinary circumstances of life. The welcoming disposition, which leads one to make the respondent's problems one's own, the capacity to take the persons and understand them just as they are in their distinctive necessity, is a sort of *intellectual love . . .* (Bourdieu 1999: 614)

The portraits I have offered are themselves outlined through love; these pages are written with it. Making the "respondent's problems one's own" in this case contains an immediacy because it has, through thinking, involved a healing and reckoning with personal loss and bereavement: Ken is my brother and his father was my father. But I hope that this discussion also resonates with Bourdieu's contention that sociology should be about a process of *conversion* and transformation in the way we look at other people and their bodies.

The paradox of working-class tattooing is that it can, and does, mark out the painted body as a target for class stigma and prejudice. My argument throughout has been that contained within these inscriptions are complex emotions and affinities. Sue Benson has argued that the conception that the body can be remade and fashioned is a powerful one today. Yet the tendency to think of the body as something that can be styled and controlled contains a broken promise. Tattooing and other forms of body culture bring this paradox into clear view:

> For in truth we do not own our bodies, they own us, that the only thing that is certain about our bodies is that they will let us down, that in the end they cannot be mastered or bent to our will. In this sense what these practices bring into sharp focus is the *impossibility* of Western ideas about body and self, and of these fantasies of permanence, control autonomy that they seek to negotiate. (Benson 2000: 25)

The lines in these tattoos touch permanence but cannot grasp eternity. This has a double consequence for working-class expression because this is often the only medium through which their stories are told. There is no place for them, and no prospect of what Jacques Derrida calls a "hospitable memory" (1994: 175). As the cadavers disappear, the traces of their embodied history, of life and love, are lost – they become The Nameless. They pass through hospital wards to the crematoria, to be remembered in the inscriptions made on young flesh that will in turn grow old.

Acknowledgments

Thanks to Paul Halliday for the contribution of his extraordinary images for this article and for providing such great company on various photographic trips through London's "deep south." A special thanks to Mickey, Darren, Vicki, and Ken for their patience and generosity in allowing us to photograph them. Many thanks also to Stephen Dobson, Claire Alexander, Fran Tonkiss, Kirsty Campbell, Vic Seidler, Celia Lury, Roxy Harris, Ben Gidley, Sue Benson, and Michael Keith for providing bibliographical clues and useful insights that helped me along the way. A special "thank you" to Judith Barrett for her critical and literary judgment.

Notes

1   Debbie Back treated this patient in the Winter of 2000 and I am grateful to her for sharing his story.
2   BBC Radio 4, *The Sunday Papers*, Sunday, August 4, 2001.
3   *Nil by Mouth* (1997), Twentieth Century Fox Film Corporation, written and directed by Gary Oldman.
4   *Croydon Advertiser*, June 22, 1956.

References

Back, L. (2001) "Out of the Shadows," in D. Bravenboer (ed.), *Contagious*. London: Croindene Press.

Bale, J. (1994) *Landscapes of Modern Sport*. Leicester: Leicester University Press.

Benson, S. (2000) "Inscriptions of the Self: Reflections on Tattooing and Piercing in Contemporary Euro-America," in J. Caplan (ed.), *Written on the Body: The Tattoo in European and American History*. London: Reaktion Books.

Berger, J. and McBurney, S. (1999) *The Vertical Line*. London: Artangel.

Berman, M. (1999) *Adventure in Marxism*. London: Verso.

Bernstein, B. (1979) "Social Class, Language and Socialisation," in J. Karabel and A.H. Halsey (eds.), *Power and Ideology in Education*. New York: Oxford University Press.

Bernstein, B. (1990) *The Structuring of Pedagogic Discourse*. London: Routledge.

Bourdieu, P. (1986) *Distinction: A Social Critique of the Judgement of Taste*. London: Routledge.

Bourdieu, P. (1999) "Understanding," in P. Bourdieu et al., *The Weight of the World: Social Suffering in Contemporary Society*. Cambridge: Polity Press.

Bradley, J. (2000) "Body Commodification? Class and Tattoos in Victorian Britain," in J. Caplan (ed.), *Written on the Body: The Tattoo in European and American History*. London: Reaktion Books.

Burchill, J. (2001) *The Guardian Columns, 1998–2000*. London: Orion Publishing Group.

Campbell, K. (1999) "The Slide in the Sign: Lacan's Glissement and the Registers of Meaning," *Angelaki: Journal of the Theoretical Humanities* 4, 3: 135–43.

Caplan, Jane (2000) "Introduction," in J. Caplan (ed.), *Written on the Body: The Tattoo in European and American History*. London: Reaktion Books.

Connerton, P. (1989) *How Societies Remember*. Cambridge: Cambridge University Press.

Derrida, J. (1994) *Specters of Marx: The State of the Debt, the Work of Mourning, and the New International*. London: Routledge.

Foucault, M. (1977) *Discipline and Punish: The Birth of the Prison*. London: Allen Lane.

Foucault, M. (1994) "Nietzsche, Genealogy, History," in M. Foucault, *Aesthetics, Method, and Epistemology*. London: Allen Lane, pp. 369–91.

Geertz, C. (1979) "From the Native's Point of View: On the Nature of Anthropological Understanding," in P. Rabinow and W.M. Sullivan (eds.), *Interpretive Social Science: A Reader*. Berkeley, Los Angeles: University of California Press, pp. 225–41.

Geertz, C. (2001) *Available Light: Anthropological Reflections on Philosophical Topics*. Princeton, NJ: Princeton University Press.

Gell, A. (1993) *Wrapping in Images: Tattooing in Polynesia*. Oxford: Clarendon Press.

Glatzer, N.N. (ed.) (1988) *The Collected Stories of Franz Kafka*. Harmondsworth: Penguin Books.

Guest, H. (2000) "Curiously Marked: Tattooing and Gender Difference in Eighteenth-century British Perceptions of the South Pacific," in J. Caplan (ed.), *Written on the Body: The Tattoo in European and American History*. London: Reaktion Books.

Gustafson, M. (2000) "The Tattoo in the Later Roman Empire and Beyond," in J. Caplan (ed.), *Written on the Body: The Tattoo in European and American History*. London: Reaktion Books.

hooks, b. (2000) *All About Loving: New Visions*. London: The Women's Press.

Jones, C.P. (2000) "Stigma and Tattoo," in J. Caplan (ed.), *Written on the Body: The Tattoo in European and American History*. London: Reaktion Books.

Lacan, J. (1977) *Ecrits: A Selection*. London: Tavistock Publications.

Levi, P. (1987) *If This is a Man/The Truce*. London: Abacus.

MacQuarrie, C.W. (2000) "Insular Celtic Tattooing: History, Myth and Metaphor," in J. Caplan (ed.), *Written on the Body: The Tattoo in European and American History*. London: Reaktion Books.

Maxwell-Stewart, H. and Duffield, I. (2000) "Skin Deep Devotions: Religious Tattoos and Convict Transportation to Australia," in J. Caplan (ed.), *Written on the Body: The Tattoo in European and American History*. London: Reaktion Books.

Merleau-Ponty, M. (1962) *The Phenomenology of Perception*. London: Routledge & Kegan Paul.

Merleau-Ponty, M. (1968) *The Visible and the Invisible*. Evanston, IL: Northwestern University Press.

Modiano, P. (2000) *The Search Warrant*. London: The Harvill Press.

Phillips, S.A. (2001) "Gallo's Body: Decoration and Damnation in the Life of a Chicano Gang Member," *Ethnography* 2, 3: 357–85.

Pratt, A.C. (2000) "New Media, the New Economy and New Spaces," *Geoforum* 31: 425–36.

Randall, H. and Polhemus, T. (1996) *The Customized Body*. London: Serpent's Tail.

Rediker, M. (1987) *Between the Devil and the Deep Blue Sea: Merchant Seamen, Pirates, and the Anglo-American Maritime World*. Cambridge: Cambridge University Press.

Robson, G. (2000) *No One Likes Us, We Don't Care: The Myth and Reality of Millwall Fandom*. Oxford: Berg.

Schwarz, D.R. (ed.) (1994) *James Joyce: The Dead*. Boston & New York: Bedford/ St. Martin's Press.

Skeggs, B. (1997) *Formations of Class and Gender*. London: Sage Publications.

Tagg, J. (1987) *The Burden of Representation*. Basingstoke: Macmillan.

Tonkiss, F. (2002) "Between Markets, Firms and Networks: Constituting the Cultural Economy," in A. Warde and S. Metcalfe (eds.), *Market Relations and the Competitive Process*. Manchester: Manchester University Press.

Tuan, Yi-Fu (1976) "Geopiety," in D. Lewnthal and M.J. Bowden (eds.), *Geographies of the Mind: Essays in Historical Geography*. New York: Oxford University Press.

Weil, S. (1977) "Human Personality," in George A. Panichas (ed.), *The Simone Weil Reader*. New York: David McKay.

Williams, R. (1977) *Marxism and Literature*. Oxford: Oxford University Press.

Chapter 2

From Catwalk to Catalog: Male Fashion Models, Masculinity, and Identity

Joanne Entwistle

Introduction

Modeling is not typically "masculine" work. In *Glamorama*, Bret Easton Ellis's (1998: 110) tale of models and celebrities in New York, Victor, the central character and a young male model, meets an old friend, Lauren, and their encounter comically captures this:

"Where are you going?" asks Lauren.
"Todd Oldham show," I sigh, "I'm in it."
"Modeling," she says, "A man's job."
"It's not as easy as it may look."
"Yeah, modeling's tough Victor," she says. "The only thing you need to
    be is on time. Hard work."
"It *is*," I whine.
"It's a job where you need to know how to wear clothes?" she's asking.
    "It's a job where you need to know how to – now let me get this
    straight – *walk*?"
"Hey, all I did was learn how to make the most of my looks."
"What about your mind?"
"Right," I snicker. "Like in this world" – I'm gesturing – "my mind
    matters more than my abs. Oh boy, raise your hand if you believe that."

Unlike other display work men do that involves being looked at (such as dancing or acting, for example) modeling is work that has men solely as objects of display – they merely have to "be on time," "walk," and "wear clothes" but nothing more. This apparent lack of activity, the assumed passivity of modeling, make it seem an inappropriate job for a man since a "real" man is supposed to "do" rather than "appear" (Berger 1972). However, the growth of male modeling in recent years, evidenced by the wide usage of male models selling fashion and non-fashion products, and the increasing number of male models represented by model agencies, seem to challenge these assumptions and suggest that, at least for younger men, modeling has lost some of its stigma as "unmanly." Since the 1980s there has been an expansion in male modeling, brought about as a result of the opening up of the "men's markets" in retail and grooming products (Mort 1996; Nixon 1996). This expansion has continued apace in recent years: over the 1990s there was a considerable increase in the numbers of male models represented by model agencies in London and New York.[1] Today, modeling may even represent a very desirable job for some young men. Thus, while older prejudices surrounding male models still linger (as in Easton Ellis's quote above), it would seem that ideas about masculinity are shifting. Men born in the late 1970s and early 1980s have grown up surrounded by images of men selling all kinds of commodities, as well as celebrities, such as British soccer player David Beckham and the pop star Robbie Williams, who both display a quite feminine interest in fashion, the body, and their appearance.[2] It would seem, then, that the taboo that men should not be interested in fashion or in looking good has been eroded to some extent, at least for a younger generation of men.

Thus, one major indication of this change within contemporary understandings of masculinity has been an increased emphasis upon the commodified male body, which has become an established part of contemporary commercial culture. Since the 1970s, and perhaps more significantly, the early 1980s and the rise of the "new man," attention in the media and popular culture has been focused upon the male body as something to be toned, dressed, groomed, and generally attended to as an object "to be looked at." Although, as Gill et al. (2000: 100) note, men have been presented as sexually desirable before, what is different today is that codes for the presentation of the male body "give permission for it to be looked at and desired." This, they argue "is a *new* phenomenon, which is culturally and historically specific" (ibid.: 100) and they point to a number of developments, which have helped establish a "cultural milieu" in which a "new man" could emerge and "flourish" (ibid.: 102). These include the rise and influence of feminism and new social movements, which have put gender under scrutiny, the rise of the "style press" such as *Arena*, *GQ*, and *The Face*, and the expansion of retailing for men. These developments have helped to promote a qualitative shift in representations of men: the displayed male bodies since the 1980s are unlike previous male bodies – young, muscular, sexy, self-consciously narcissistic, and offered for the gaze of women and heterosexual men in the new men's magazines and fashion magazines. This trend is significant because it suggests that the aesthetic appreciation and display of the male body, for a long time associated with gay men and black men, has extended into mainstream commercial culture to include white, heterosexual men. There is growing evidence to suggest that this expansion in images of men is having some impact upon young men, stimulating them to take an interest in how their bodies look (Gill et al. 2000). Younger men appear to invest in their bodies more than previous generations of men and this may also go some way to explain why some of them consider modeling as a career. In "this world," as Victor in the quote above puts it, a man's "abs" (or "six-pack") have become important.

Taking these developments as evidence of a noticeable change in contemporary masculinities, it is my contention that male modeling is one prominent arena in which these transformations have been played out and can thus be examined. In this paper, I examine the work of male fashion models in order to explore how young men at the fore of these developments negotiate their masculinity identities. I have several overlapping questions about the nature of male modeling as work for men, which focus attention upon the body. The central question is: How is gender performed and reproduced through aesthetics and strategies of embodiment? Recent work on gender has demonstrated how it is inscribed on, and reproduced through, the body (see for example, Butler 1990; Gatens 1996). For Butler, gender has no ontological reality; it is an effect of codes of performance which are endlessly and compulsively repeated within the hegemonic framework of "compulsory heterosexuality." Gender, according to Butler, is in fact a product of endless incitements which serve to maintain the appearance of "difference." However, despite their theoretical importance, Butler's arguments are largely abstract and fail to examine how gender is performed and reproduced at the mundane level of everyday social and cultural practices. This research extends Butler's work, focusing on how gender is reproduced in everyday situations by examining how bodies are constantly at work in reproducing themselves as gendered bodies through routine performances in "situated practices"

(Entwistle 2000a). In other words, I am interested in how bodies "do" gender through various investments in, and techniques of, the body, and through particular embodied performances. Given the nature of male models' work, focusing as it does on appearance, I am particularly interested in how they manage and maintain their body. This raises two particular questions. First, in what ways do male models invest in the body; how do they come to see their body and how do they maintain it? Secondly, in what ways do they "do" masculinity and how is it reproduced through particular bodily performances in a context, which, as I will argue, potentially disrupts dominant (hetero-sexuality) masculinity? I contend that male modeling opens up a contradiction between gender and work identities: fashion modeling is dominated by gay men, and is both "feminine" and "queer" work that contradicts, or potentially disrupts, what it means to be a "real" man as defined by the "regulatory framework" of heterosexuality (Butler 1990, 1993). I am interested in how male models manage this contradiction and orientate their body in order to adapt to the habitus (Bourdieu 1984) of this sphere of work.

Through analysis of these two aspects of embodiment, I examine how, on the one hand, performances of masculinity by male models highlight some of the ways in which dominant masculinity has been (and continues to be) recoded or modified through strategies of embodiment. Unlike other forms of work for men, male modeling requires particular investments in the body: it has to be shaped in terms of a "look" and thought of as a commodity. However, on the other hand, these performances of gender can also be said to reproduce dominant ideas about heterosexual masculinity, albeit in a modified form. In this way, male modeling sheds light on some contemporary problems and contradictions inherent in contemporary styles of masculinity as it is embodied through the actions and practices of these particular young men.

The World of Fashion Modeling

Before discussing these issues, I want to say a word or two about my sample and methodological approach. I have conducted interviews with 22 male fashion models and six bookers in five different agencies in New York and London. Bookers are the people who "book" the models for jobs and effectively shape their careers. As influential people within the agencies, bookers were my key informants and it was largely through their cooperation that I was able to interview most of my models. In addition, over a two-month period, I spent some time at one of the London agencies, sitting in the open reception area, observing models and their bookers *in situ*. During this time I not only conducted many of my interviews, but I had the opportunity to observe models and bookers at work, witnessing the regular interactions between them, and also with photographers and clients who passed through the agency. On a number of occasions I was at the agency when clients were casting for models and this afforded me the opportunity to see how models deal with this routine part of their job. In addition to these accounts and observations, I also draw on the performances within the interview situation, itself a source of qualitative data. Interviews are performative: the interview situation is an interaction which, in terms of my research concerns, provides evidence of the ways in which male models "do" masculinity in the context of a heterosexual encounter with me (a young, heterosexual woman). Finally, having befriended a couple of models, I have been able to maintain regular, informal contact over a longer period of time and this has enabled me to gain a long-term perspective on modeling.

The age range of my models was between 15 and mid-40s; however the majority of my sample were between 19 and 22 (only one model was 15, and only one in his mid-40s) and are known as "New Faces" by the agencies because they are just starting out. The reason I have so many new faces has to do with access: younger models are more likely to stop by the agency where I've been recruiting for interviews and so are easier to get hold of than more successful models who are often traveling and rarely visit the agency. The young age of these men has to be factored into findings and analysis since their experiences of modeling will differ from those of older, more experienced models. So, too, will their relationship to their bodies, to which I shall now turn my attention.

The Body of the Model/Modeling the Body

Fashion male modeling demands a particular kind of body, one that is largely ascribed by genetics rather than attained through care and work.[3] The male fashion model's body is a very standard one in terms of size and shape: the required height for most agencies is between 180 and 191 cm (5 ft 11 in.–6 ft 3 in.) and the standard measurements are, usually: chest, 96–107 cm (38–42 in.), and waist, 76–81 cm

(30–2 in.). Fashion models are, without exception, very slim, even skinny by everyday standards. One booker described male models as "genetic freaks," although he meant this not in any pejorative sense, but as a description of these men as taller and leaner than most men in the west. Fashion models (male and female) can sometimes look quite unusual, with large or exaggerated features, such as a large mouth or very strong jaw line, although it is essential that these features are "photogenic." The quite distinctive bodily features required in male modeling make it something that only a very small minority are "naturally" predisposed to. The model's body, his look, is the product of nature, although his "beauty" is most definitely cultural, produced as "beautiful" by being chosen and valued within the fashion modeling world. Modeling is an aesthetic practice producing some bodies as "attractive" or "beautiful," which is *internally valorized* within the modeling and fashion industries. These bodies are, by definition, rare or unusual. Since, as I have argued elsewhere (see Entwistle forthcoming), this aesthetic discourse is internal to these industries, the definitions of male (and female) beauty produced do not necessarily correspond to definitions of beauty outside: fashion models are sometimes quite unattractive by conventional standards of beauty found outside of fashion modeling. An obvious example of this is the rise of "heroin chic," which, since the 1990s, has produced extremely thin bodies and often quite extreme or strange looks. This aesthetic for female models has attracted considerable criticism by the press and politicians in the UK, but can also be found, less controversially, in contemporary aesthetics in male modeling since the 1990s as well. The lack of correspondence between the male fashion model's "beauty" and ideas of male beauty outside is evidenced by the negative reactions, particularly from female students, to footage of male models in the seasonal runway shows which I have shown in class.

The very specific bodily requirements of fashion modeling may account, at least in part, for the surprising lack of body maintenance by a significant number of the models I talked to. Most male fashion models have to do very little to their body in order to become a model. However, age is a factor here since fashion models are very young compared to "lifestyle" models: they are generally men who have a naturally low body weight and may therefore not need to diet or exercise to maintain it. In a number of interviews some models referred to their age when discussing their body: for example, some argued they are "lucky" in that they do not need to "work out" or watch what they eat as they have a fast metabolism. A couple of younger models noted that their body is still changing, as they are still not yet through puberty. Others were aware that as they got older they might have to watch their weight more carefully. Whether these descriptions of the body are entirely true or not, it is interesting that so many male models drew on the notion of the "natural" body rather than admit to having "cultivated" their bodies. This may be, in part, a rhetorical strategy to obscure or distance themselves from associations with the cultivation of the body, which might be construed as "vanity." This attitude was prevalent among the British models, as discussed in more detail below.

A small number of models did describe how they had to watch what they ate to keep their weight down, and a couple of models had been told by their booker to lose some weight. Only a few models told me they had to "work out" and of these, the majority were not from the UK. Indeed, many of the British models I spoke to laughed when I asked them about exercise and gym membership and seemed almost proud to say they had never been inside a gym: for example, one model, Simon (in London), told me, "I don't go the gym, I keep as far away from it as I can." This attitude, prevalent in the UK, may explain why the London-based models tend to have skinny and "undeveloped" bodies compared with many of their US counterparts. Indeed, this difference in body styles was noted by a booker in a London agency, who described how UK men are much less sporty than men from the US, South Africa, or Australia, countries renowned for active, outdoor, and sporty lifestyles. According to him, models from these countries have better bodies than UK models and are therefore more likely to do underwear or swimwear jobs. Of the models who do work out, there is still a real concern to maintain a very slim look. Contrary to the perception of male models as muscular "hunks," the fashion aesthetic favors a very lean look, with some, but not too much muscle, and definitely not "developed." "Fitness" models, for sportswear, may be quite large and developed, but fashion models are advised to maintain a very slim silhouette. Some models described how they had to ensure they did not build up too much, and this might run counter to what they would like to do with their body if they were not a model: for instance, one of these models, Ben, described being a little annoyed to have been told by his booker not to "build" his arms when he told her he would like to do this.

A cultural variation between UK models and others in terms of body management and aesthetics was also reflected in attitudes to tanning. In New York quite a number of models were concerned to acquire a good color over the summer and one New Zealand model used sun-beds while in London to acquire a tan. In contrast, the London models took great pride in their pallid complexion and skinny, undeveloped bodies. Indeed, quite a significant number of the UK models claimed to pay little or no attention to how they look, something which may be linked to a particular "laddish" performance amongst the London models. Two models, Simon and Robbie, interviewed together at a casting in their London agency, typify this. When I referred to Robbie's stubble in many of the images and asked him if he cultivated it, his reply was, "No, generally I just leave it, because I am so fucking lazy." When I asked them to talk about their body maintenance, they laughed and joked about their lack of it and appealed, once again, to the "natural" body:

Q:	Do you take much care with your hair and skin?
ROBBIE:	I've always had good skin. I dunno, no I don't. I smoke far too much, I drink far too much [chuckles], I do fuck all exercise. (You don't go to the gym at all?) No.
Q (to Simon):	What about you?
SIMON:	I don't go the gym, I keep as far away from it as I can. I do the same as Robbie: I smoke and drink too much. And I don't have any problems with my skin.
Q:	You are both very lucky then, are you not?
SIMON:	Yeah.

This cultural variation can, to some extent, be explained in terms of a difference in attitudes toward the cultivation of appearance between models in the UK and the USA. In the UK there is a reticence to appear to take too much interest in your appearance and to appearing like "you love yourself." Another London model, Gary, exhibited this attitude when he quite forcefully condemned the sort of men who use gyms. He told me he used to work out "about four times a week" at home before becoming a model, but after moving to London, he no longer has the space to do this. Although describing himself early on in the interview as "a bit of a poser," he was critical of any public signs of narcissism and gave this as his reason for disliking gyms:

> I haven't got the motivation to go down to the gym 'cos I hate people like that. You know, if you want to pose and love yourself in front of your own mirror in your own bedroom, that's fair enough. But when you're doing it in front of other people it just makes me feel sick. So that is why I'm not really a great fan of gyms. I go swimming from time to time.

The distinction he draws between the private posing which he deems "fair enough" and the public posing he describes as making him "feel sick" seems strange given that his occupation as a male model means he must pose "in front of other people" all the time. If he sees "posing" as part of the job of being a model, his relationship to it is obviously quite ambivalent. Comments may be read as a rhetorical strategy to disavow the content of much of his work and perhaps also his enjoyment of it. However, there is more going on here: vanity, posing, and "loving yourself" are considered moral failings, as Gary's comment indicates. It was frequently noted by the models that people assume models to be narcissistic and arrogant, assumptions these young men try hard to debunk. It would seem, however, that these are particularly "feminine" failings, since many models described how they encountered female models that were arrogant and vain (or "love themselves"). Thus, it could be argued that these particular models are keen to distance themselves from any signs of narcissism, and from any possible "feminization" that may be associated with their work, by disavowing body maintenance altogether. This "laddish" attitude may therefore be a moral performance to try not to appear as "vain" or too "feminine," produced for the benefit of the interview. It may also be read as part of the models' overall performance of "masculinity," produced through denial of the overtly "feminine" aspects of the job.

However, these men may also be in denial about the attention they actually do pay to how they look, since how they look is essential to their careers as models. Although male models may not always be dieting or exercising, this does not mean they are oblivious to their appearance and do not work at it in some way. Most, if not all, models are aware of the importance of cultivating or maintaining a particular look and develop some distance from their body and the image, objectifying both as part of their career development. Of particular significance to many models, in terms of shaping a look, is hair. Many models described having their hair regularly cut at top salons in London or New York, usually for free in return for modeling. In one instance, Ben, who had very short hair when he was "discovered," had been told by his booker that he could not grow it longer since this was felt to be "working" for him at present. However, as hair trends change, canny models will adapt their hair too. Over the time I was conducting the interviews, a number of the models described how many top models in the major shows and campaigns were wearing their hair quite long. In some cases, the models said they were growing their hair to keep pace with this trend and help them get work over the summer, when the castings for major campaigns take place. Gary, for example, said, "I am growing it 'cos long hair is very in at the moment. Therefore, I think it will benefit me 'cos I'll be more versatile." Since hair is very malleable, it is one aspect of appearance that can be frequently changed as part of an ongoing process of self-promotion. When asked about how he can cultivate a look appropriate for more fashion (as opposed to commercial) work, Gary returned to the issue of hair, noting that one can transform oneself with different hairstyles: "A lot of it is to do with the hair at the moment . . . long hair is quite in at the moment. If I have hair coming over like this [pulls hair over his face] it changes the appearance completely." The aim here is to get a more weird or "edgy" fashion look, as opposed to the "clean-cut" look required for commercial work. "Edgy" is the description often given as appropriate to high fashion: it is "weird" or "quirky," as opposed to the more conventionally good looks required for commercial work.

A more radical story of self-transformation was told to me by Tony, an older, experienced model based in New York, who told me he was planning to meet with his booker the following week to totally overhaul his image: his hair, clothes, and the images in his "book" (his portfolio of images). It was, he said, a "strategic" way to separate himself from "all the other models coming through." He was considering reverting to an earlier hairstyle from a few months previously, a photograph of which he showed me, and described as "mo-ho," i.e., "mohican." The look he was aiming for was "edgy." He intended to try this look for a month for two to see if the 1980s made a return to fashion (which it did in the Fall and Spring 2000–1, although I lost track of this model and therefore do not know if this hairstyle was a success as a result).

While such changes in image may be required to renew a model who has been around for a few years, it takes quite a lot of effort and a considerable degree of commitment on the part of the model to reinvent himself so completely. Such a total overhaul demands effort not only in terms of thinking about one's image and making changes, but also in terms of the images in his "book," which also have to be changed to reflect the new look. A model's book is his main tool for self-promotion and it will contain his best jobs and strongest images. When a model starts out he will only have a few Polaroids to take to clients along with some "tests" with photographers. These give the model a chance to practice in front of the camera, try out with photographers used by the agency and to collect some images for his book. However, as a model gains valuable work experience, his book will be made up of prestigious jobs, good editorial and commercial work, and any campaigns: experienced models do not do "tests." If the model's appearance changes significantly, as in Tony's case, a whole series of new "tests" will need doing to update his book – a considerable investment in terms of time, which he was prepared to make to reinvent himself.

Such an active shaping of one's image requires the model to see his body as a commodity. The model's body is *the* commodity traded by the agency, model, and clients: a model is booked because he has the right look for the client. This point I will return to in a moment. However, important also in male modeling is "personality." Many models and bookers argued that male models must be "nice guys" – friendly, confident, and professional – if they are to become successful. A very arrogant, bad-tempered male model will not last long in a business that is so competitive. In contrast, bookers and models described how female models can get by on looks: a number of very successful female models have reputations for very bad behavior, which would not be tolerated of male models. As one booker in New York, James, put it, it is "easy enough to get a good-looking guy booked: what is harder is getting him rebooked," and this will only happen if he has shown himself to be decent and professional. James explained this discrepancy between male and female models in terms of the different values placed on male and female beauty, which has women's beauty more highly valued.[4] As this booker put it to me, guys are not meant to be "too good-looking" and should not be rewarded for it.

However, while the emphasis on "personality" is stronger in the case of male models, having the right look/body is still paramount, making modeling a quite unique occupation for men in its total focus on the body. Of course, modeling is not the only occupation in which the body is traded as part of the job: acting and dancing, as well as prostitution, are the other obvious examples. What is different about modeling is the degree of emphasis on the body: in modeling the body is the foremost object of the model's career and his identity as a model. An actor may shape his body as part of his career development, either in order to land work, or as part of his job to develop a particular character, as in the case of Brad Pitt's muscular and toned body for the film *Fight Club*, which he fashioned especially for the role. However, the acting body's appearance is part of a larger commodity transaction, namely acting ability (or celebrity), and alone is not generally enough to ensure an actor's success. Similarly, the dancer's body is a primary tool in his career but, here again, it is shaped as part of a broader concern to make it move and perform in particular ways. In both instances, the body is a body to be looked at, which may also be eroticized in the process, but this attention, and the possible libidinal excesses provoked by it, are by-products of a body that is *also doing something*.

Mulvey's (1975) classic analysis of the female body in Hollywood realist films argues that the woman's body functions primarily "to be looked at" and in ways that frequently halt the flow of the narrative to allow for erotic contemplation. Men's bodies are rarely photographed as disruptions in the narrative (although, of course, this does not mean they may not sometimes be read in this way). However, the contemporary male model's body displayed in fashion advertisements for Calvin Klein underwear and some commercial advertisements, such as the Diet Coke television advertisement (in which numerous women huddle around a window to watch a male worker outside take off his T-shirt and drink a can of Diet Coke), is a body which functions as a pure (and often erotic) image. This makes modeling a unique occupation for men and this is one reason, I argue, that it serves as a cultural marker of a new kind of masculinity, one that is more self-consciously narcissistic and erotic.

Getting models to talk about this objectification of their body was difficult, if not impossible, in some cases. Most models were quite inarticulate when it came to talking about their relationship to the body and some seemed embarrassed when asked about their images and how it feels to be looked at all the time. It is also the case that being looked at constantly becomes so taken for granted that it is not consciously reflected upon by models. The most visible and ubiquitous object, the body of the model, is everywhere, and yet it is almost impossible for models to describe what it feels like to be looked at and objectified in this way. Having said this, I suspect that for the majority of male models, the fact that their bodies, and indeed, their sexuality, are commodified is not a problem: most spoke of enjoying their work and, although pay is not nearly as high as many people imagine, they are paid well enough most of the time and get to travel to interesting places as well. Ben's comments on the commodification of his body probably speak for a good many of the models I interviewed:

I think if the money was a lot less and the images weren't so great, you would realize you were a commodity, but it's really weird because it's like, Model's 1 is using you, but you then you're using Model's 1, but then the editorials and campaigns are using you, but then you are using them because you're getting so much money off them for doing nothing, posing in front of a camera!

Sexuality at Work

Having examined the ways in which male models invest in their bodily appearance, I want to consider another important aspect of their embodiment by examining the ways they "do" masculinity through particular bodily performances in a context which, as I will argue, potentially undermines the conventions of dominant (hetero-sexual) masculinity. In contrast to increasing numbers of professional women, who must muffle their sexuality at work (see Entwistle 1997, 2000b), and other men whose sexuality is a repressed feature of their work (Collier 1998), male models are sexualized beings at work. Indeed, a model's career prospects may depend upon his ability to project sexuality at work in routine day-to-day interactions: as one model put it to me, models are often asked by a photographer to give "sex, sex, sex." Thus, male models have to adapt to a visual arena in which they are the focus of attention that can be quite desirous. Models frequently told me stories of how they were the recipients of sexual advances while at work on the part of the photographer, stylist, or other onlooker. The body of the model, exposed to the gaze of bookers, photographers, and stylists, is an erotic object. The visual arena in which they work is orchestrated predominantly by gay and bisexual men, since most of the bookers, clients, photographers, and stylists in the fashion industry are either openly gay or bisexual, or are commonly thought to be, even if they are not "out." Some of the most powerful players within fashion today, such as Calvin Klein, have a reputation as bisexual, while other big names are thought to be gay by models, even though they may have wives and children.

The role played by the homoerotic gaze in defining the codes of masculinity stretches back centuries, as George L. Mosse (1996) has suggested. Since the 1980s, gay photographers, stylists, and designers have been very much at the fore in changing representations of masculinity (Bordo 1999). The body aesthetics of fashion have served to produce gay aesthetics of the male body that have become part of mainstream commercial culture and the iconography of contemporary masculinities. Thus, while Bordo celebrates the intervention of men such as Calvin Klein for producing images that can be enjoyed by heterosexual women, frequently the look for male fashion models does not correspond to dominant ideas of heterosexual male beauty outside the world of fashion modeling: it is often young, boyish, and quite "feminine," with features such as a large mouth favored. These looks are quite different from the style of male models in commercial and "lifestyle" advertising, which favor a more conventional "masculine" look that is generally older and more ruggedly "masculine."

However, in contrast, male models are predominantly heterosexual. The majority of the models I interviewed self-identified as heterosexual in the course of the interview, referring to their sexuality in comments unsolicited from me. For example, one model told me he was only doing it "for the girls," while other models told me about their girlfriends. In a couple of interviews, the model alluded to his sexual identity through references to the gay men he encounters at work, sometimes making quite homophobic remarks (for example, telling me that they don't like "them" but have to "get on with it"). One model, Gary, summed up this situation:

> A lot of people think male models are gay. But not at all, a lot of male models are really big lads if you know what I mean: they want to go out and get laid and whatever. This is where people misinterpret it. A lot of the bookers and stylists and photographers are the gay ones, it's not the models.

The domination of gay men, and the control they have within modeling and fashion, raises interesting questions in terms of the ways in which these (largely straight) male models negotiate their masculinity in an environment where they are frequently the objects of a gay gaze. I therefore argue that male modeling is work with a "queer" dimension, and the work identity of the male model is, potentially at least, a "queer" one (Butler 1993). Modeling "queers" masculinity because of the way it confounds the conventions and expectations of dominant heterosexual masculinity. On the one hand, male models are frequently called upon to perform heterosexual masculinity through poses, gestures, and dress, in the production of images that are often hyper-masculine. On the other hand, beyond the image, references to male models as "poofs" or "poncers" (see, for example, Freedman in *Guardian*, March 5, 2002) demonstrate the assumptions people outside the fashion industry have of these men. A male model's "masculinity," defined as it is in terms of sexuality framed within the "regulatory framework" of heterosexuality, is compromised or undermined by his work identity, which is associated with homosexuality and effeminacy, and this may partly explain why so many models told me of their reluctance to tell people they model for a living. Given this, how do models handle this contradiction between gender identity and work identity? How do they manage the potential "threat" posed to their heterosexual masculinity by their work? I want to examine these questions by exploring the accounts given by models of their interactions at work, focusing on the ways in which they describe their performances in routine situations. I also want to consider the peformances of gender witnessed in my observations of models at work and in the interview. Two narratives commonly recurred in the interviews and detail two performances drawn on by models to handle their encounters with gay men at work, such as photographers or clients. Both narratives illustrate how male models are sexualized in the process of their work as models and how they respond to this accordingly.

Flirting

The first narrative concerns the way in which models interact with those they work with, especially the clients they meet at castings. I am calling this narrative "flirting" because it describes how models attempt to win over clients in order to increase their chances of landing work. Models, especially new models, spend a considerable part of their work life going to castings, where they meet clients casting for shoots or new campaigns. At any casting there may be 20, 30, or many more models, and the issue is how to stand out from the crowd. Canny or "cynical" models say they exploit their good looks and sexuality by flirting to charm clients; indeed, to make the clients "fancy" them. This inevitably means a model has to flirt with male as well as female clients, using his sexuality either by "queering" it or by overperforming heterosexuality. Simon, a London model, is one such model who is happy to flirt with clients, male and female. Indeed, he demonstrated for me in the interview how he interacts with clients at castings according to their gender. If the client is a woman he will give her a very firm handshake and throw her a direct and confident gaze. If the client is a man, he assumes that he is gay and adopts the stereotypical image of the gay man, camping up his performance, with limp wrists, fey manner, and effeminate voice. Although he claimed not to do this himself, Gary, a model in London, also described this:

GARY: Some of the guys play up to the gay thing, you know so they get the job: they go to the casting [puts on a camp voice], "oh hi, yeah," make their voice a bit higher, or whatever, be a bit kinda like that [strikes an effeminate pose]. But it's not really me to do that. If they don't like my look, you know, then they're not going to use me.

Q: So you're not going to play to it?

GARY: Yeah, of course not.

Other models similarly described how they used their good looks as a tool to charm clients, regardless of gender. James said he had no qualms about using his sexuality to get work and spoke quite openly and confidently about being comfortable with his sexuality as a commodity. Although he drew the line at nudity, as do most of the models I spoke to, often the images in a model's book will be quite sexual. On shoots models are required to act sexy by photographers and, here again, they may adopt a flirtatious performance with their photographer. In some cases, models talk about flirting with photographers, especially big names in the industry, many of whom are men reputed to be homosexual. Photographers can be very influential in promoting a new model and thus it makes sense to win them over by being sexy and flirtatious. Here, the aim is, as Simon put it to me, to "keep them guessing" as to their sexuality. While I have no observational evidence of these performances in the clients' casting or on shoots, I observed models flirting with others at the agency and also found myself on the receiving end of these flirtatious performances in the interview itself, as models would often joke and banter with me in the course of the interview.

It would seem, therefore, that flirting represents a positive adaptation by some models to the sexualized nature of their work. These men are realistic about the work and its erotic content and are not afraid of the gay gaze. This reminds me very much of David Beckham, who has appeared in some highly homoerotic shoots in magazines, such as *Arena Homme Plus* (Summer 2000), and talks of being very comfortable with the idea of himself as a gay icon.[5]

Sexual Danger

The second narrative I call "sexual danger" because it describes instances where models find themselves in sexual situations that are threatening or problematic. These situations generally occur on shoots, where models may be the recipients of unwanted erotic attention from either stylists or photographers, all of them male (although one model did describe how his booker made sexual advances). Almost all the models I spoke to have been on the receiving end of such attention and it would seem that this is accepted as an occupational hazard. Given the highly sexualized nature of the relationship between model and photographer, as well as the potentially sexual encounter between the stylist and model, it is not surprising that these situations occur. Moreover, as discussed above, there is much room for misunderstanding if models flirt or in other ways use their sexuality while on the job. Narratives of sexual danger describe what happens when the situation becomes untenable for the model. Models told me how they had been "felt up" by stylists while being dressed, or been asked to strip down or wear provocative or revealing clothes by the stylist or photographer. For example, Simon told of how he once arrived on a shoot, to be handed a set of wings and nothing else to wear. A couple of models in New York described this behavior on the part of photographers as "pushing the envelope" (pushing things a bit too far). Indeed, one model made a very particular point of complaining about the sexual advances of certain photographers, describing his anger at being asked to "play with himself" on a shoot so as to make himself semi-erect.

Sometimes these instances are contained by the model's insisting on the boundaries within which he wants to work: Simon insisted on wearing a pair of trunks and was given them. A model may also threaten to call his agency to complain if he feels the behavior is inappropriate. A more radical response came from Emanuel, a model in New York, who described how he handled the unwanted attentions of his desirous booker by punching the wall next to his head. However, sometimes the advances are made after the shoot and may be less overt, implied rather than made directly. Models told me how they handle shoots where they believe the photographer or stylist fancies them: they described imaginary telephone calls to friends in which they brag about a sexual conquest with a woman the night before, or talking to their real girlfriends. Gary described this clearly:

GARY: I've got the vibe, yeah, but I make it quite clear that, you know, if they start I just make a phone call, pretend to make a phone call to my mate sayin' "Yeah I got laid last night, gorgeous bird," and then they get the message. It happened once and I did do that yeah.

Q: What happened to make you reach for the telephone?

GARY: I was getting changed and he said, "Oh you can get changed here if you want." I don't really care, like. It was him, me, and a girl and a guy so although he wouldn't have done anything I went to the loo and just as I was coming out, he was coming in to the loo and I've noticed, I dunno, I took note that he'd gone to the toilets about five minutes before that. When I come out he's like, "Oh I'm sorry" and he kinda like brushed up against me and I am like, right, so I got on the phone.

Q: And made that call?

GARY: Yeah, yeah, I haven't been home since last night.

However, sometimes it may come down to saying something directly to the photographer. Byron described how he handled such situations either by just telling them "Look, I'm not that way inclined" or ". . . in the politest way, to fuck off." Some may go as far as to describe their distaste at these experiences, possibly to ensure that I am in no doubt over their heterosexuality. It would seem, therefore, that models manage these situations by overperforming heterosexuality, in an attempt to reassert their masculine heterosexual identity.

These two narratives may be told by the same model in some form or another: in other words, models may be happy to flirt at work but may also describe situations where the sexual nature of the inter-action goes far beyond anything they feel comfortable with. In these situations they may switch from a "queer" performance to one in which they reassert their heterosexual masculinity. In this way, these performances describe two strategies used by models which, in the case of the first narrative, demonstrate how far removed modeling is from more conventional masculine occupations which do not routinely involve heterosexual men flirting with gay men. However, the second narrative demonstrates how the sexuality of modeling can sometimes threaten a model's heterosexuality, which is reclaimed by overperforming it.

Conclusion

To conclude, I have noted how modeling has opened up to men in recent years, affording some young men the opportunity to undertake work that has previously been regarded as "feminine." It is work that highlights some important directions within contemporary culture that have taken mainstream masculinity into spheres of activity, in this case new forms of work, which are unconventional and which challenge the straitjacket of conventional white masculinity. It is work that has white, heterosexual men sexualized and commodified in ways that have been associated with women, and to some extent with gay and black men. In addition, it is work which demands men to be sexual beings at work and places them at the center of attention as erotic objects. Through analysis of the various strategies of embodiment employed by male models, I have argued that these men have to adapt to a habitus which has traditionally been both "feminine" and "queer." This work is not without its problems and contradictions and heterosexual masculinity may be reasserted or overperformed in some situations. Being a male model may involve greater investment in how the body looks, although this investment is often downplayed or disavowed by models, especially those working in London. It would seem that, for some models at least, appearing to care about your appearance is still taboo: either unmanly or too arrogant. It is also the case that while this work has extended or challenged, to some extent, the dimensions of dominant heteorosexual masculinity, this asserts itself through the ways in which many models perform their identities while at work, with clients, photographers in particular, and especially with regard to gay men with whom they routinely work.

Notes

1 Evidence of this was provided by model agencies, who said they represented significantly more male models in the late 1990s than previously.
2 For example, Beckham is famous for changing his hairstyle (first to a skinhead in 2000 then a mohican in Summer 2001) and this always attracts the attention of the press, who see it as evidence of his vanity. See C. Porter, "A Cut Above," *Guardian*, May 25, 2001 for a discussion.
3 There are a number of distinctions between fashion models used in fashion shows and campaigns, such as Versace or Calvin Klein, and commerical or "lifestyle" models, for furniture, beer, and the other commodities. Fashion

modeling uses very young models (teens to early 20s) and some of these may be described as "edgy," i.e., unusual or distinctive. Commercial models are older (late 20s–30s or 40s) and may be more conventionally "good-looking." Fashion models may cross over into commercial work, especially as they get older, but commercial models generally do not do fashion. This project is based on interviews with fashion models.

4 These values are reflected in pay. Modeling represents one of the few occupations where women are paid significantly more than men (pornography is another). A standard commercial day rate for women starts around £5000, while shows pay between £5000 and £20,000. The figures for men are closer to £2000 for commercial work and a few hundred to perhaps £1000 for a show appearance.

5 See *OK!* issue 228, September 2000.

References

Berger, J. (1972) *Ways of Seeing.* Harmondsworth: Penguin.

Bordo, S. (1999) *The Male Body: A New Look at Men in Public and in Private.* New York: Farrar, Straus and Giroux.

Bourdieu, P. (1984) *Distinction: A Social Critique of the Judgement of Taste.* Cambridge, MA: Harvard University Press.

Butler, J. (1990) *Gender Trouble: Feminism and the Subversion of Identity.* London: Routledge.

Butler, J. (1993) *Bodies That Matter.* London: Routledge.

Collier, R. (1998) "'Nutty Professors,' 'Men in Suits' and 'New Entrepreneurs': Corporeality, Subjectivity and Change in the Law School and Legal Practice," *Social and Legal Studies* **7**, 1: 27–53.

Easton Ellis, B. (1998) *Glamorama.* New York: Pimlico Books.

Entwistle, J. (1997) "Power Dressing and the Fashioning of the Career Woman," in M. Nava, I. MacRury, A. Blake, and B. Richards (eds.), *Buy this Book: Studies in Advertising and Consumption.* London: Routledge.

Entwistle, J. (2000a) "Fashion and the Fleshy Body: Dress as Situated Practice," *Fashion Theory: Dress, Body and Culture* 3, 4: 323–48.

Entwistle, J. (2000b) "Fashioning the Career Woman: Power Dressing as a Strategy of Consumption," in M. Talbot and M. Andrews (eds.), *All the World and Her Husband: Women and Consumption in the Twentieth Century.* London: Cassell.

Entwistle, J. (forthcoming) "The Aesthetic Economy: Fashion Modelling and the Production of Value in the Field of Cultural Production," *Journal of Consumer Culture.*

Freedman, H. (2002) "Hello Girls," *Guardian*, March 5, London.

Gatens, M. (1996) *Imaginary Bodies: Ethics, Power and Corporealities.* London: Routledge.

Gill, R., Henwood, K., et al. (2000) "The Tyranny of the 'Six-Pack'? Under-standing Men's Responses to Representations of the Male Body in Popular Culture," in C. Squire (ed.), *Culture in Psychology*. London: Routledge.

Mort, F. (1996) *Cultures of Consumption: Masculinities and Social Space in Late Twentieth-Century Britain*. London: Routledge.

Mosse, G.L. (1996) *The Images of Man*. Oxford: Oxford University Press.

Mulvey, L. (1975) "Visual Pleasure and Narrative Cinema," *Screen* 16, 3: 6–18.

Nixon, S. (1996) *Hard Looks: Masculinities, Spectatorship and Contemporary Consumption*. London: UCL Press.

Porter, C. (2001) "'A Cut Above,'" *Guardian*, May 25.

Chapter 3

Reading Racialized Bodies: Learning to See Difference

Suki Ali

Introduction: Does "Race" Matter?

It don't matter if you're black or white.

Michael Jackson

Is Michael Jackson black or white?
Joshua, aged 10

Throughout the 1980s and 1990s there have been significant changes in the configuration of "race." Western histories of "race" show how the body has borne the burden of "race," and how it continues to be the site for struggles over control and containment of racialized divisions in societies. "Race" is inevitably lived and experienced through the body. The border of self and other, between internal and external – the skin – has been one of the most tenacious markers of "race" throughout western history. Skin is the visible reflection of raced ideologies, the mutable surface of the "racialized self." In spite of the academic rejection of the biological "truth" of "race" based on phenotypes, the *ideas* of the corporeality of "race" still provide the basis for social tensions in everyday life.

The concept of "race" invokes, as a counterpart, specific and responsive forms of "racism" and is one of the most persuasive examples of Foucauldian discourse operating in contemporary British society. Foucault suggests that "regimes of truth" arise through power/knowledge matrices, that discourses speak of a rule and that "the code they come to define is not that of law but that of normalisation" (Foucault 1980: 106). The process of the discursive normalization of raced difference is a result of responsive, situated regimes of truth about "race."

In order to foreground the dynamic and contingent nature of these terms as they relate to raced embodiment, I will use the term "racialization." Miles suggests that racialization is:

> a dialectical process by which meaning is attributed to particular biological features of human beings as a result of which individuals may be assigned to a general category of persons which reproduces itself biologically. (Miles 1989: 76)

It is this process of racialization, attached to the expression of ethnic, national, and cultural distinctions, that contemporary readings of bodies illuminate. It is also indicative of the ways in which certain "preferred readings" (Hall 1993) come to be more or less powerful in the constitution of individual dis/identifications. This chapter looks at the "signs" of "race" as read from the body.

> In fact, it is already one of the prime effects of power that certain bodies, certain gestures, certain discourses, certain desires come to be identified and constituted as individuals. (Foucault 1980: 98)

By investigating the taken-for-granted processes of reading bodies, we can perhaps learn how to break the stranglehold of the dominance of visible "race," as it appears to (form) individuals and groups. Despite (or it may be because of) the idea that all visualizations of raced bodies have to be learned and discursively re/produced, it is in the so-called ruptures and disjunctures between the dominant and counter-readings of embodied raciality that space for change can be created.

Using data from an ethnographic study,[1] this chapter shows the ways in which young children (aged 8–11) are negotiating their own and others' racialization through readings of bodies in popular culture. The processes by which children choose their terminologies as they work through their readings reveal the mechanisms which enable normalizing discourses of racialization. Children in the study show the evasive and arbitrary meanings attached to interlocking terminologies of "race," ethnicity, and culture as they are used in everyday cultural contexts. These terms are notoriously problematic, and it was essential that some shared meanings were established between the children and myself. In using popular culture and images of contemporary "stars," I facilitated discussion of the terms to be used, especially "mixed race." The results of this part of the research were both illuminating and perplexing on many levels.

The children in the study were all "learning" how to read "race" through their social relations both inside and outside the school environment. Within the schools, children created shared social spaces through their collective re/readings of the popular (see Ali 2002; de Block 2000). In so doing they also began to work through complex interpretations of racialized bodies and style. By asking children about popular culture, I discovered some of the ways they began to form associations of visible markers of "race" with ideas about nation and ethnicity, as well as some more interesting and unexpected links between gendered style, sexuality, and attractiveness. The readings of "race" were all inflected with children's attempts to develop within frames of normative, gendered heterosexuality, and with the "regulatory schemas that produce intelligible morphological possibilities" (Butler 1993: 14). The regulatory matrices of (heterosexed) gender are also constitutive of the intelligibility of racial distinctions. In learning to read "race" children are also learning to read gender and sexuality, and are challenging the dominant discourses of "beauty standards" that are inflected with raciality. Contrary to the discourses that stress the "centrality of whiteness," children showed themselves to be forming identifications that avoided simple racial hierarchies in appearance.

Changing "Race"

Many of those who work in the social sciences have argued for some time that the forms that racism takes have to be understood as contingent in order for there to be any hope of countering it. It is not the purpose of this paper to rehearse the arguments in any detail here: texts such as the excellent work by Solomos and Back (1995) deal with these debates in detail (see also Goldberg 1990 and Mac an Ghaill 1999 for overviews). It is also important to note that this paper is set within British frameworks, which are distinct from those in other locations, having specific intellectual, historical, and material trajectories. Combating discrimination and inequality has therefore to be situated within a framework of multiply figured projects that challenge the discursive registers that continue to produce and authorize them. "Anti-racist" work then has moved through a series of conceptual and organizational shifts. Of these, three are important to this paper: the rise and fall of "identity politics" in the 1980s; the increasing use of the term "ethnicity," especially new ethnicities, and finally, development of analyses of "new racism" and ethnocentrism.

These three are, of course, interlinked, and the strands of intellectual and community activity that hold them together are what might be loosely termed as ongoing engagements with "the politics of race." Briefly, the politics of racial activism that gave rise to political struggle based upon "racially authentic" blackness and Asianness gave way in the early 1990s to a call for a more inclusive understanding of racism. The "new racism" of the late 1980s was as likely to be based on ethnic and cultural differences as it was on skin color, and the work of academics was to understand the ways in which ethnicities themselves become racialized (Anthias and Yuval-Davis 1992). For Anthias and Yuval-Davis (1992) all analyses of "race" should be conducted on the axis of ethnicity, and are always classed and gendered. One example of this "new racism" that mobilizes different kinds of "difference" can be identified in the rise of "Islamophobia" and increasing demonization of Muslims:[2]

> it is quite possible that we shall witness in the next few decades an increasing deracialisation of, say, culturally assimilated Afro-Caribbeans and Asians, along with, *simultaneously*, a racialisation of other culturally "different" Asians, Arabs, and non-white Muslims. (Modood 2000: 164)

Prejudices come in many forms, and a simplistic notion of, for example, blackness, failed the stated political project of countering all kinds of racism, in that it diminished the impact of the heterogeneity of black populations in Britain.* In addition, "black community/ies" found themselves digressing into disputes over inclusiveness and authenticity. From the early 1990s, there has been a rise in studies into "whiteness," with a commitment to taking the ethnic inevitabilities out of the term "British." From the recognition that "there ain't no black in the Union Jack" (Gilroy 1987) to the development of theories of "new ethnicities" (Hall 1992), the mundane and extraordinary experiences of being British have been reformulated as ethnically and culturally diverse.

---

* For the most part I do not capitalize the terms "black" and "white." I do occasionally use capitals to indicate a particular commitment to politicize the term or where I quote others who use capitals.

In social and cultural studies, we witness ongoing attempts to develop more nuanced theorizations of what becoming racialized involves, and an increasing interest in postraciality; what might be termed a deconstruction of "race." Gilroy (2000) has controversially called for a "planetary humanism" and an end to the ultracertainty of "race." In a recent lecture, he suggested that we should look to the future in the everyday multiethnic urban sites where "race" is already "ordinary and mundane" (Gilroy 2002). His choice of terms is strikingly similar yet markedly different to those written above for this chapter, some weeks before his lecture. This research shows how the minutiae of these existences are not "beyond" raciality, nor is this simply "race" as "ordinary," existing in an unremarkable form of mixedness. With frequent and depressing (read mundane) regularity, incidences of racism are reported across Britain (and elsewhere). In urban areas, racism is no longer the domain of whites only. We are told of black-on-white, Asian-on-white, black-on-Asian attacks, which in some cases have resulted in full-scale violent protest. All kinds of "black on black" violence have been a particular cause for concern in urban environments. Whether or not these incidents are racially or ethnically motivated hate crimes, the fact that young people are increasingly involved in them shows the insidious nature of antagonistic identifications, in these "ordinary" sites. It is both the *problems* as well as *potential* pleasures of multiethnic and "multiracial" living that are ordinary.

Nowhere are these struggles more obvious than in the micro-environment of schools. Rattansi (1992) argues that there have been two main strands to educational, teaching, and activist approaches to "race" in Britain throughout the 1980s and into the 1990s. He conceptualizes them both as essentialist. First, he identifies multiculturalism, as an "additive model." From this position one can see that there are many cultures within society and one should learn about them and respect them all. The focus here is on "culture" not "race," which he calls a form of ethnic essentialism (ibid.: 39). Secondly, he cites "anti-racist" approaches, which disallow heterogeneity amongst groups and try to maintain a "black community" struggle, a "reification of community." This latter position tends to marginalize groups that do not fit into such a category easily: he mentions Greeks, Turks, Jews, and Irish positions (ibid.: 40). In the late 1990s there were calls for "intercultural education" as a means of countering such essentializing tendencies (Gundara 2000). It was obvious that one of the key influences on children's understandings of "race" would come from the school, not only through the formal curriculum, but also through the work that children undertake within their relationship cultures in the informal spaces in schools.

Even a cursory glance at much of the literature on multicultural-ism in schools reveals the kind of containment approaches Rattansi identifies. From the "saris, samosas and steel bands" approach, to "show and tell" kinds of "tolerance," to the decision to include discussions about racism in aspects of Personal, Social and Health Education, the common understandings of "race," ethnicity, and culture were often entangled with a range of other school discipline issues (Ali 2000). Despite an ongoing concern with "bullying" of all kinds, none of the schools included in the study had a clear idea of the perceptions *children* had of specifically racial matters.

The children's own accounts were heavily influenced by locatedness.[3] In multiethnic areas, racism based upon very crude markers of phys-ical difference – that is, the commonsense version of physical "race" – was an everyday part of their lives. This is not to say that they did not draw on those other "Othering" differences connected with ethnicity – such as language, religion, dress, food, and so on – just that they privileged "color" in the first instance. Crucially, in the mainly white, semi-rural school, Fairsham, the concepts of "race" and racism were mediated through consumption of television and radio. For children, the terminologies of "race" were often learned, then, from the media; thus the visualization of "race" as embodied was also part of the media experience.

Popular culture, consumption, and globalizing media are currently the source of many of the anxieties about "childhood." Whether con-tributing to "the disappearance of childhood" (Postman 1994), to the cautious optimism of the freedoms that media can bring for children (Buckingham 2000), there is no doubt that children are increasingly immersed in the consumption of images and signs, which are there-fore sources of learning about their social world (Kenway and Bullen 2001). It was upon this basis that the work of trying to understand children's perceptions of "race" as visible difference, often related to the color of skin, proceeded.

"We're all the Same under our Skin"

[T]he skin marks and polices the boundary between inside and outside. It is a boundary that guarantees a separation.

Ahmed 2000: 45

A significant finding was that there was a distinction between comprehension of the terms "race" and racism, and how this is influenced by location. In inner-London schools, where the pupils came from a range of ethnic backgrounds, the term "racism" was often understood immediately. But even those who knew what this entailed, hesitated when it came to "race." Only the most politicized children could easily answer this question. One of the key prompts, which seemed to have the most successful answers, was to invoke the term "the human race." Despite little "diversity" within their social geographies even the children in Years 5 and 6 at Fairsham could respond to this idea, having been taught it during their lessons. In one conversation with the only South Asian girl within Fairsham, she responded that there were different "races" within the "human race" like Chinese, black, and so on. She suggested that this had been discussed in class, but I did not corroborate this with her teachers.

For children, "race" was both a fact of life, and a fiction that they knew to be untenable, a very complicated matter of bodies. Asked about the meaning of "race," responses ranged from "it's something you run in" (Fairsham) to the more sophisticated, which incorporated some notion of kinship and cultural and national heritage. The single most commonly held idea across all locations and ages was that "race" was about "the color of your skin." In addition, however, they argued that although we are all separated by our skin color, that was no reason for racism because we are also all the same inside. This contradiction of the body – different on the outside, same on the inside – was held in place by all the children throughout. The skin in this case is indeed a site, a border, a boundary which needs policing. Its ambiguous role in the maintenance of separations is a source of confusion and certainty.

Quoting her class teacher, Maria's words are rather graphic, but show this logic in action:

> [My teacher] said that it doesn't matter what color you are, that you're all equal and all the same, in different ways. That you're different in different ways, that if you were to cut someone in half, um, if you were to cut two people in half they'd be exactly the same. (Maria: May 1998)

For Maria, the surface skin of the body may imply confusing difference, but it contains the sameness of the "human." In this formulation, the borders and boundaries are unimportant compared with the interiors.

Skin, then, betrays at all turns and requires narrative interventions such as biographic details in order to make sense of it and this will be explored below (see Ali 2000; Bell 1996). Skin is indeed a site of the materialization of "race" and as such is paradoxically often in a state of flux, requiring fixity in order to make sense of it (Butler 1993). Seeing skin as the source of "race" is a process which involves an understanding of the significance of skin color to collective identities; as the boundary not only of self to other, but also between and within "us" and "them," as shown in the readings made by the children.

In/visible "Race" and Nation

If we are to understand how ethnicities and cultures are racialized we have to consider the ways in which they become visualized, not only as bodies but also within broader social contexts of cultural expression. In contemporary culture, it is argued that we are now in an age of dynamic translation and syncretism. There are no true original and pure cultures; rather there are creative fusions that provide endlessly new forms of expression. In addition to this, we are living in a period of heightened visibility in which "human experience is now more visual and visualized than ever before" (Mirzoeff 2002: 4). For many children, learning and leisure are dominated by the visual media.

In mainly white areas, children often learned about racial distinctions via visual media. In an area with few minority ethnic families, they rarely encountered diversity in their town, and as a result many of them told me that they learned about "race" from the news. During some of the data collection there was a great deal of publicity surrounding the first attempted trial of the defendants in the murder of Stephen Lawrence, and this was a source of discussion in some homes. In a more opaque example, a boy aged ten (Giles), told how he had learned about racism in a comedy program. This program was under fire for reinforcing anti-Irish prejudices, featuring as it did three Irish Catholic priests. In the episode he described, the main character was accused of being "racist." In a "comedy of errors" he had offended the local Chinese community. The humor was doubled, as the priests' own ignorance and stereotyping were as profound as that which they directed toward the Chinese people. For Giles this was a key source of learning about the term "racist." He saw this as straightforward, despite the intended ironies of the script. The expressions of difference in the program were based on a range of visual cues about "race," and relayed through what is perceived as a dominantly visual medium.

In addition to this kind of televisual encounter, one of the chief sources of "edutainment" for these white middle-class children was the experience of popular music. In this they are no different from any number of others, including those from multiethnic areas (see for example, Bazalgette and Buckingham 1995). In British youth culture, the dominance of African-American musical forms has been noted by a number of writers (Back 1996; Frith 1996; Gilroy 1993b). It would appear that the same is true for the preadolescent age group. In one session, a group of white middle-class boys discussed the fact that not only were all the best runners black but that "all the blacks were American." They later qualified this by saying that the vast majority of people they encountered in popular culture who were black, were also American. The powerful allure of the glamour industries, which now extend to sporting arenas, was evident in all areas of their relationship cultures, and it was these areas that provided more detailed information on the reading of racial bodies.

So far the discussion has revealed that for the children in this study, "race" still matters. For those in inner-city, multiethnic areas it is part of the struggles of identification in everyday life. What became clear very quickly was the importance of bodies to the understanding of "race," which required a more detailed reading of how children actually learned the codes that imposed racialized meanings upon bodies and style, and the relationship between terminology and visual codes. One of the main reasons for investigating the terminologies used in racialization processes was that the ambiguities of occupying "mixed" positions are impossible to articulate other than through the list of "comma-ed" factors that include "race," nationality, and kinship affiliations. The research into these multiply held affiliations framed a question through the readings of popular culture about "who is raced by whom: who can be identified, which bodies are intelligible?"

Who is Scary?

Reading the visible in "race" was difficult for children, and reading the ambiguous and unstable mixedness of people such as Scary Spice was a rich source of information on the workings of the regimes of truth that produce coherent narratives of "race." At the time of data collection, the Spice Girls were just at the end of their reign as the queens of "Girl Power." Like other major stars of the teens and pre-teens, they provoked responses of absolute extremes amongst children, who were either fans or "anti." Melanie Brown (or Mel B a.k.a Scary Spice) was particularly famous for being one of the most flamboyant in the already over-the-top personas projected. "Scary Spice" spent much of her time cultivating her larger-than-life personality through her style and behavior. The band were all "white" apart from Scary, who named herself as black, whilst openly discussing the fact of her "mixed parentage." The group was never out of the papers or off the television, and Mel B had been on several television programs, including *Black Britain* (BBC 1998), talking about her "mixed race" identity which came, she said, from her having one black Jamaican parent and one white British parent. She was one of the prominent "mixed" figures the children were asked to discuss.

Asking for descriptions of Scary generally invoked responses about her appearance but not necessarily about her skin color, or "race." They did see her as raced, but did not say this unless I asked about it. In fact, one of the most significant findings was that children did not focus on "race" as a *primary* source of identification in their readings – they drew upon a range of resources, visual, verbal, and cultural. Stuart Hall has argued that it is not where we come from but where we are going that is important when thinking about the move from theorizing identities to thinking through identification (Hall 1996). In the case of children between eight and 11 years old, it would appear that "where you come from" matters more than where you are going. To make sense of the ways in which they did make (raced) identifications, I resorted to using the terminologies, including the language of "where you come from," that they had used with me in other areas of conversation. In order to work out "race," questions of heritage, family, nationality, and location were all raised to varying degrees by all children.

In this example, Dawud [D], Raizal [R](both South Asian), and Aaron [A](Zairean), three boys in Year 6 at Barnlea School in London, work through their understanding of Scary in ways that are very typical of the form of many of the interviews:

S[SUKI]:   How would you describe Scary Spice?
D: She's kind of scary and she's got her tongue pierced and everything.
S: Do you know anything about her background? Could you describe it?
R: She's black.

D:	She's kinda weird.
	[someone unidentified says "crazy"]
S:	Could you describe her family?
A:	Er . . . Her Mum's white and I think her Dad's white too.
S:	So you think both her parents are white?
A:	Yes.
S:	So how is she black then?
R:	'Cos her Mum is white and her Dad is black.
S:	Have you heard of the expression "mixed race"?
D:	Yeah, I knew she was "mixed race" 'cos of her skin color . . .
S:	Because of her skin color, is that how you can tell if some-one is "mixed race"?
R:	No.
A:	No.
S:	So it's quite confusing as to how you would tell?

In this conversation, the children begin by drawing on what they consider to be the most interesting and salient features of Scary – that she is indeed "scary" and this is in part to do with the fact that she has her tongue pierced. In response to a question about her "background," which is often code for "family," or "nationality," one of the boys responds by describing her as racialized – "black" – whilst another perseveres with the "weird" theme, which may be an obtuse reference to her not being black or white, or a continuing reading of her "unnaturally" boisterous and flamboyant persona. At this point, I began to guide the children to talk more about her racialization through her family in order to understand what they meant by both aspects of her appearance that were so interesting to them. However, their problems with identification came from the limited information they had about her. In order to make her "racially" intelligible, the children needed to narrativize her family history.

Having described both of her parents as "white," Aaron had to back-track in order to agree with his friend that she was, after all, black. The two possibilities were incommensurate. However, the revelation of her mixedness seemed to be a satisfactory resolution to her (visually) uncertain ethnicity and ambiguous "race." For the knowledgeable Dawud a hint of superiority accompanied his revelation that he had known that Scary was "mixed race" because of her skin color. This is such a common way of thinking of white/black mixed-race positions that, in one school, the Acting Head had walked along a corridor look-ing into classrooms to see which contained children who would fulfill the research focus! It is no wonder that these young children were also learning that "brown skin" meant "mixed." What was more surprising was that they could also know when asked if this was always true, that it was, paradoxically, a useless way of trying to categorize someone, given the other possible meanings attached to "brownness."

The research has shown that children do see "race" as important, yet also in certain situations unremarkable; thus it was never the *first* way to describe a person. If asked about "race" directly, children could show how it was signified and the attendant difficulties in fixing people such as Scary Spice into a raced position. Although there is a recognition of this difficulty, children can do this only by using the limited terminologies available, and by drawing on narratives about individuals. Despite evidence of multiplicity and syncretism in their cultural experience, the "race" of a person still determines skin color, and vice versa. So children show some evidence of "postracial" thinking, where race is too mundane to mention, but the relentless need for fixing people into categories which include "race" means that they struggle to learn how terminologies relate to seeing ambiguities in "race."

Beauty is in the Eye

What these children were working through is common to the everyday experiences of people dealing with the ubiquity of raciality: that is, its manifestation, its materialization as embodied, despite attempts to reduce its (negative) impact in society. The ways in which this is part of the *gendering* processes of identification was central to the way children talked about seeing "race." In addition, the value attached to gendered "racial" markers became more evident throughout the research. If racism is the expression of superiority and inferiority, it is simultaneously the expression of gendered discourses. Again, the processes of visualization are central to these debates.

Despite the dominance of a syncretic form of African-American "cool" in the youth scene and amongst the youth-wannabes, who were the subjects of the research, there was a significant finding which forces us to reconsider the ways in which "whiteness" is held as a beauty norm, along with the resistances to such a norm as found in research into monoracial (*sic*) positions. It is a commonly held belief that white femininities are the (beauty) standard against which all others are held: they are the norm and all others are more or less deviant from them. These kinds of femininities are expressed as physical characteristics but also reflect behavioral characteristics that

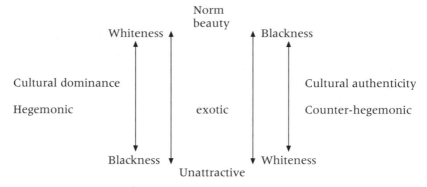

Figure 3.1 Normative racialized beauty standards

are somehow held within the whole that is the embodied persona. There is nothing new about this kind of visual categorization; in fact femininities have been constructed through comparisons of embodied characteristics since the processes of classifying humans gained ascendancy during the eighteenth and nineteenth centuries. Madness, criminality, lewdness, and hysteria could all be detected through studying both physiognomy and demeanor (e.g. Gilman 1992; Showalter 1987). Femininity and heterosexuality are linked in the realm of attractiveness; "beauty is as beauty does."

Conventional studies of racialized beauty standards produce results which I suggest form a constraining continuum for both conventional *and* so-called counter-hegemonic readings (see figure 3.1).

For authors investigating such issues there are a number of reasons for the operation of these norms and how they are mediated through bodies. In the mid-range of skin tone femininities take on a vague form of indeterminate exoticism. Skin color, hair texture, facial features, such as thickness of nose and fullness of lips, are invoked as the markers of blackness.[4] Debbie Weekes (1997) studied the attitudes of young "Black" women between the ages of 14 and 16 years old to beauty and attractiveness.[5] Her findings showed practices of exclusion by those of darker skin against those with paler skin and more European features, including those of "mixed parentage." She argues that the discourses of "colorism" and "essentialism" have become intricately woven, resulting in a form of essentializing as a means of claiming a position of power in the face of the normative standard of European beauty (Weekes 1997: 122). Young women appear to be resorting to such narrow "definitions of Blackness" as a form of strategic essentialism, which is a result of the construction of "Whiteness as the yardstick by which beauty is judged" (Weekes 1997: 124). Cultural representations of selves and readings of bodies and images in popular culture are validated through authenticating racialized biographies. Whilst recognizing the validity of this position, I would argue for another interpretation of it.

In common with the other theoretical works cited above, Weekes's analysis leaves us with no room to explore "the Thing" (ibid.) that "does" the constructing, despite a desire to reclaim the work of the young women as active responses to cultural hegemony. As Butler (1993) suggests, in taking this position, discourse becomes the subject of the sentence, and in the process creates the passive object. The tension between activity and passivity within a knowing subject is one that plagues discussions of racialization and Othering processes in general. The analysis of representations of blackness by writers such as bell hooks (1991) holds to and, I would argue, *reinforces* the "centrality of whiteness" position. hooks's use of the terms "black folks" and "brown folks," who often become "nearly white," in her analysis of the British film *Sammy and Rosie Get Laid*, authorizes and even reinforces the hierarchical additive models of racialized oppression. In her account, the only worthy folks are black and those who are brown inhabit a twilight zone of disidentification and inauthenticity, resulting in their alignment with the dominant whites. Whether this is a matter of choice or the fault of the filmmakers is unclear, the illegitimacy of the position is stressed regardless of intention. This research set out to investigate whether such sentiments are witnessed in daily life or if children were exploring resistances and subversions to such hierarchies in their cultural practices, whether knowingly or not.

Pretty Nice, Ugly Nasty

It's that blacker-than-thou mentality you have to face, that's the reality of a Woman of Colour.
        Julietta Hearne, cited in Mason-John and Khambatta 1993: 34

One of the phases of the research was to ask children about who they thought was attractive, both in personality and appearance. The purpose was to assess the relevance of both the "blacker-than-thou mentality," and the "blonde is beautiful and best" discourse and whether it affected choice of identifications. The answers were wide-ranging, children selecting favorites from people who were known personally as well as the more familiar "pin-ups" from the popular. It became clear from the outset that there was a common stated concern with the visibility of character as a form of beauty. Thus children were almost unanimously concerned with connecting the two. Those who were pretty were also nice, those ugly also nasty.[6] Unlike other studies, as above, the children were using the markers of beauty and attractiveness that *traversed* racialized categorization and identification. This may not be "postracial" thinking but is certainly not a hegemonic form of racialization.

The conversation below is typical of many I had. Both Leila and Sima were bright and articulate middle-class children of "mixed" (black Jamaican/white English and Asian Chinese/white Scottish) backgrounds. When talking about who they would like to meet and who displayed good humor and a "fun" character, Scary Spice (Mel B) came up again:

> SI: That's who I was thinking of, 'cos she seems like a really good person to know and she's not like all in love with herself.
>
> L: Yeah, she helps people. Like Diana she helped people but unfortunately she died, boo hoo.

Sima in particular is very concerned with people being "nice to know" and here Leila elevates Scary to the role of the pseudo-saint on the same level as Princess Diana, whom they both decided was a "really nice person." The idea that Scary is "nice" in turn makes her a good person with a desire to help others. This is in stark contrast to the imagery of wild sexiness she worked to cultivate on television, or the weird, crazy woman described in the first extract. Seeing Scary as mad, bad, or sexy was one of the ways children read her as raced.

A group of (self-named) black Caribbean and British children aged ten to 11, both boys and girls, spent much of the time in their taped video session ridiculing the Spice Girls, including Scary, insisting that they were the "ugliest group on the planet" – so much so, they considered them to look like "aliens." This view of the Spice Girls was by no means limited to the children who identified as "black." Conversely, the liking of African-American artists such as Will Smith crossed all boundaries of class and location.

The positions are obviously intricately tied to "taste" and taste itself is, of course, highly culturally inflected. Kenway and Bullen argue that "cultivating the fine distinctions of 'taste' is a disciplined and difficult educational process" with which children must engage (Kenway and Bullen 2001: 18). Within Cultural Studies, taste has been linked to a sense of style, and style has in turn been used to categorize people into dominant cultural and subcultural groups. Style is one of the greatest arbiters of taste, and within popular culture and popular music in particular, the cross-over between style, appearance, and musical content is inseparable (Hebdige 1979). In the words of the children, style and appearance provide a clear correlation with character and often a strict form of morality at odds with their inevitable curiosity and explorations of hetero/sexuality. Complexity was shown in the array of readings that could come from the same image, and, more importantly, how they defied neat forms of (racialized) cultural identification.

None of the female artists escaped sexualization and yet again the Spice Girls provided a fine example of this. The young women in the group were carefully manufactured to embrace and display a range of femininities. At the time of the research they presented their images in line with their nicknames at many of their major appearances: Sporty in gymwear, Baby in pink gingham with her hair in bunches, and so on. Yet just as Scary could be read as ultra-"masculine" and "nasty" as well as "good fun" by children occupying a range of ethnic positions, so too could the "white" women in the group, such as Baby Spice.

Cain (Anglo/Turkish) and Jamal (African Asian/black African), aged nine and eight years old respectively, were friends at an inner-city London school. Both of these boys thought that Baby Spice, Emma Bunton, was "very pretty" and chose her as their favorite person, as well as their most attractive female. They clearly read her style in a wholly unproblematic way. Baby wore short "feminine" low-cut dresses, a lot of pale pink gingham and frequently had her long blonde hair in two bunches to make her look young; hence "Baby." For these boys she was "nice" and "sweet" as well, despite the fact that she wore clothes that were just as revealing as those of Scary. Her style was, in fact, a form of "hyper-femininity," which distorts and exaggerates the fetishes of young female sexuality through a middle-aged white male gaze. It is clear that for these boys the readings were multilayered and informed by heterosexualized gender aspirations which read Baby as cute, unproblematically feminine, infantilized, and sexy, and Scary as scary "masculine," that is, independent and assertive – and therefore of necessity unsexy.

These readings show such a heterogeneity as to defy recourse to a "dominant" position, a preferred reading, and are certainly *not* linked to strict forms of racialized identification. Neither do they privilege either whiteness or blackness.[7] Some children showed a preference for black music and stars, knowing it has a kind of authenticating kudos; however, the majority of children chose to idealize an array of people. It is therefore not possible to argue that the children are simply valorizing blackness in opposition to whiteness, or vice versa. However, although they could think through "coffee-colored," they were clear that they did not recognize other minority groups in music.[8] The children were in this sense locked into the binaries of black/white thinking without using them in simplistic linear continuums, as expressed in the diagram above. In relinquishing straightforward identifications, yet finding themselves working within representational straitjackets in the arena of popular music, they reveal many of the ways in which the processes of normative racialization work.

There appears to be a greater degree of freedom for children at this age than for those who reach the adolescent minefield of sexual and cultural "maturity" in social relations. Many people have detailed the ways in which claims to cultural authenticity often mask a form of racialization in music.[9] Children in all locations used their re/readings of popular culture to negotiate friendships based on a form of expert knowledge of their chosen favorites (Ali 2002). They were less invested in the process of authorizing their own "racialized" positions through their readings of others in the media and so were able to read across lines of racialization.

Conclusions: Believing is Seeing

> *Power operates for Foucault in the* constitution *of the very materiality of the subject, in the principle which simultaneously forms and regulates the "subject" of subjectivation.*
>
> Butler 1993: 24, original emphasis

The move to eradicate the compulsion of "race" continues in the academy. Meanwhile, empirical studies show that the conceptual frameworks that create the conditions for visualizing difference still revolve around the crudest of embodied racialized characteristics. Despite the attempt to reduce the levels of ocularcentrism in everyday life, children in this study show that they are central to them in their processes of identification. What they also show, however, is that whilst some of the most obvious kinds of visual associations are being made between, for example, skin color and "race," there are as many doubts and creative rereadings that challenge the hegemonic ideas of racialized beauty and attractiveness and the dominance of "white is best" in racist discourse. The children are clearly showing the tensions between the erroneous yet tenacious notion of "race" as an ontological certainty – something that one simply is – and the processes of embodied and encultured racialization into which they are interpellated. Interestingly, they do this by resorting to visualizing character, but also do this through creative readings of bodies and style.

The implications are clear. Racialization processes are normative and, within a few years, children will be approaching the age of "youth culture," when their resistances and subversions will take far more conventional and predictable turns. It appears that at this age children feel free to experiment with the logics of visibility in order to make sense of their everyday world. Pop stars can be nasty, nice, ugly, and pretty all within the same reading. In the examples above, "race" was not the *first* way to assess a person. The children are already part of the matrices of subjectivation that are materializing racialized bodies. In their attempts to "read" correctly, to make sense of nonviable or unintelligible bodies (Butler 1993), they help to make such processes transparent. It is surely a moment at which potential changes to the associations of "race" and power can be challenged.

Much of the writing on childhood argues for placing the voices of children themselves at the heart of the work. In this aspect of the research the children are showing how it is possible to maintain contradictory readings quite comfortably. However, children are not able to "authorize" their own accounts and so are forced back into the normalizing frameworks. I do not claim the "authority" to authorize their accounts for them, but suggest they are important and informative. The power which is attached to the "truth" of "race" is not fixed and so leaves space for their creative insertions, even in the face of the all-consuming fascination with skin color and other bodily indicators. These interventions are, however, temporary, as the recuperative effects of the discursive frameworks of "race" are ultimately constraining.

In order to find a way out of this theoretical and practical dead-end we need to find resolutions for some of the current problems: first, a new language that moves beyond binaries such as either black or white; secondly, a recognition of the operation of "webs of power" that lock us into racialization, such as those in schooling; and finally, freedom from the dominance of the visible in categorizing through "race." It is these measures that may allow us to truly experience the potential fluidities in cultural production, in identification, and in thinking.

To find these answers requires the political will to find ways to change at the level of the academy. Barring a few notable exceptions, academic work is most often "top down." I believe that (especially) in the area of "race," this needs to change so as to bring together some of the more interesting poststructuralist theories with the pragmatism of the "uneducated." "We" can learn a great deal about the everyday worlds of those who are currently disadvantaged by the manifestation of racialized social relations of power, but it is unfortunate for us that the structural and institutional constraints upon what counts as knowledge, and useful knowledge at that, remain within the hands of the few. Most importantly, the process of "translation" between knowledgeable and knowledge-less is one which continues to disadvantage the insights of the latter, and worse, to result in the loss of much of what is most startling and unsettling for the former. The most positive aspect of this difficulty is that communication continues to result in unexpected pockets of change, and thus possibilities for the future. In this research, children have shown that the body is an important site for the translation of what may become "postracial" thinking across fields of cultural and intellectual production.

Notes

1 The central theme of the broader project was an investigation into the formation of self-claimed "mixed race" identities in children. Data collection took place during 1997 and 1998.

2 This phenomenon was recorded to be on the increase throughout the later 1980s and into the 1990s. It has, of course, increased since the events of September 11, 2001.

3 I will use this term throughout to foreground the importance of social and geographic positioning to the responses children gave.

4 Numerous "Black feminist" writers have written about this phenomenon, such as Hill Collins (1990/3), Mama (1989), hooks (1992), and Morrison (1994).

5 In her first footnote, Weekes writes that of the 31 black women she interviewed, 13 of them were of mixed parentage. "All mixed-parentage

women interviewed categorised themselves as such, and many of the sample considered their ancestry African" (Weekes 1997: 125). However, having established separate categories, the conflation of them becomes problematic, with black and "mixed parentage" becoming interchangeable.

6   The use of the word "ugly" for someone who was perceived to be "nasty," that is, too sexualized, too loud, or too vain, was used by many of the London children.

7   It is true that the black children in the multiethnic environments were more likely to utilize a specific form of cultural expertise based on forms of black music, but this was part of the general dominance of black music and admiration for black stars from all the London children.

8   In film, Jackie Chan came out as a hero for young boys from a range of ethnic backgrounds. He was considered "cool," clever, and good-looking because he "got all the girls" (see Ali 2000).

9   See Negus (1996) for a summary of debates about "racial essentialism" in popular music.

References

Ahmed, S. (2000) *Strange Encounters: Embodied Others in Post Coloniality.* London and New York: Routledge.

Ali, S. (2000) "Who Knows Best: Politics and Ethics in Research into Race," in S. Ali, K. Coate, and W. Wa Goro (eds.), *Global Feminist Politics: Identities in a Changing World.* London and New York: Routledge.

Ali, S. (2002) "Friendship and Fandom: Ethnicity, Power and Gendering Readings of the Popular," in D. Epstein and V. Hey (eds.), *Discourse: Studies in the Cultural Politics of Education. Special Edition on Friendship* 23, 2: 153–65.

Anthias, F. and Yuval-Davis, N. (1992) *Racialized Boundaries: Race, Nation, Gender, Colour and Class, and the Anti-racist Struggle.* London: Routledge.

Anzaldúa, G. (1987) *Borderlands/La Frontera: The New Mestiza.* San Francisco, CA: Spinsters/Aunt Lute Foundation.

Back, L. (1996) *New Ethnicities and Urban Culture: Racism and Multiculture in Young Lives.* London: UCL Press.

Bazalgette, C. and Buckingham, D. (1995) *In Front of the Children: Screen Entertainment and Young Audiences.* London: British Film Institute.

Bell, V. (1996) "Show and Tell: Passing and Narrative in Toni Morrison's *Jazz,*" *Social Identities* 2, 2: 221–36.

Bhabha, H.K. (1990a) "The Third Space: Interview with Homi Bhabha," in J. Rutherford (ed.), *Identity: Community, Culture and Difference.* London: Lawrence and Wishart.

Bhabha, H.K. (1990b) "Nation and Narration: Introduction," in H.K. Bhabha (ed.), *Nation and Narration.* London and New York: Routledge.

Black Britain Special (1998) *Scary Spice.* BBC Television Productions.

Block, L. de (2000) "Television, Friendship and Social Connections," Paper presented at Education for Social Democracies, CCS Conference 2000, Institute of Education, London.

Buckingham, D. (2000) *After the Death of Childhood: Growing Up in the Age of Electronic Media.* Cambridge: Polity Press; Malden, MA: Blackwell.

Butler, J. (1993) *Bodies that Matter: On the Discursive Limits of "Sex."* London and New York: Routledge.

Foucault, M. (1980) "Power and Strategies," in C. Gordon (ed.), *Power/Knowledge: Selected Interviews and Other Writings, 1972–1977, by Michel Foucault* (trans. Colin Gordon, Leo Marshall, John Mepham, and Kate Soper). Hemel Hempstead: Harvester Wheatsheaf.

Frith, S. (1996) *Performing Rites: The Value of Popular Music.* Oxford: Oxford University Press.

Gilman, S. (1992) "Black Bodies, White Bodies," in J. Donald and A. Rattansi (eds.), *"Race," Culture, Difference.* London: Sage.

Gilroy, P. (1987) *There Ain't No Black in the Union Jack.* London: Hutchinson.

Gilroy, P. (1993a) *Small Acts: Thoughts on the Politics of Black Cultures.* London: Serpent's Tail.

Gilroy, P. (1993b) *The Black Atlantic: Modernity and Double Consciousness.* London: Verso.

Gilroy, P. (2000) *Between Camps: Nations, Culture and the Allure of "Race."* Harmondsworth: Penguin.

Gilroy, P. (2002) "There Ain't No Black in the Union Jack: Fifteen Years On," Unpublished lecture, Goldsmiths College, University of London, March 22, 2002.

Goldberg, D. (ed.) (1990) *Anatomy of Racism.* Minneapolis and London: University of Minnesota Press.

Gundara, J. (2000) *Interculturalism, Education and Inclusion.* London: Paul Chapman Publishing.

Hall, S. (1992) "New Ethnicities," in J. Donald and A. Rattansi (eds.), *"Race," Culture, Difference.* London: Sage.

Hall, S. (1993) "The Television Discourse – Encoding and Decoding," in A. Gray and J. McGuigan (eds.), *Studying Culture: An Introductory Reader.* London: Edward Arnold.

Hall, S. (1996) "Introduction: Who Needs 'Identity'?" in S. Hall and Paul Du Gay (eds.), *Questions of Cultural Identity.* London: Sage.

Hebdige, D. (1979) *Subculture: The Meaning of Style.* London: Methuen.

Hill Collins, P. (1990/3) *Black Feminist Thought: Knowledge, Consciousness and the Politics of Empowerment.* London: HarperCollins.

hooks, b. (1991) "Stylish Nihilism: Race, Sex and Class at the Movies," in b. hooks, *Yearning: Race, Gender and Cultural Politics.* London: Turnaround.

hooks, b. (1992) *Black Looks: Race and Representation.* Boston, MA: South End Press.

Kenway, J. and Bullen, E. (2001) *Consuming Children: Education–Entertainment–Advertising*. Buckingham: Open University Press.

Mac an Ghaill, M. (1999) *Contemporary Racisms and Ethnicities: Social and Cultural Transformations*. Buckingham: Open University Press.

Mama, A. (1989) *The Hidden Struggle: Statutory and Voluntary Sector Responses to Violence Against Black Women in the Home*. London: Race and Housing Research Unit.

Mason-John, V. and Khambatta, A. (eds.) (1993) *Lesbians Talk: Making Black Waves*. London: Scarlet Press.

Miles, R. (1989) *Racism*. London: Routledge.

Mirzoeff, N. (ed.) (2002) *The Visual Culture Reader*. London and New York: Routledge.

Modood, T. (2000) (first published in 1997), "'Difference', Cultural Racism and Anti-Racism," in P. Werbner and T. Modood (eds.), *Debating Cultural Hybridity: Multicultural Identities and the Politics of Anti-Racism*. London: Zed Books.

Morrison, T. (1994) *The Bluest Eye*. London: Picador.

Negus, K. (1996) *Popular Music in Theory: An Introduction*. Cambridge: Polity Press.

Postman, N. (1994) *The Disappearance of Childhood*. New York: Vintage Books.

Rattansi, A. (1992) "Changing the Subject? Racism, Culture and Education," in J. Donald and A. Rattansi (eds.), *"Race," Culture and Difference*. London: Sage.

Showalter, E. (1987) *The Female Malady: Women, Madness and English Culture, 1830–1980*. London: Virago.

Solomos, J. and Back, L. (eds.) (1995) *Racism and Society*. Basingstoke: Macmillan.

Weekes, D. (1997) "Shades of Blackness: Young Female Constructions of Beauty," in H.S. Mirza (ed.), *Black British Feminism*. London: Routledge.

Chapter 4

Narratives of Embodiment: Body, Aging, and Career in Royal Ballet Dancers

Steven P. Wainwright and Bryan S. Turner

Introduction

In this chapter we develop a sociological framework for the study of classical ballet that examines the sociology of the body as a productive orientation toward dance and ballet careers. In particular, we adopt the approach of the French sociologist Pierre Bourdieu (1930–2002) to understand the intimate connections between body, dance, and identity. By concentrating on the embodiment of the dancer, we depart from the contemporary emphasis on dance as a "discursive practice" within which the dancer becomes strangely disembodied. Contemporary writings in the discipline of dance studies have often been influenced by postmodern readings of "dance as texts" (Adshead-Lansdale 1999; Desmond 1997; Fraleigh and Hanstein 1999). We argue that this textual approach neglects the fact that embodied performance lies at the core of the aesthetic practice of dance (Shusterman 1992). Although there is a long tradition of anthropological and ethnographic work on dance (Hanna 1979; Kaeppler 1978), there is a dearth of specific empirical work on the sociology of western theatrical dance and especially ballet (Thomas 1995). A notable exception is Helen Wulff's international ethnographic study of the culture of some of the world's great ballet companies – the Royal Swedish Ballet, the Royal Ballet, American Ballet Theatre, and Ballet Frankfurt (Wulff 1998). Unfortunately, Wulff's emphasis on breadth inevitably means that

Table 4.1 Summary table of Royal Ballet interviews

Interview number	Pseudonym	Age	Gender	Role
1	Jessie	52	F	Administrator
2	Casper	64	M	Administrator/Performer/ Teacher
3	Oscar	64	M	Administrator/Performer/ Teacher
4	Georgina	43	F	Teacher
5	Lisa	53	F	Teacher
6	Dexter	63	M	Teacher
7	Rudolf	47	M	Administrator
8	Percy	33	M	Administrator/Performer
9	Dudley	63	M	Teacher
10	Dominic	63	M	Performer/Teacher
11	Megan	59	F	Teacher/Administrator

her study lacks the depth often associated with ethnographic research (Hammersley and Atkinson 1995). Moreover, the body receives little specific attention. Given the centrality of embodiment to dance, this lacuna is unfortunately all too characteristic of contemporary research in cultural sociology (Turner and Rojek 2001).

This chapter draws on aspects of an ongoing qualitative research study of the embodied dancer that we have conducted at the Royal Ballet in London. Our focus here is on 11 interviews with ex-dancers who now work as teachers, administrators, and "character dancers" at the Royal Ballet.[1] All our informants for this chapter have retired – in a very narrow sense – as they no longer dance "classical ballet roles" (table 4.1). The authors conducted all of the interviews in the field – that is, at the Royal Opera House, London.

Ballet, Body, and Bourdieu

In describing ex-dancers' perceptions of their bodies, of aging, and of their careers, our argument works on three levels. First, we provide an account of ex-dancers' "lived experience" of embodiment through in-depth interviews. Secondly, we explore the fruitfulness of Bourdieu's theoretical schema in empirical research, especially research that considers the relationships between personal identity, the human body, and social practices; and finally we consider the relevance of our research to the philosophical debate around the so-called "social constructionist of the body" (Turner 2000). We turn first to the notion of embodiment. Research on the body has been chastised for privileging theorizing, bracketing out the individual, and for ignoring the practical experiences of embodiment (Turner 1996). Moreover, little attention has been focused on the ways that specific social worlds shape human bodies (Wacquant 1995). One productive way to animate these concerns is via the social theory of Bourdieu. We draw upon an array of concepts developed by Bourdieu – habitus, capital, and field – in our empirical investigation of the dancer's body and embodiment.

Bourdieu's corpus of work is widely viewed as a productive approach to both theory and research on the body (Fowler 1997, 2000; Turner 1992). His work attempts to take full recognition of human agency, including the idea of strategy through the notion of practices, but it also recognizes the determining role of institutions and resources (or capital) in shaping and constraining human agency. This emphasis on practice lends itself conveniently to an understanding of dance as a social performance, but in order to understand Bourdieu we need to start with some basic definitions. Ballet in Bourdieu's sociology can be described as a specific social field of cultural practice, that is, "a network, or a configuration, of objective relations between positions objectively defined, in their existence and in the determinations they impose upon their occupants" (Bourdieu 1990: 39). The institutional structure of ballet, like any field of social activity, determines a range of social positions in terms of their authority and prestige. The structure of the field shapes the career of the ballet dancer. The field is the context within which the habitus of individuals is formed. We can define "habitus" loosely as the attitudes, dispositions, and taste that individuals share as members of a field. In Bourdieu's terms, taste is neither individual nor random, but organized by reference to social positions, practices, and institutions. Habitus is an "acquired system of generative dispositions" (Bourdieu 1977: 95) within which individuals think that their preferences are natural and taken-for-granted. Individuals in their everyday world are not typically reflexive about their dispositions, because "[w]hen habitus encounters a social world of which it is the product, it is like a 'fish in water': it does not feel the weight of the water and it takes the world about itself for granted. . . . It is because this world has produced me, because it has produced the categories of thought that I apply to it, that it appears to me as self-evident" (Bourdieu and Wacquant 1992: 127, 128). For Bourdieu, tastes and dispositions are clearly related to our embodiment, and, for example, things or ideas that we forcefully reject cause us disgust. In colloquial English, things for which we feel a natural attraction are "just my cup of tea," whereas things that are annoying make us feel "fed up." These basic patterns of classification are aspects of a "practical taxonomy" that is associated with the body, and they help us to arrange the world through a set of dichotomies: hot/cold, dexterous/clumsy, handsome/ugly, tall/small, and so forth.

Habitus and embodiment are entwined. Bourdieu writes that "the way people treat their bodies reveals the deepest dispositions of the habitus" (Bourdieu 1984: 190). Bodies embrace and express the habitus of the field in which they are located. For example, in his famous study of French status systems, Bourdieu argued that differences in preferences for sports were closely related to different social classes, and different social classes express different preferences for body weight and shape. Whereas weight lifting and heavy bodies are part of the habitus of the working-class male, mountaineering and tennis are more closely associated with the dispositions of the educated middle and upper classes. In *Distinction* (Bourdieu 1984: 190) he argued that there are important connections between social class and preferences for food and body shape, because "[t]aste in food also depends on the idea each class has of the body and of the effects of food on the body, that is, on its strength, health and beauty; and on the categories it uses to evaluate these effects, some of which may be important for one class and ignored by another, and which the different classes may rank in different ways." Because different types of bodies (strong and squat, lithe and athletic, or curvaceous and sexual) have different values in their respective fields, we can talk about the physical and symbolic capital of bodies.

People in high-status positions have better access to valued goods than people in low-status positions. These "goods" are heterogeneous and include physical goods such as commodities, but they also include intangible qualities such as honor. These goods represent different forms of "capital." Bourdieu has identified social capital (the social relations that people invest in), cultural capital (such as educational qualifications), and symbolic capital (the honor and prestige that people enjoy). The human body itself is part of the capital to which human beings ascribe values. In the sexual field, we might say that Marilyn Monroe enjoyed considerable physical capital, that is, the prestige flowing from bodily "investments." Because aging tends inevitably to reduce our physical capital, we can argue that this form of capital is not renewable and is characterized by its scarcity. By contrast, aging is or can be associated with increases in wisdom, respect, and influence. The power that comes with aging in patriarchal societies is associated with symbolic capital, that is, honor and social status. Thus, physical and symbolic capital of the body stand in a contradictory relationship. Sporting careers can be analyzed in terms of these contradictory pressures, where retired athletic stars can retain their symbolic capital by becoming celebrities in related fields, for example on television or in films. Bourdieu's work has been particularly useful in the study of sport and sporting bodies, and our aim here is to build on the exploration of physical capital in ethnographic studies of boxing (Wacquant 1995) to study the body and ballet. The habitus of classical ballet produces dispositions (or tastes) toward the body that emphasize beauty, youthfulness, and athleticism, and hence aging, injury, and retirement are aspects of the ballet career that are deeply problematic within the field of classical ballet.

Embodiment and the Dancer's Habitus

In modern sociology, it is often said that the body has become a project in contemporary society, where diet, exercise, lifestyle, and even cosmetic surgery are employed to produce a body consistent with our self-definition. The body can be "seen as an entity which is in the process of becoming; a project that should be worked at and accomplished as part of an individual's self-identity" (Shilling 1993: 5). For the professional dancer, Shilling's claim is, perhaps, too moderate, since to become a classical ballet dancer requires the body to be the very essence of self-identity. The discipline of ballet produces and maintains a particular type of body that cannot be separated from the identity of the dancer. As Rudolf Nureyev said: "I am a dancer" (Solway 1998). Bull (1999: 275) argues: "[I]f the body can talk, then the language of classical ballet should be the most articulate which exists." However, fluency in this particular language of the body is only gained through a punishing body schedule. The Royal Ballet prima ballerina Darcey Bussell (1998: 46) comments that daily "[c]lass is like brushing your teeth – if you don't do it your body starts to rot!"

The purpose of ballet schooling is to make the unnatural natural, to acquire an unconscious ballet habitus. Another Royal Ballet principal dancer, Deborah Bull, writes: "The problem with classical ballet, the sort of dancing I do for a living, is that it is second nature to me: I must have learnt it at some time, in the way that once upon a time I must have learnt to speak. But I don't remember the process at all. . . . The ability to learn movement, to recognize patterns and memorize sequences, is something I take so much for granted. Yet for non-dancers, getting movement 'into their bodies' has the nightmare quality of wading through treacle" (Bull 1999: 140, 264). The steps are literally inscribed into the dancer's body. In Bourdieu's terms, this taken-for-granted choreography is the dancer's habitus.

Dancers take their particular social world and their embodiment in it for granted. They do not think about their ballet habitus unless they have to, that is until they are forced to as a consequence of some traumatic event or radical change of circumstance. Our research is focused upon a series of epiphanies such as aging, retirement, and injury that all, potentially, require the dancer to become reflexive about their habitus. The fruitfulness of this approach is illustrated in the account of one ex-principal dancer who, on her return to the stage after being off with an injury for nine months, commented:

> *Megan*: I walked on as a court lady in the first performance of *Swan Lake* and couldn't curtsy when I got onto the middle of the stage because my legs were shaking so much. I was really, really scared and horrified that I could have so totally lost everything that I'd taken for granted before. Performing with the company had never bothered me. And now, suddenly, I found that I was this alien person. I would say it was easily over a year from the accident before I was really back on form.

We see here how the taken-for-granted habitus of dancing on stage is disrupted by injury, and that, perhaps surprisingly, it took over a year for this performance dimension of the dancer's habitus to be restored. The unconscious and unreflective nature of the dancer's habitus is also revealed in the following comment by Rudolf, who speaks of the rigors of professional ballet, and how this embodied discipline now helps him in his role as a ballet company administrator:

> *Rudolf*: One of the things that I discovered early on is that the mental strength that you have from being a dancer is amazing – the strength to put behind you the negative aspects of anything that's happened, and

to actually go for "the performance." You have a tremendous amount of self-discipline. That side of my training, which one didn't actually realize was training, it was how you evolved, has been a tremendous strength really.

Similarly, the career shift from being a dancer to becoming a dance teacher requires the acquisition of a new habitus:

Megan: I think the hardest thing of all, obviously, was looking at other people and seeing what other people were doing. I was determined to get to grips with handling a room full of people and not being terrified of it.

Megan has now made this career transition from performance to coaching, and we can think of this career change as involving different forms of capital. The physical capital of the performing dancer has been replaced by the cultural capital of the status of a professional coach. This shift, from the use of physical to cultural capital, may also occur for established dance teachers:

INTERVIEWER: How has growing older affected the way you think about your body?

DUDLEY: Well, dramatically. I had no problems at all until about five years ago when I was teaching. I taught four classes a day, I taught seven days a week. Then all of a sudden – crash. Then I thought, "Well you see people worse than you, barely able to walk. Really, don't complain – there are a lot of people worse off than you and if you really want to do it you'll find a way to do it." But it is traumatic, in a way, because your body is a means of expression. What I've had to learn to do now is to express myself verbally. Which I've always been able to do, but now I've had to do it more. I've had to describe it more, and describe the feelings of what's involved, rather than say, "Well this is what it looks like."

In this case the teacher gave up dancing, at the age of 28, following a back injury, and became a famous ballet teacher. However, a series of injuries in his late fifties has now forced him to reinvent himself for a second time and to adopt a less physically demonstrative and more verbally elaborate dance-teaching habitus.

Schooling and discipline are key processes in the acquisition of a balletic bodily habitus. In order to acquire the turn-out of the hips, which is a basic physical requisite for acquiring a ballet technique, schooling has to begin by around the age of ten (Karsavina 1973; Koutedakis and Sharp 1999):

Rudolf: You can't decide to become a dancer at 21!

Although large numbers of people start ballet as children, very few become professional dancers, and those who become classical ballet dancers need considerable physical and mental strength (Greskovic 2000; Hamilton 1998). A dancer's discipline is embodied. Retirement from dance can result, almost inevitably, in a loss of this physical and emotional discipline, and this loss of control and regulation can have potentially dramatic effects on the body:

Jessie: It can be absolute hell: the biggest disappointments, the biggest heartaches that can come from it, and also wonderful things. It's a very tough profession, very demanding, physically and emotionally, and it takes all your life. It's given me great tenacity, because I don't really think you can be a professional ballet dancer without a large degree of tenacity. A lot of dancers do have to be absolutely rigid about their diet when they're working. Sometimes when people do stop, they kind of blow up, because they've all their careers just had an iron discipline.

Pain is routinely part of the habitus of professional dance, and training for that habitus involves the management of pain and injury. The mental toughness to work through the pain was seen as one feature that distinguished those who became professional dancers. Lisa, who now coaches leading dancers of the Royal Ballet, recalled her time teaching young nonprofessional dancers at the Royal Ballet School:

Lisa: Obviously some people were never going to make it in dance, because they didn't have the guts to come in every day and get on with it. They always had pain and it affected them; whereas some people had pain and it didn't affect them. So you could tell the people that were really going to make good company members.

Familiarity with pain and its acceptance is part of what we might call the institutional habitus, and a professional belief that "the show must go on" becomes quite literally embodied in those dancers who are seen as the most likely to succeed in a professional ballet company. This ability to dance through the pain is a leitmotiv of many ballet biographies (Bull 1999; Fonteyn 1975; Newman 1986; Solway 1998; Villella 1992). These examples illustrate how the habitus is a collective and shared set of dispositions rather than simply an aspect of individual psychology, because the habitual nature of the experience of pain is a product of the discipline, training, and values of the ballet as both a company and a community. Moreover, occupational success itself reinforces this physical and mental toughness, which has to become part of the ballet habitus. The physicality of dancing is clearly addictive:

> *Dexter*: I think that if you make it you tend to want to go on longer than if you don't. I always remember Margot [Fonteyn] saying to somebody once that if it's such hard work then why do you go on so long? And she said, "Well you don't realize, you're given success very early and you don't want to give it up." But you have to work to keep that success. No, I was driven, and that's why I've worked so hard because I thought I've got to prove it. I wasn't living anybody else's fantasy. I was doing it for myself and I didn't want to be a failure. I didn't like giving up dancing, so I kept going to class. 'Cos it would have been like coming off drugs.

> *Megan*: What scared me enormously was when somebody said to me, when I was 30, "You're already past your peak, you know." I said, "I beg your pardon. Passed my peak! I haven't peaked yet!" And they said, "Oh yes you have! Physically you are past your peak at 30." I remember being so cross, and thinking, "Why didn't I know? Why didn't I enjoy my peak!" I think now I find old age scary, from the point of view of being physically decrepit. I don't like the idea. It scares me, having really built a life based on physical fitness. We're surrounded by beautiful, talented, young people. Unusual people. We all have the same identity in a sense. We love being pushed. We love being challenged. We don't mind getting hot and sweaty and killing ourselves. We get a buzz from being exhausted, and still managing to get up and do it again. It's a drug. All of us have that in common.

These two examples illustrate the way in which the social world of the professional ballet company becomes embodied in its dancers. We have so far explored this professional embodiment through the sociological notion of the habitus and the body. We now turn to our third theme, which is the interrelationship of aging and career in ballet. We will argue for the salience of Bourdieu's notions of physical capital and cultural capital in illuminating the career trajectory of aging dancers.

Aging and Career in Ballet

The inevitable process of aging prompts dancers to confront the vulnerability of their bodies and the precarious features of their professional careers (Hamilton 1998). We focus on this potential epiphany, which encourages dancers to reflect on their bodily habitus. Moreover, we suggest that the decline in a dancer's physical capital, what we describe as the ontology of aging, provides a critique of radical social constructionism in the social sciences. There is a widespread argument in sociology, which has been developed in particular in feminist research, suggesting that the body is a product of social and historical processes rather than simply a given fact of nature. There are many versions of this argument (Hacking 1999). To take one influential study (Laqueur 1990), it is claimed that, because there has been considerable difficulty in the history of medicine in settling on an unambiguous definition of the physical characteristics of men and women, the sexual body is socially constructed by the political struggles over sexual identity in the wider society. The differentiation of male and female is not unambiguously decided by the growth of scientific anatomy, because gender is a politically contested category. These arguments, which are powerful and convincing, have unfortunately often been generalized, with the result that the body is rendered invisible by becoming simply a cultural artifact. We do not deny that the representation of the human body is culturally defined and socially produced, but we argue that, for example, pain and injury can only be understood sociologically by taking human embodiment seriously. Old age is socially constructed, but the experiences of the constraints of aging are also a consequence of physiological and biological changes. We want to restore the importance of the phenomenology of the body in everyday life through understanding the role of embodiment in the careers of professional dancers.

CASPER: I did daily class for a few years afterwards because it's ingrained into you. It's not a thing that is easily given up. It's a discipline that's there. You feel rather like you're playing truant if you don't do it! You feel guilty, even if you don't have to do it. I mean

	there's one guy who's the same age as me [64] who religiously does class every day! I got out of the habit! I don't expose myself the way the dancers look now!
INTERVIEWER:	Is that partly because you see these young beautiful things doing class effortlessly, and that was something that you could no longer do?
CASPER:	Yes. It's demoralizing. Well you thought you could do it, but you can't. The ability has gone. Of course you can go on doing class forever, but it doesn't mean to say that the audience is going to appreciate it! There are certain standards that must be kept up. And the standards are continually getting better and better.

We see here how the physical decline of the dancer's body, the ontology of aging, is a threat to both a dancer's career and their very identity. Professional ballet is in particular such an all-consuming and demanding career that it is inevitable that self-identity is, essentially, determined by it. From a sociological point of view, ballet is an occupation like professional football, but it has an additional dimension, namely that it is a vocation, or a calling. In the terminology of Max Weber (2002: 312), whereas a job is simply a means of making a living, a calling is an end in itself that requires no further justification. Somebody with a religious vocation has been called out of the everyday world to undertake a special task or duty, a task that they experience as a compulsion. A calling is not exactly a personal choice but an obligation. Now professional dancing as a vocation often assumes this compulsory character, and hence one can talk about a dancer as "driven." This calling to dance involves more than the acquisition of a good technique. Obviously, dance is something that the ballet dancer's body can do, but being a ballet dancer is also embodied. In other words, being a ballet dancer is not just something that you do, it is something that you are. This invariably means that there is a pressure, we might say "habitual force," to delay the final termination of a dancing career by retirement:

> *Jessie*: You can see that a dancer's powers are declining, and you can see that it's going to be downhill from here on in – and not uphill. Some people are going to have to hear things that they don't want to hear, and cannot see for themselves. So for some people it is very painful and very difficult.

Casper: Dancing is not easy. You have to go through a certain amount of pain, through the pain barrier, and if you can't do that, you don't have the ambition and the drive to rise above all that, there's no point. I just wish one's body didn't deteriorate! It would be great to be able to do it all still. In fact you feel in here [points to his head] that you can. You have to believe what people tell you, and normally people in this company are very truthful – they try to let you down gently. But one always feels one can still do it. It's like the run to catch the bus, and then you realize that you are not going to catch it!

This belief (that the mind thinks it can do it, but the body no longer can) is also developed in a quotation from Rudolf below. Both examples can be recast within the debate about the social construction of the body. The notion that "they think they can do it" chimes with a radical social constructionist view of epistemology where, essentially, "the world" is little more than a social construction. The aging process itself has often been studied within the framework of social constructionism. For some, aging is wholly socially constructed (Katz 1996), but we argue that such a radical position is limited unless it can include an understanding of embodiment and aging (Turner 1992; Wainwright 1997). The world acts back on our epistemological claims about it, by forcing us to modify our epistemological assumptions about reality. Sayer (1992: 70) argues that "although the nature of objects and processes (including human behaviour) does not uniquely determine the content of human knowledge, it does determine their cognitive and practical possibilities for us. It is not thanks to our knowledge that walking on water doesn't work, but rather the nature of water." Similarly, with the notion of the ontology of aging, we are arguing for the view that there is an inevitable physical decline in the capacities of the human body that clearly modifies the nature of our embodiment as social actors. For ballet dancers, this aging process means that their careers as performing classical ballet dancers are invariably over by early middle age (Greskovic 2000):

Rudolf: I retired at 38. I would say the last three years [I was] increasingly aware of aches that hadn't been there in the past, and also the fact that you take a little bit longer to recover from a particular exertion. When I first did that [points to a photo on his wall of himself as Tybalt in *Romeo and Juliet*] I was fine. But as I got a little older my wife would always notice when I got out of bed and creaked! When you talk about aging, the danger that happens to people in their late thirties is that their brain thinks they can do it and the body doesn't, and that's when you run the risk of hurting yourself. There are suddenly things that you could do last year and you threw yourself into but gravity takes over and you hit the floor a little earlier than you thought! It's a young person's job, it always has been.

With aging, aches and pains gradually become more common. There is also an increased chance of injury. The extreme physical demands of ballet can, literally, wear your body out (Hamilton 1998):

Megan: I said, "Well Kenneth [MacMillan; then Director of the Royal Ballet], I've absolutely got to stop soon. I just hurt everywhere and I'm 39!"

Moreover, with the aging of the body, recovering from injuries takes longer and the outcomes are uncertain. This increasing vulnerability of the dancer's body requires a wariness that often interferes with performance, and requires various compensating strategies, for example by favoring one side of the body:

LISA:	It takes longer to warm up properly. You also have standards, and you can't go below a certain standard and it takes a longer time to get there. So more energy is going into reaching the same level. It's a bit like an alcoholic, isn't it? You have to drink a little more to get the same effect!
INTERVIEWER:	I wouldn't know!
LISA:	Well nor would I but that's what they say. You just have to spend longer getting to the same point!

Megan: I danced less and less, yes. I remember giving up *Swan Lake* with a huge sense of relief. Because as time went on the only way to cope with something so demanding was to wrap myself in cotton wool and to be so precious that it was horrible! You took care of every little toenail and every little blister on your foot. Every pair of *pointe* shoes was worked in miraculously. You planned your rehearsal, and you planned what you ate and when you ate it and how many hours sleep you had. It was unbelievable. The dedication. There was no other way I could do it. I remember saying to my husband, "Oh you haven't agreed to go to a cocktail party and reception for your company on Tuesday! I've got *Swan Lake* on Thursday." He'd say, "But this is Tuesday!" I'd say, "But darling, I'm 35! Ten years ago I could have done that. Don't ask me to come to a cocktail party and stand in high heels on Tuesday." All that sort of rubbish. So, a huge sense of relief when you actually think, "God, I was so obsessed with my body and myself and now I can actually live." I never walked from Covent Garden to Leicester Square [5 minutes] because it was too far! So I think there is a huge sense of relief when you let go of that preciousness.

These physical changes in the strength and resilience of the dancer's body can begin to appear well before middle age. For example, the youngest person we spoke to was 33 years. Percy was still doing some classical dancing but even he acknowledged that this involvement was becoming much harder. At the time of the interview he was also a part-time administrator. He was retiring from dancing and becoming a full-time administrator at the end of the season. What is striking here is the way that much greater care had to be taken to avoid injury, even with a "30-year-old dancing body":

INTERVIEWER: Do you find class is physically harder now that you are getting older?

PERCY: Oh God, yes! Going into arabesque is a struggle now. [When I was younger, in class] I was right at the front! I'm not now, you'll find me at the back! I hide in the corner now!

INTERVIEWER: Is the pain just part of your everyday life, as it were?

PERCY: Yeah, like I said, as you get older it gets worse. There's more niggles, things hurt a lot more. I'll come off stage, or I'll wake up the next morning and my Achilles tendons feel like the first few steps they are going to snap, and I never had that before. My body tightens up a lot quicker than it used to do.

INTERVIEWER: Does the warm-up take longer?

PERCY: I never warmed up when I was younger! We used to just go and do a quick warm-up five minutes before and then go on. I can't do that now. I have to do a full 25 minutes' warm-up. Ten years ago there is no way I would have done that. Two pliés and I was on! And my body could get away with it. You think, "Oh God, if I don't do this now I could be injured," whereas I never thought that as a young dancer.

In contrast, one teacher, who is 63, was very positive about his physical abilities:

INTERVIEWER: How do you think growing older has affected the way that you see your body?

DEXTER: Not at all. I'm still fit. I don't [do] ballet exercise. I mean I obviously demonstrate, and I can still lift. I can lift Darcey Bussell up there [points above his head]. I can do it all.

However, another dance teacher, who is also around 60, disagrees:

INTERVIEWER: Do you think that when you come to teach classes that dancers accept that their physical prowess is on the decline? Because the impression we get from talking to some people is that they almost feel that, even though they're now in their sixties, they could go out on the stage and still perform as they did when they were 19.

DUDLEY: That's in their mind! The mind is a funny thing because the mind thinks it's doing it, and it's not. Ballet is definitely for the young. [Natalia] Makarova, who I worked with a lot, she said to me one day, "Just when you are beginning to realize how it all should be done, your body packs up." One day, when she was going to retire, she had a little party. She sat there and she said, "I'm going to retire," and we all cried. And she said, "Why are you crying? Why aren't you happy for me that I can move on? You have to move on in life. And anyway, everything I've done, most of the good things, are on film. And if I do it now the doing it, well, is in your imagination, it's not actually happening." She was like 44. Gels [Gelsey Kirkland] walked away from it at 35. Cynthia Harvey at 39. Maya Plisetskaya is still dancing, unfortunately, at 72 and in a way it's sad. It's a sickness. It's a mental sickness. They cannot get off the stage. You have to take a hook and pull 'em out!

As we have already argued, our sample had effectively offset their declining physical capital by drawing on and developing their stock of symbolic capital (prestige) and cultural capital (their practical knowledge of dance):

Jessie: Of course I knew all the people here because we'd been at school. I came back and it's been wonderful. It is a marvelous way of being able to, sort of, capitalize and use all of the things.

In fact, Jessie had been asked by the Director of the Royal Ballet to rejoin the company as an administrator. In Bourdieu's terms, we can see that an amalgam of social, symbolic, and cultural capital is being employed here. This heritage of ballet becomes sedimented into the dance teacher's body. For some, developing the artistry of current dancers offsets to some extent the loss of "the performing self." However, the embodiment of being a dancer, of "dancing in a world of pain and magic" (Villella 1992), is inevitably lost once an artist can no longer dance on stage (Hamilton 1998):

INTERVIEWER: You said that you danced for the sheer joy of dancing, and you no longer have that joy of dancing.
LISA: No you don't. There's no real replacement for being a performer. But there's a wonderful transition of helping others to do it. I remember coaching Belinda Hatley, on Giselle. When I watched her I was just so thrilled because she was really exactly how I would have liked to have looked. There was something very rewarding about that.

There is some evidence that great dancers continue to develop their major roles through coaching the next generation of dancers, even though they themselves no longer dance their former roles (Newman 1992). That said, retirement was generally not something to which our interviewees were looking forward:

Dexter: I've got to retire in a year's time, which I'm not very happy about. I've been here for 46 years and I've done all the roles and I've coached for a long time. Peter Wright [former Director of the Royal Ballet's sister company] said to me: "People like you shouldn't retire. You've got too much to offer. Lavatory attendants should be forced to retire at 65, not people like you!"

Unfortunately for Dexter, Jeremy Isaacs, the former head of the Royal Opera House (or ROH, by which the Royal Ballet staff are employed), brought in compulsory retirement of all ROH employees (Isaacs 1999), and now three of our ex-dancers have websites as "legendary ballet stars." Another member of our sample, Dudley, continues to be respected in the United States:

Dudley: By the time I was 28 I decided that, having been at it since I was ten, I was burned out. I was having certain problems with my back and I went to see an orthopedic surgeon and they said, "If you don't stop you're going to have trouble." So I stopped. I had some back problems and then a knee problem and then a foot problem. Those injuries caused me to rethink and I had to – and I use the word very strongly – I had to reinvent myself. I had to come back and reinvent myself. And fortunately in our business the older you get, if you survive, you become legendary. In the States now they call me "This legendary star maker."

This is an example of the evolution, perhaps revolution, in a dancer's habitus that we discussed earlier in this chapter. As we have seen, coaching dancers is one way to utilize the accumulation of cultural capital after retirement. Another strategy is to become a principal character dancer, but such a move can be too demeaning for dancers who have enjoyed "stellar careers":

Dominic: It's very difficult, very difficult. Irek Mukamedov [Royal Ballet principal, and widely regarded as the world's great male dancer in the 1980s and early 1990s] would be fantastic in the sort of roles that I'm doing. He'd be absolutely wonderful. But the ego gets in the way. "I'm Mukamedov" [in a swaggering Russian accent]. Once one's been at that height, then it's very difficult to graciously go into the cameos and subsidiary roles. I asked to do Dr Coppelius (*Coppelia*), as I'm the right age, but I was told I couldn't [by the Director]. Perhaps the new Director will see things slightly differently. You don't run out of ambition, you see!

The aesthetic of classical ballet, its requirement for perfect bodies coupled with outstanding ballet technique, means there are no classical dancing roles for dancers once they reach the age of around 40 years:

DOMINIC: There is still an ageist thing in dance. Some people do use older people and there are some outstanding examples of that. I mean dancing, using their bodies, not just wandering around acting, which is what I do nowadays, dancing in their seventies and eighties. You get these companies specializing in old people like White Oak [a modern dance troupe for "older dancers." Mikhail Baryshnikov is the most famous member; see Craine and Mackrell 2000], and Jiri Kylian's group [NDT3, Netherlands Dance Theatre troupe for "older dancers"].

INTERVIEWER: But that is modern dance rather than ballet, isn't it?

DOMINIC: Yes, modern dance. You can't do classical dance. With modern dance then Merce Cunningham can brood impressively in a corner at 80. Tragically, if you're trying to do classical stuff – and Rudolf [Nureyev] destroyed his own legend – then you mustn't go on. It is difficult, but it is something we should be tackling. If you've got a company of 80 people and you've got 10 percent – eight – who are "of an age," let's say, and you create for them then that is important. The influence in the company tends to be quite good because it [the dancer's heritage] gets passed on.

Because ballet is an art that is literally inscribed on the body, both ballet technique and, especially, ballet artistry is handed from one generation to the next (Bland 1981; Guest 1988). Retirement from the Royal Ballet Company is usually viewed with dread:

INTERVIEWER: How are you thinking about retirement?

OSCAR: I'm absolutely petrified. I've got to retire next year. I'm absolutely petrified.

INTERVIEWER: Will they allow you to come back and dance your Ugly Sister [in *Cinderella*]?

OSCAR: I wish they would, darling! They might say, "He's too old." I would love to!

As we saw earlier, giving up dancing on stage can be very difficult, because performing is a calling and it is an addiction:

INTERVIEWER: So how did you feel at the end when there was some decline in your physical abilities? You seem to have been almost pushed, if that's the right word, into giving up dancing.

LISA: Well, that is the right word. And let's face it, if I hadn't been then I'd still be here now. Because some people just don't know when the right time is to give up.

For some, there was a deep sense of loss of their performing selves:

INTERVIEWER: Did you feel any sense of loss when you gave up dancing?

DEXTER: Oh I did, because that was all I ever wanted to do. I've had a wonderful life really. If I lived my life again

I would be an actor, not a dancer, because I could still be doing it now. Be doing big stuff now. I didn't come into it to teach. I came in to perform, and that's all I ever wanted to do. I had a good innings; 23 or 24 years is quite a good innings for a dancer. But for an actor, it's no time at all really. You are halfway through it then. I think I was lucky that I've turned out to be a good coach. I wouldn't be here if I wasn't, would I? So I must be quite good. But it's not the same. I mean, I've been going to Barons Court since 1951, till we came here a year ago. I didn't know anything else. It's been all my life. That's why I'm not all that keen on retiring.

Discussion

Our next quotation synthesizes the themes in this chapter: embodiment, habitus, physical capital, cultural capital, aging, and career in ballet:

Megan: I still feel some days as if I'd love to be able to jump up and move. There's suddenly a piece of music playing in the studio or there's a particular role. I mean, in the ballet we are doing at the moment – God, I loved it so much and just have such vivid memories of the joy of that ballet and those performances. I think all of us do that did leading roles in that ballet. But in a sense you just think what would it be like to wind the clock, and do it now with all the knowledge one has now. And there is something so sad that dancers' careers really are relatively short. Because just at that point when you are in your mid-thirties, I think, you just begin to understand so much more about the world, and yourself and life and other people and emotions. But you can no longer dance like you could when you were 25. So it's a cruel business. It has wonderful rewards for probably very few people to go on in the business in the way they'd like to.

Dancers often speak of "muscle memory," the ability of their bodies to remember particular sequences of dance steps perhaps years after their original performance. Similar everyday, embodied practices include riding a bike, swimming, and playing the piano. The inevitable physical decline of the aging dancer is to some extent offset by their growing practical, cultural knowledge of the ballets they danced in. There comes a point, however, when cultural capital can no longer supplement the deterioration in the dancer's physical prowess. Retirement from dancing the classical roles of the ballet repertory is then inevitable. Yet this retirement often occurs at a time when most professional careers are still in some sense developing. "It's a cruel business," indeed. Very few people become professional ballet dancers, and of those that do only a tiny fraction get the chance to stay within the social world of a ballet company and to cash in their cultural, social, and symbolic capital as administrators and teachers. Our sample in this chapter is, therefore, an elite one.

The evolution of self-identity is a common theme in the sociological literature. Variations on this theme include the notions of turning-point experiences (Strauss 1959); biographical disruption (Bury 1982); epiphanies (Denzin 1989); fateful moments (Giddens 1990); transformational experiences (Wainwright 1995); and disrupted lives (Becker 1997). These sociological sources all have a resonance with our account of aging and career change in ballet. A recent paper (Gearing 1999) on narratives of identity in ex-professional footballers provides an interesting comparison with our narratives of the embodiment of ballet. Gearing found that the past history of individual ex-footballers continues to give meaning to their contemporary lives as they move through middle and old age. More generally, the life story is our self-identity (McAdams 1993). Retirement from an occupation that is often surrounded by public acclaim and celebrity status is clearly disruptive to self-identity, but with both ballet and football retirement also brings with it important transformations of embodiment that challenge existing self-definitions. Embodiment and identity are linked together by a habitus that is shattered with retirement.

One of our aims in this chapter has been to embed a critique of radical social constructionism in empirical research on the aging dancer. Our critique is consistent with the argument that:

> it is not sufficient to change language or theory to change reality. . . .
> While it never does harm to point out that gender, nation, or ethnicity
> or race [or ageing] are social constructs, it is naive, even dangerous, to
> suppose that one only has to "deconstruct" these social artefacts, in a
> purely performative performance of resistance, in order to destroy
> them. . . . One may . . . doubt the reality of a resistance which ignores
> the resistance of reality.   (Bourdieu 2000: 108).

We suggest that any attempt by "aging ballet dancers" to dance the classical roles of their "youth" would be an example of the absurdity of ignoring the resistance of reality.

In conclusion, our aim throughout our chapter has been to embed theory within empirical research. We believe that ballet is an important topic in the broader project of making sociology more cultural and cultural studies more sociological, and in producing more comprehensive social research on the reciprocal relationships between the body and society. We also believe that Bourdieu's concepts are especially salient in this broader quest.

Note

1 Ten of the ex-dancers trained at the Royal Ballet School. All of the ex-dancers currently work for the Royal Ballet at the Royal Opera House, Covent Garden, London.

References

Adshead-Lansdale, J. (ed.) (1999) *Dancing Texts: Intertextuality in Interpretation.* London: Dance Books.
Becker, G. (1997) *Disrupted Lives: How People Create Meaning in a Chaotic World.* Berkeley, CA: University of California Press.
Bland, A. (1981) *The Royal Ballet: The First Fifty Years.* New York: Doubleday.
Bourdieu, P. (1977) *Outline of a Theory of Practice.* Cambridge: Cambridge University Press.
Bourdieu, P. (1984) *Distinction: A Social Critique of the Judgement of Taste.* London: Routledge.
Bourdieu, P. (1990) *In Other Words: Essays Towards a Reflexive Sociology.* Cambridge: Polity Press.
Bourdieu, P. (2000) *Pascalian Meditations.* Cambridge: Polity Press.
Bourdieu, P. and Wacquant, L. (1992) *An Invitation to Reflexive Sociology.* Cambridge: Polity Press.
Bull, D. (1999) *Dancing Away: A Covent Garden Diary* (revised edn.; first published in 1998). London: Methuen.
Bury, M. (1982) "Chronic Illness as Biographical Disruption," *Sociology of Health & Illness* 4: 167–82.
Bussell, D. (1998) *Life in Dance.* London: Century.
Craine, D. and Mackrell, J. (2000) *The Oxford Dictionary of Dance.* Oxford: Oxford University Press.
Denzin, N. (1989) *Interpretive Interactionism.* Newbury Park, CA: Sage.
Desmond, J.C. (ed.) (1997) *Meaning in Motion: New Cultural Studies of Dance.* Durham, NC: Duke University Press.

Fonteyn, M. (1975) *Autobiography*. London: W.H. Allen.

Fowler, B. (1997) *Pierre Bourdieu and Cultural Theory: Critical Investigations*. London: Sage.

Fowler, B. (ed.) (2000) *Reading Bourdieu on Society and Culture*. Oxford: Blackwell.

Fraleigh, S.H. and Hanstein, P. (eds.) (1999) *Researching Dance: Evolving Modes of Inquiry*. London: Dance Books.

Gearing, B. (1999) "Narratives of Identity Among Former Professional Footballers in the United Kingdom," *Journal of Ageing Studies* 13: 43–58.

Giddens, A. (1990) *Modernity and Self-Identity: Self and Society in the Late Modern Age*. Cambridge: Polity Press.

Greskovic, R. (2000) *Ballet: A Complete Guide*. London: Robert Hale.

Guest, I. (1988) *The Dancer's Heritage*, 6th edn. London: Dancing Times.

Hacking, I. (1999) *The Social Construction of What?* Cambridge, MA: Harvard University Press.

Hamilton, L.H. (1998) *Advice for Dancers: Emotional Counsel and Practical Strategies*. San Francisco, CA: Jossey-Bass.

Hammersley, M. and Atkinson, P. (1995) *Ethnography: Principles in Practice*, 2nd edn. London: Routledge.

Hanna, J.L. (1979) *To Dance is Human: A Theory of Nonverbal Communication*. Austin, TX: University of Texas Press.

Isaacs, J. (1999) *Never Mind the Moon*. London: Bantam Press.

Kaeppler, A. (1978) "Dance in Anthropological Perspective," *Annual Review of Anthropology* 7: 31–49.

Karsavina, T. (1973) *Classical Ballet: The Flow of Movement* (first published in 1962). London: A. & C. Black.

Katz, S. (1996) *Disciplining Old Age: The Formation of Gerontological Knowledge*. Charlottesville, VA: University Press of Virginia.

Koutedakis, Y. and Sharp, N.C.C. (eds.) (1999) *The Fit and Healthy Dancer*. Chichester: John Wiley.

Laqueur, T. (1990) *Making Sex: Body and Gender from the Greeks to Freud*. Cambridge, MA: Harvard University Press.

McAdams, D.P. (1993) *The Stories We Live By: Personal Myths and the Making of the Self*. New York: William Morrow.

Newman, B. (1986) *Antoinette Sibley: Reflections of a Ballerina*. London: Hutchinson.

Newman, B. (1992) *Striking a Balance: Dancers Talk About Dancing*, rev. edn. New York: Limelight.

Sayer, A. (1992) *Method in Social Science: A Realist Approach*, 2nd edn. London: Routledge.

Shilling, C. (1993) *The Body and Social Theory*. London: Sage.

Shusterman, R. (1992) *Pragmatist Aesthetics: Living Beauty, Rethinking Art*. Oxford: Blackwell.

Solway, D. (1998) *Nureyev: His Life*. London: Weidenfeld & Nicolson.

Strauss, A.L. (1959) *Mirrors and Masks: The Search for Identity*. Glencoe, IL: Free Press.

Thomas, H. (1995) *Dance, Modernity and Culture: Explorations in the Sociology of Dance*. London: Routledge.

Turner, B.S. (1992) *Regulating Bodies: Essays in Medical Sociology*. London: Routledge.

Turner, B.S. (1996) *The Body & Society: Explorations in Social Theory*, 2nd edn. London: Sage.

Turner, B.S. (2000) "An Outline of a General Theory of the Body," in B.S. Turner (ed.), *The Blackwell Companion to Social Theory*. Oxford: Blackwell, pp. 481–501.

Turner, B.S. and Rojek, C. (2001) *Society and Culture: Principles of Scarcity and Solidarity*. London: Sage.

Villella, E. (1992) *Prodigal Son: Dancing for Balanchine in a World of Pain and Magic*. Pittsburgh, PA: Pittsburgh University Press.

Wacquant, L.J.D. (1995) "Pugs at Work: Bodily Capital and Bodily Labour Among Professional Boxers," *Body & Society* 1: 65–93.

Wainwright, S.P. (1995) "The Transformational Experience of Liver Transplantation," *Journal of Advanced Nursing* 22: 1068–76.

Wainwright, S.P. (1997) "A New Paradigm for Nursing: The Potential of Realism," *Journal of Advanced Nursing* 26: 1262–71.

Weber, M. (2002) *The Protestant Ethic and the Spirit of Capitalism*. New York: Penguin.

Wulff, H. (1998) *Ballet Across Borders: Career and Culture in the World of Dancers*. Oxford: Berg.

Part II
Theory

Being a Body in a Cultural Way: Understanding the Cultural in the Embodiment of Dance

Sally Ann Allen Ness

Introduction

Dance presents the analyst of human movement with a distinctive opportunity for cultural study, given the content of its choreographic symbolism. However, this opportunity is contingent to a great extent on the method employed in the study of dance movement. In this chapter, I explore the question of what kinds of cultural understanding of human movement can be gained through embodied methods of studying dance, calling on the discipline of philosophy to characterize this understanding.

Embodiment and Dance Ethnography

Much has been made in the last decade of culturally focused research on dance, about the importance of embodied practice as a methodology for the cultural study of dance.[1] Cultural studies dance scholar Barbara Browning, for example, writes in her award-winning volume, *Samba*:

> For a time, while I lived in Brazil, I stopped writing. I learned to dance. I also learned to pray and to fight – two things I had never felt called upon to do. I did them with my body. I began to think with my body. That is possible and, in the case of Brazilian dance, necessary. (1995: xxii)

The cultural aspect of human movement in Browning's perspective is *necessarily* studied via thoughtful, intellectual bodily practice. Cynthia Novack, as well, in her landmark ethnographic history *Sharing the Dance*, makes a similar case in somewhat more universal terms. In the introduction to this study of the counter-cultural American dance form, contact improvisation, Novack argues:

> Culture is embodied. . . . Movement constitutes an ever-present reality in which we constantly participate. We perform movement, invent it, interpret it, and reinterpret it, on conscious and unconscious levels. In these actions we participate in and reinforce culture, and we also create it. (1990: 8)

Novack posits an essential role for embodied practice in achieving a self-consciously hermeneutic understanding of culture. Most recently, dance ethnologist and performance studies scholar, Deirdre Sklar (2000), has identified a shift toward embodied practice as one of two "trajectories" that distinguishes contemporary culturally focused research on human movement from earlier, standard twentieth-century approaches.[2]

In short, a methodological conversion or paradigm shift, away from an emphasis on "objective" observation and toward one on embodied participation, currently characterizes the leading work in the cultural and cross-cultural study of dance. However, what is considered "cultural" about the movement at issue varies from study to study and is conceived in diverse terms. Body movement in dance may be understood as the embodiment of history, of existential givens, of social value systems, of symbolism, and/or of thought per se.

As to reasons why this practice-orientated methodology has been championed, they are multiple as well, but one seems to stand out – an epistemological justification. It suggests that there is something new to be learned, some otherwise inaccessible understanding to be gained of human movement as a cultural phenomenon, through the methodological shift to embodied practice. It is this epistemological shift that I want to look at more closely in the remainder of this essay and ask: How far have we *really* come via the shift away from the observationally weighted approaches? How, in philosophical terms, might we characterize the "advance" that has been made in the discourse, if so?[3]

With regard to the latter question, it is phenomenology, amongst a variety of philosophical orientations, that has received the most attention in the literature as the philosophical orientation best defining this new trajectory in cultural and cross-cultural dance research. At least in general terms, phenomenology appears to characterize the methodological shift most aptly (away, as it might be summarized, from empiricism of a less radical sort). Phenomenological approaches recognize experience as *the* way of gaining knowledge and provide a basic rationale for embodied methodology in so doing. Phenomenology, however, looked at more closely, may seem paradoxical as the orientation of choice, since the cultural significance of human movement, at least from some phenomenological perspectives, can be understood as an imposed framework, a symbolic overlay that is "read into" the movement "itself," as human beings learn or acquire a given cultural competence. From this perspective, the cultural aspects of human movement might appear as relatively superficial dimensions of movement practices and constitute precisely what the phenomenologist would attempt to strip away, neutralize, or "bracket" in order to approach and reflect upon the lived body in an "untainted" manner.[4] In this regard, the characterization of the shift to embodied methodology as a shift toward phenomenological forms of inquiry, in the context of *culturally* focused research on dance, might seem problematic. The symbolic character of this cultural dimension would preclude a phenomenological approach, or at least some phenomenological approaches.

To address these questions, I present a few representative examples characterizing the "Before" and "After" stages of the new trajectory of embodied practice in culturally focused dance research. Here, I focus on the textual representations of human movement given by a small array of scholars who have studied dance for cultural purposes. I have chosen to let the authors' descriptions of human movement stand as the main indicator of their understanding of the movement, assuming that what they have put into writing to document the movement conveys as well as any other measure the philosophical foundations of their understanding of it.

Observation-driven Descriptions

First, let me cite two observationally orientated (relatively "disembodied") accounts that illustrate some common themes of the earlier research period.[5] It is important to remember throughout this discussion that there has never been an absolute division between approaches relying primarily on observation and those relying on participation or embodied practice. Observation and participation were invariably co-present in culturally focused dance research of this period. It is more accurate to assume a methodological spectrum characterizes the literature, which, at opposite ends, tends toward minimizing, to a greater and greater extent, one or the other of the paired strategies.

The first example presented comes from the work of James Mooney, a nineteenth-century ethnologist working for the US government on Native American affairs. In his report of the Ghost-Dance religion (1896), Mooney provided detailed descriptions of the movements of the Ghost-Dance as part of his account of this ritual's political import. His example may be considered at the far end of the spectrum of objective, "dis-embodied" understanding of the body movement at issue and its cultural significance. Speaking of the Ghost-Dance action sequence, Mooney writes:

> When all is ready, the leaders walk out to the dance place, and facing inward, join hands so as to form a small circle. Then, without moving from their places they sing the opening song, according to the previous agreement, in a soft undertone. Having sung it through once they raise their voices to their full strength and repeat it, this time slowly circling around in the dance. The step is different from that of most other Indian dances, but very simple, the dancers moving from right to left, following the course of the sun, advancing the left foot and following it with the right, hardly lifting the feet from the ground. For this reason it is called by the Shoshoni the "dragging dance." (1965: 185)

Mooney's account characterizes movement in "present perfect" terms, using action verbs in a declarative mood. Movement is represented in this way as an accomplished fact. Moreover, the observations are made in relation to a set of generic body parts and person. The definitive article, "the," modifies body parts and/or bodies identified: "leaders," "hands," "feet," etc. Agency is understood in terms of these preexisting and enduring individual bodies and/or subindividual body parts. The movement is observed as contained or delimited to them.

The second example of a predominantly observational approach is taken from A. R. Radcliffe-Brown's classic text *The Andaman Islanders* (1948), in which the movements of the Andaman Islander style of dance are characterized in general terms. Radcliffe-Brown assumed an observer's stance in relation to the dancing, again a relatively non-participatory "disembodied" approach. Of Andaman dancing, Radcliffe-Brown writes:

The bending of the body at the hips and of the legs at the knees, with the slightly backward poise of the head and the common position of the arms held in line with the shoulders with the elbows crooked and the thumb and first finger of each hand clasping those of the other, produce a condition of tension of a great number of the muscles of the trunk and limbs. The attitude is one in which all the main joints of the body are between complete flexion and complete extension so that there is approximately an equal tension in the opposing groups of flexor and extensor muscles. Thus the whole body of the dancer is full of active forces balanced one against another, resulting in a condition of flexibility and alertness without strain.

While the dance thus brings into play the whole muscular system of the dancer it also requires the activity of the two chief senses, that of sight to guide the dancer in his movements amongst the others and that of hearing to enable him to keep time with the music. Thus the dancer is in a condition in which all the bodily and mental activities are harmoniously directed to one end.   (1948: 248)

Radcliffe-Brown's interpretation of this movement in terms of its cultural significance reads as follows:

Yet, the dance, even the simple dance of the Andamans, does make, in the dancer himself, partly by the effect of rhythm, partly by the effect of the harmonious and balanced tension of the muscles, a direct appeal to that motor sense to which the contemplation of beautiful forms and movements makes only an indirect appeal. In other words the dancer actually feels within himself the harmonious action of balanced and directed forces which, in the contemplation of a beautiful form, we feel as though it were in the object at which we look. Hence such dancing as that of the Andaman Islanders may be looked upon as an early step in the training of the esthetic sense, and to recognize all that the dance means we must make allowance for this fact that the mental state of the dancer is closely related to the mental state that we call esthetic enjoyment.   (ibid.: 250–1)

Finally, Radcliffe-Brown adds this functionalist interpretation of the movement:

As the dancer loses himself in the dance, as he becomes absorbed in the unified community, he reaches a state of elation in which he feels himself filled with energy or force immensely beyond his ordinary state, and so finds himself able to perform prodigies of exertion. This state of intoxication, as it might almost be called, is accompanied by a pleasant stimulation of the self-regarding sentiment, so that the dancer comes to feel a great increase in his personal force and value. And at the same time, finding himself in complete and ecstatic harmony with all the fellow-members of his community, experiences a great increase in his feelings of amity and attachment towards them.

In this way the dance produces a condition in which the unity, harmony and concord of the community are at a maximum, and in which they are intensely felt by every member. It is to produce this condition, I would maintain, that is the primary social function of the dance. . . . For the dance affords an opportunity for the direct action of the community upon the individual, and we have seen that it exercises in the individual those sentiments by which the social harmony is maintained. (ibid.: 252)

Radcliffe-Brown's account is of particular interest because it vividly illustrates an observational approach that identifies the integration of mental and physical aspects of the participants, as it is produced in and through movement. The observational stance Radcliffe-Brown assumes in relation to the movement analyzed does not result in a dissociative understanding of the minds and bodies of the dancers he observes. The "disembodied" methodology employed does not project itself into the observation process in this respect. Moreover, Radcliffe-Brown's analysis focuses on the felt experience of the movement processes, not simply on their visual form. It recognizes an articulate (as opposed to irrational, mysterious, or inchoate) relationship between the design of the movement, the felt experience produced, and the cultural understanding that results.

Also of interest in Radcliffe-Brown's account is the characterization of movement as achieving a balance of active forces and a "harmonious" condition. The description does not take such a balance as a natural given. Rather, the account identifies a balancing act as a specific outcome of certain types of movements, *synchronized* movements.

Like Mooney's account, however, Radcliffe-Brown's description locates movement in relation to generic body parts: "the" hips, legs, knees, head, arms, shoulders, elbows, hand, trunk, limbs, etc. Even more pronounced than in Mooney's account is the ascription of movement to these body parts. Radcliffe-Brown uses the genitive case repeatedly to represent movement as belonging to or originating in these members, identifying such "internal" features as joints and muscles as the agents of movement. While Radcliffe-Brown's description does not assume that the human body is somehow naturally connected or harmoniously integrated, it does assume that the source of human movement is a preexistent, generic, individual human body.

The two examples given present accounts written by anthropologists who were personally not participating, not only in the performances they were documenting, but in the whole subject of dancing itself more generally speaking. For these anthropologists, dance was a means to understanding other anthropological subjects, such as social structure and organization, aesthetic judgment, and political action. The key common features identified in the description of human movement that emerge as characteristic of this observationally weighted ("disembodied") "far end" of the observation–participation spectrum can be summarized as follows:

1 The representation of the body involved in the movement occurs in generic terms: "the" heels, knees, heads, etc.
2 Movement is represented as originating in, belonging to, and being contained by individual, generically defined bodies.
3 Movement is represented as mobilizing, in some cases in an integrative manner, parts of these individual bodies, which exist prior to the movement's occurrence and which remain essentially unaltered as a consequence of participating in it.
4 Movement is represented as absolutely "present," expressed by the use of a declarative and present-tense grammar.
5 Movement is represented as occurring in both abstract as well as contextually specific spaces.

Human movement, in sum, is described as a relatively elemental source of positional change in human beings, universally conceived. It is energetic and transient in character. Bodies and body parts are its agents, or objects. Space is its environment. Movement thus serves as the relatively colorless "juice" that animates the givens of a rule-governed collective structure.

Not all observationally weighted accounts, however, fall this far out on the disembodied or nonparticipatory end of the observation–participation spectrum. The following example evidences an orientation that gradually approaches a more participation-orientated embodied methodology. In this example, in a study focusing specifically on ritual performance, anthropologist Edward Schieffelin writes a description of the movement of the Kaluli *Gisaro* ceremony that is also derived from largely nonparticipatory/observational methods. His understanding of the dance movement, however, is of direct relevance to his main interest in understanding social action as it creates a basis for social structure. With regard to the dance movements of the *Gisaro* ritual, Schieffelin writes:

> Through it all the dancer seems oblivious. He remains downcast and sad, singing of ridge tops and sago places. Despite the flamboyant splendor of his bobbing feathers and streamers, he seems curiously remote. He does not address those around him. He bounces in place, rhythmically bending his knees, his body bent slightly forward, arms held at his sides, eyes on the floor. He is withdrawn, unnoticing, absorbed in his singing . . . In the Gisaro, the feet are held together (legs apart is bad form), and the motion is graceful and controlled, self-consciously beautiful throughout the ceremony.
>
> The appeal of the dance lies in more than the motion of the man himself; it is in the whole bobbing and flowing motion of his regalia. The split palm leaf streamers at his back move with a waving, falling motion, reminiscent to Kaluli of forest waterfalls. Other feathers and leaves bob and beckon with motions familiar in the forest; the waving of the sago fronds or banana trees the dancers often sing about. The movement has an abstract appeal that sometimes leads people to bob a blade of grass or a weighted feather, in idle moments, just to watch it move.   (1976: 176)

Schieffelin's account employs a generic third person singular, present perfect, declarative grammar, similar to those presented above. However, the description also begins to move beyond the present tense at certain points, noting what the dancer "does not" do (address those around him) and what the dancer in general is not *supposed* to do (stand with legs apart). The description also introduces some uncertainty into the observational process, noting how the dancer "seems" as well as what the dancer does. Finally, the description includes the observation that the movement is not wholly contained by or internal to individual bodies and body parts, although it does assume bodies and body parts as originative of the movement. The account emphasizes the integrative character of the movement with respect to "nonbodily" (nonanatomical) co-presences. For example, the movement is observed as animating the dancer's regalia, an observation that also leads to a discussion of imagined and remembered associations inspired by the movement as well. In all of these respects, the account differs from those cited above.

In sum, this "mid-spectrum" example presents some characteristics identified for the observational end of the spectrum, illustrating that an increased interest in and identification with embodied practices does not appear necessarily to alter the understanding produced from an observationally orientated approach. However, the example also illustrates that observational approaches may present different kinds of understanding regarding the cultural character of human movement, depending on the researcher's purposes and interests.

Participation-driven Descriptions

Let me now turn to descriptions generated from embodied practice. At this end of the observation–participation spectrum, it is not so easy to separate out methodological consequences. While the reliance on observation in culturally focused research has tended historically to coincide with diminished participation or embodied practice of the movement described,[6] a reliance on participation and embodied practice has more often than not resulted in an *increase* not a decrease in observation of the movement practices at issue.[7] The embodied practitioner, in this regard, does not necessarily sacrifice the role of observer in choosing to participate in an embodied manner.

Perhaps as a result of this combinatory effect occurring at the participatory end of the observation–participation spectrum, authors employing embodied practice as a methodology in many cases describe the movement they have studied in a manner that preserves and retains an observational orientation. Their accounts of the movement practices at issue are in some cases written as though derived from observation alone, exhibiting many or all of the characteristics identified above for observationally weighted description, even though participation may have been a main, or even the primary, method of learning to understand the movement. Embodied practice, in effect, appears to act as a methodological "silent partner" as far as the description of human movement is concerned in these cases, and there is no evidence of any "gain" in understanding with regard to the specific type of evidence I am assessing in this essay. Nor is there evidence of a philosophical or conceptual shift or advance resulting from the methodological approach. The change in methodology simply reinforces, or, it could be argued, enhances the more standard, long-established orientations used in observationally weighted, non-participatory methodologies.

It is interesting to look at the work of the pioneering dance ethnographer Gertrude Prokosch Kurath in this regard, as Kurath was a most influential scholar in dance anthropology during the mid-twentieth century and a specialist in describing and documenting dance movement, particularly with regard to Native American dance practices. Kurath's 1957 article on the game animal dances of the Rio Grande Pueblos is cited here as an example of her documentary writing of dance movement. Kurath, unlike the anthropologists cited above, was extensively trained as a dancer, and embodied practices of various sorts were constitutive of her understanding of dance movement in general. The description of the Deer Dance presented below, a dance that Kurath learned and performed, was accompanied by a blueprint of the dance space, showing the placement of dancers and key buildings in the dance performance space. With regard to the San Juan Deer Dance of February 15, 1957, Kurath writes:

> The performers assemble in the practice kiva, which serves the combined moieties. The game priest, *pinken* (mountain lion), leads forty men and boys into the south plaza and halts near one of two small spruce trees holed in for the occasion. The dancers line up between these trees, with the *pinken* north of the first dancer and a drummer south of the *sawipinge*, the coveted position of best singers in the middle of the line. After a complete performance the dancers migrate to the north plaza for a repeat, then to the east plaza which is a tight squeeze. Finally they crowd into the practice kiva for a fourth repeat, invisible to the public.
>
> During each performance the dancers remain in place and stamp and lift the right foot in the so-called *antege* or "lift-the-foot" step.[8] They keep time with a gourd rattle in the right hand. After each set of four songs they face about. For the fifth repeat of a set they conclude in the original position. During each face-about the game priest moves along the line, to the middle (B), rear (C), middle (B), and front (A) as indicated in Figure 1 . . .
>
> During the dawn approach and in *antege* the Deer lean on sticks as forelegs, but during the plaza dance they stand upright without mime. The same procedure and stylization characterize the Santa Clara Deer dancers, who also blacken their faces with sacred mud, *naposhun*. (1986: 187–8)

Kurath's description employs the third person plural, present perfect, declarative grammar seen previously. In some instances the action vocabulary represents a more integrative capacity of movement with regard to nonbodily environmental co-presences, characterized as the abstract environmental givens of space and time. For example, Kurath describes the dancers as "lining up" and "facing-about" – human movements that originate and constitute spatial configurations through bodily actions as opposed to occurring in abstract spatial environments. Likewise, Kurath observes the dancers "keeping time" with hand-held rattles, employing a verbal construct that indicates the integration of temporal and bodily characters through human movements that constitute time patterning. In other respects, however, the account is very similar to Mooney's cited earlier, particularly with regard to the description of body movements.

Kurath's work illustrates that embodied practice does not necessarily yield an understanding of movement that is fundamentally different from observationally weighted methodologies. The generic representation of body parts, the reliance on standardized action vocabulary, and the assumption of movement as internal to the body are all evident in her example. Participation, in this regard, may simply lead to a more detailed, more articulate understanding of human movement, or it may produce no apparent difference whatsoever in the account.[9]

Recent work undertaken from an embodied practice approach, however, has made a concerted effort to integrate the participatory experience into the ethnographic description of the movement studied and the cultural understanding of human movement that it represents. Two such cases cited below indicate that fundamental differences in understanding may potentially result from the new trajectory of embodied practice in culturally focused dance research, although this result is by no means guaranteed.

John Chernoff, one of the most deeply committed participation-based ethnomusicologists, taken here as a first case in point, presents the following account of an African dance performance in his phenomenologically orientated study, *African Rhythm and African Sensibility*:

> I was amazed when I saw some Congolese dancing to one of their popular Rumba tunes; in spite of their reputation for lively dancing, it seemed that they were not even moving. One dancer raised his knee as if he intended to take his foot off the ground, but he never lifted it. He stayed poised to move. Gideon said, "Wow! Look at him dance!" and had a beer sent to the man's table. The beauty of the dance was in the expression of calm on the man's face as he heard the music. The collectedness of mind which distinguishes the great drummers can be seen in the head of a dancer. When Africans dance, the head seems to float apart from the body, becoming the center of balance and control. Even when the shoulders and feet are violently active, the head is stable. If the head is cool, the body is cool. The first evening

I went dancing in Accra, I had sweated through my shirt before the first number was over. Later I could dance every dance and keep a dry forehead. (1979: 149)

Chernoff's description, as it shifts into the first person, reports the difference between the individual and the ideal movement process, although it also reports the sustained achievement of a masterful practice of that ideal as well. In the earlier portion of the description cited above, Chernoff's description also illustrates two other characteristic consequences of embodied methodology: the employment of a subjunctive mood and the adoption of an instrumental or purpose-orientated processual descriptive strategy (contrasting with the mechanistic or what I would characterize as "organismic" strategies apparent in the examples above). The description reports the cultural significance of the movement of one dancer's knee as resulting from its "as if" character, its having been apparently intended for one effect but not actualizing it. Later, when focusing on the use of a dancer's head, the description, again using a subjunctive "seems to" construction, describes how the head serves a purpose in the dancing, becoming instrumental as a stable locus in contrast to other parts of a dancer. The "how to" nature of this description differs fundamentally from the "what-where" strategy typical of observationally weighted approaches.

Of African dance in general, Chernoff again describes movement within a nonpresent, futuristic frame, in terms of variations between "good," "best," and other performance instances. Chernoff writes:

The African dancer may pick up and respond to the rhythms of one or more drums, depending on his skill, but in the best dancing, the dancer, like the drummer, adds another rhythm, one that is not there. He tunes his ear to hidden rhythms, and he dances to the gaps in the music . . . Just as they listen to the supporting drums in a drum ensemble, African dancers listen to the rhythm section of a band – drums, bass, rhythm guitar, perhaps piano – and put some part of their bodies into a steady and relevant rhythmic pattern so that they can better hear and enjoy the melody or the improvisations. . . . Throughout a dance, a good dancer will maintain a correspondence between certain rhythms and certain movements, thus building a coherent unity into the dance by organisation of the music. When there is a significant shift of emphasis or accentuation in a musical arrangement, a good dancer will change his entire style of movement to fit the changing rhythmic motifs. He shows how the beat moves . . . (ibid.: 144–6)

In this passage, the descriptive strategy again is instrumental, explaining how the purpose of "adding rhythm" to a performance is accomplished. Chernoff goes even further in this regard in locating the source of movement, not in a predetermined, generic body part but in the incorporation of a noncorporeal phenomenon, "the beat," into an open-ended array of possible bodily members, idiosyncratically designated on the part of every dancer.

A second case in point, Barbara Browning's description of rhythmic movement in Brazilian samba dancing, provides another illustration of the new trajectory. Browning's description, taken from *Samba*, focuses on a rhythmic practice similar to that described by Chernoff above. Browning writes:

> The basic samba step appears to articulate the triplets. It requires levity, speed, and dexterity: it also requires accuracy, but not in the sense of hitting the rhythm on the mark. It must locate itself *between* rhythms. The dance is on a three-count – right-left-right/left-right-left – but it also weights one count, either the first or the second triplet. It may accentuate or contradict the weighting of the triplets in the music. As one triplet is heavier, the step slides toward the first line of rapid sixteenth-notes. The stronger step gives almost two sixteenths to itself and hints at the doubleness by, in an instant, shifting the weight from the ball of the foot to the heel: a double articulation or flexing at the joint. The step is *between* a triplet set and four sixteenth-notes. (1995: 12)

In this description, the abstraction of "the basic samba step" appears to follow an observationally weighted strategy. However, despite the generic characterization, the movement is nonetheless described in purposeful terms, and the description notes what it doesn't do (hit the rhythm on the mark) as well as what it does. Moreover, Browning's description also illustrates the integrating of bodily and nonbodily co-presences in movement, in this case of temporal patterning and the actions of the feet. As with Chernoff's concluding summary remark above ("he shows how the beat moves"), and Kurath's "keeping time" observation noted earlier, Browning's graphic description of the samba step characterizes movement in detailed terms that integrate bodily and temporal, nonbodily co-presences.

Interestingly, Browning notes at the end of the passage cited above that the description developed is not designed to facilitate embodied practice, which raises the question as to what extent it represents Browning's own embodied understanding. In a later section of *Samba*,

Browning provides one of a very few descriptions of her own movement practice given in this text, narrated in the context of an interaction with one of Browning's Brazilian candomblé teachers. The excerpt reads:

> My mother of saints . . . performed the same choreography, but the movement had become completely abstracted. Whereas my brutally referential thwacking of arm against arm would have been recognizable as a striking of blades, her gesture was a fluid vague crossing and uncrossing that might have been read as suggestive of anything from water to wheat.   (ibid.: 48)

In this passage, not only is an individual/ideal distinction emphasized, but the description also employs imagery in order to depict the energy quality and spatial form of the performance. This strategy is even more pronounced in a section of Browning's volume entitled, "Divine Choreography," which is devoted to describing the body movements of candomblé dancing. This is the section of *Samba* devoted most extensively to body movement description. Of the movements of the orisha goddess Yemanjá, Browning writes:

> Yemanjá, for example, the goddess of salt waters, dances with a shimmering, shivering motion in the shoulders which resembles the sea's surface. Her ample arms out-stretched, her ample breasts shaking with her fulsomeness, she steps forward and back on her right foot, the left nearly still, just skimming the surface on which she dances. She begins to pull her arms toward her in a gesture of collection: drawing her waters in as she does at low tide. Sometimes she bathes herself, scooping up the air-become-water which surrounds her and dousing herself in herself. In this sense she both *is* and *is in* water. Water in water disappears. But the principle of water makes herself manifest in the dance.   (ibid.: 65)

In this account, movement description integrates bodily action, characterized in terms of present perfect action, with the imagined, nonpresent substance of water.

Summarizing from the above descriptions of movement resulting from the use of embodied methodology, when differences in the description of human body movement in dance do emerge in studies relying more heavily on embodied practice, they present the following contrasts to the observationally weighted descriptions of such movement:

1   The embodied understanding is temporally complex or *plastic*, sometimes conditionally subjunctive or futuristic, as opposed to declarative in mood, framed more often by "as if" characterizations and modal "supposed to" clauses or negating contrasts. Chernoff's nearly-but-not-done knee gesture exemplifies this understanding. The present movement is described with reference, both to what it is not, and to what it should or should not be, to a subjunctive, conditional, or yet-to-be-fulfilled cultural given.

2   The embodied understanding is explanatory or "how-to" in character, technical and attuned to the cultural purposes for which the movement is designed. Descriptions focus on how a certain movement becomes do-able as opposed to what causes a certain movement to occur. Chernoff's understanding of the head of the African dancer, and Browning's of the samba step, both exemplify this type of insight. The embodied methodology makes execution problematic as opposed to a causal result.

3   The embodied understanding foregrounds contingency, fallibility, and the uniqueness of individual performers and performance events in relation to understood norms. Browning's account of her failure to replicate her teacher's movement illustrates this characteristic, as does Chernoff's of his learning to dance with a "cool head." While the generic representation of bodies and body parts is by no means unthinkable in the methodology, embodied methodology tends to avoid representing actual performers as *perfect* tokens of some cultural type.[10]

4   The embodied understanding tends to produce an awareness of movement as a source of integrating relationships in at least two general respects. First, with respect to dissociated aspects of the mover's being – memory or imagination and corporeality most prominently. Browning's use of imagery, for example, illustrates how movement connects nonactual imagined beings and characters with present ones.[11] Second, with respect to the mover and the environment in which the movement occurs (the "not-self" regions, characters, or presences of the performance venue with those of the self). Chernoff's "showing how the beat moves," and Browning's "stepping between triplets," illustrate the understanding of movement as integrating the mover with "other" noncorporeal temporal elements of the environment. Browning's description of the manifestation of the goddess in a dancer's body also illustrates the understanding of movement as integrating "self" bodies with "nonself" ones, in this case divine bodies.

In this regard, embodied practice can be seen to produce different understandings of the cultural aspect of human body movement that is manifest in dance. "Culture" as revealed through dance is cast, not as a simple present, perfect, and definite reality, but in terms of a present understood in relation to both past oppositions and instances, and to future temporal realities and continuities. Culture is understood as a set of strategies for improving the chances of masterful conduct, rather than as instructions for an automatic or perfect manifestation. Culture here creates in human body movement an array of techniques for dealing with contingencies that over time tend to produce greater conformity, as opposed to structures guaranteed to produce uniform acts in uniform actors. Finally, culture in movement is understood as the means of integrating existential dissociates, whether they be temporal, spatial, corporeal, and/or supernatural in character.

Conclusion

Returning, then, to the questions raised in the introduction, it is evident that the methodological paradigm shift toward embodied practice has not *necessarily* produced an epistemological or philosophical shift of any particular kind. Embodied practice, as the excerpt from Kurath illustrates, may result in descriptions that are orientated by the standard empirical frameworks of observationally weighted approaches. However, it is also evident from Chernoff's and Browning's writings that the methodological shift does have the capacity to produce epistemological shifts and to yield very different forms of cultural insight as well, depending on the author's purposes.

How, then, can this shift, when it does occur, be productively characterized in philosophical terms? Is the new trajectory indeed, as suggested in the introduction, a shift toward phenomenology?

Following Maxine Sheets-Johnstone's essay on phenomenology as a way of illuminating dance (1979:124–45), a mixed result suggests itself.[12] Two points in particular bear mention here:

1 With regard to the temporal plasticity of the movement descriptions, this seems not to align with a phenomenological inquiry. The embodied methodology descriptions are in fact *less* focused than the observationally weighted descriptions are on the actuality of the movement – what is represented in phenomenological discourse as the "actually present" or "actually there" nature of the movement as it is being experienced or "lived," to use Sheets-

Johnstone's phrasing (1979: 136, 138), in some present moment. On the contrary, the descriptions emerging from embodied methodologies in culturally focused research on dance appear to be *more* focused on nonpresent, nonactual, temporal characters than the observationally weighted approaches. In this regard, the new trajectory seems actually to be moving away from a phenomenological orientation, not toward one.[13]

2   With regard to the foregrounding of uniqueness and individual performance experiences, here the embodied approach seems clearly aligned with a phenomenological project. As individual human beings become represented as something other than perfect replicants of some cultural template, their capacity for phenomenological inquiry and reflection is established.

On the other hand, in its recognition of contingency and fallibility in regard to these unique instances and performers of human movement, a sharp difference in orientation from phenomenology again seems to emerge. That is to say, both contingency and fallibility are understandable only in relation to nonpresent realities, historical and remembered, as well as potential and imagined. The recognition of fallibility in performance, in particular, is unthinkable without a judgment being made in relation to some *preconceived* knowledge of a relatively perfect alternative, existent or imagined, and such preconceptions or experiential grids are precisely what the phenomenologist seeks to edit out of an account of authentic experience. As Sheets-Johnstone summarizes the phenomenologist's orientation:

> Phenomenology is concerned with the experience itself *as it is lived* and with bringing to light the essential nature of that experience through particular reflective acts that uncover what is actually there in experience and at the same time expose *preconceptions and prejudgments which have, unknown to us, become encrusted onto the experience.*   (1979: 138; latter emphasis mine)

In this respect, a cultural understanding of human movement, and culturally focused descriptions of it gained via embodied practice, would appear to be inherently "post-" or "meta-" or even possibly "anti-" phenomenological, since such cultural study appears to be working to reinscribe and internalize or "encrust" new modes of judgment into the researcher's being as a result of embodied practice, and not to expose or somehow negate them. It is in this regard that the research does appear most clearly to be bearing out the concern articulated in the introduction of the paper – the cultural interests motivating the research are leading in directions not approached by phenomenology, even while the shift to embodied methodology would appear to be supportive of phenomenological inquiry, generally speaking.[14]

In sum, it seems apparent from the mixed results of the literature surveyed that this new trajectory of culturally focused dance research, whose hallmark is a paradigm shift toward embodied methodology, does not seem *simply* to mean that current research at the intersection of dance, embodiment, and culture is becoming more phenomenological in character. The gains in understanding, which do in some cases seem profoundly different from the insights of the earlier period of research, are not, in many or even most respects, gains in phenomenological awareness and reflection. Rather than being centered primarily on the accumulation of phenomenological awareness or insight, the new trajectory seems to be entailing phenomenology in a larger, more complex epistemological project, the philosophical outlines and foundations of which have not yet come clearly into view. In addition to phenomenology, semiotics, hermeneutics, and various approaches in "practice" philosophy all may be illuminating orientations to explore as well, in understanding where this trajectory is heading and in how to understand the "advance" in our knowledge of dance and culture that is being left in its wake.

Notes

1 The origins of this methodological shift in cultural anthropology, however – in which primary emphasis on observation gives way to an emphasis on participation – can be traced back somewhat further. I would locate its roots in symbolic anthropology, with Victor Turner's pedagogical experiments and collaborations with Richard Schechner in the late 1970s and early 1980s. See Goodridge 1999: 183.

2 I, too, have been part of this shift toward embodied practice. In the introduction to *Body, Movement, and Culture*, I characterize myself as espousing "a performer's orientation" toward the classical ethnographic method of participant/observation. Likewise, I described the text produced from this orientation as primarily an exposition and illustration of "My process of physical, subjective, and dynamic attunement to choreographic phenomena" (1992: 3). Other studies that bear mention in this same regard are: Alter (1992), Chernoff (1979), Daniel (1995), Drewal (1992), Friedson (1996), Janet Goodridge's account of Tai Chi movement in Goodridge (1999), Jackson (1989), Laderman (1994), Lewis (1992), Limon (1994), Meduri (1988), Sklar (2001), Stoller (1995), and Zarrilli (1998).

3   In turning to philosophy in this effort, I am following phenomenologist and philosopher of dance, Maxine Sheets-Johnstone (1979: 127), who has argued that philosophical awareness provides "sounder critical grounds upon which to appraise writings on dance."

4   Here I am employing the terminology of Sheets-Johnstone (1979: 133).

5   Other examples of observationally weighted approaches include: Bartenieff and Paulay (1968), essays in Boas (1944), Evans-Pritchard (1928), Jablonko (1968), Katz (1982), Rappaport (1979), and, more recently J. Goodridge's account of Maring dance in Goodridge (1999), Ness (1997), essays in Spencer (1985), and Sweet (1985).

6   A significant exception in this regard is the human movement observation methodology developed by Warren Lamb. Lamb's methodology, based in part on the work of Rudolf von Laban, emphasizes the integral role of embodied practice in developing observational skills. Lamb has coined the phrase "observation demands participation," which is a foundational principle in his pedagogical program (unpublished manuscript, "Movement Observation," p. 10 and personal communication, June 23, 2000).

7   Chernoff (1979: 146) noted this consequence of participation with regard to African dance, identifying observation as a standard aspect of embodied practice.

8   Kurath and Garcia (1970: 82) described this step as "foot lifting with emphasis on right foot: up beat of raising right knee while supporting weight on left foot: accented lowering of right foot, while raising left heel and slightly flexing knees; unaccented raising of right knee while lowering left heel" (cited in Sweet 1985: 17).

9   Daniel (1995), Lewis (1992), Ness (1992), Novack (1990), and Zarrilli (1998) are other examples of this relatively "silent" participatory approach, where predominantly observational perspectives of body movement in dance are developed in studies that involve extensive embodied participation.

10 As Zarrilli (citing John Blacking 1985: 66) has noted, in his phenomenologically orientated study of Kalarippayattu martial art, the processual understanding of the self gained from embodied practice leads to the recognition that "there is no such thing as *the body*, there are many kinds of body, which are fashioned by the different environments and expectations that societies have of their members' bodies" (1998: 6). Zarrilli rejects outright a generic understanding of embodiment in cultural performance in this regard. "The body" Zarrilli characterizes as a "palimpsest," different in every individual case, constructed through various contingent circumstances, specific practices, and experiences, all of them interpreted through multiple semiotic or representational institutions: discourses, ideologies, and other social and cultural frameworks.

11 It should be noted that Radcliffe-Brown in more general terms also observed for this type of integration.

12 Limitations of space do not permit a full discussion of this question. In particular, the "how to" character of embodied understanding and its varying compatibility with different phenomenological approaches cannot here be addressed. Also the question of whether or not some kind of phenomenological phase of research is temporarily or transiently employed in embodied approaches that ultimately align with other philosophical orientations must be set aside for the present. Finally, the integrative aspect of the descriptions of human movement resulting from embodied methodology cannot here be assessed. A more complete analysis on these issues among others must await a subsequent essay.

13 It might be argued, however, that this trend is, in fact, compatible specifically with Martin Heidegger's phenomenological notion of historicality – that embodied practice is encouraging a more authentic awareness of temporality than the observationally weighted approaches tend to do. Limitations of space will not permit an explication of this argument, but I would reject it on the grounds that it establishes a link with the existential rather than the phenomenological aspects of Heidegger's philosophy (for commentary on Heidegger's phenomenology, and on his understanding of time and being in particular, see Dreyfus 1991). The representation of temporal plasticity and the subjunctive characterization of dance movement would seem to be aligning more closely in orientation with Peircean/pragmatic semiotic theory, particularly as that approach theorizes the temporal being of symbols and the human being as essentially sign-like in character. Symbols are understood to grow through time via repeated instances of manifestation and enactment. A continuity of experience, remembered and projected – rather than a given moment of performance – is seen to define their being, and such a continuity, in this case a tradition of embodied practice, is foregrounded in the embodied methodology descriptions.

14 Again, in this regard, the shift seems to be producing a closer alignment to semiotic philosophy, in its representation of individual actors and performances as the fallible, actual, instantiating agents of a continuity of practice.

References

Alter, J. (1992) *The Wrestler's Body: Identity and Ideology in North India*. Berkeley, CA: University of California Press.

Bartenieff, I. and Paulay, F. (1968) "Choreometric Profiles," in Alan Lomax (ed.), *Folk Song Style and Culture*. Washington, DC: American Association for the Advancement of Science, Publication 88, pp. 248–61.

Blacking, J. (1985) "Movement, Dance, Music and the Venda Girls' Initiation Cycle," in P. Spencer (ed.), *Society and the Dance*. Cambridge: Cambridge University Press, pp. 64–91.

Boas, F. (ed.) (1944) *The Function of Dance in Human Society*. New York: Dance Horizons.

Browning, B. (1995) *Samba: Resistance in Motion*. Bloomington, IN: Indiana University Press.

Chernoff, J. (1979) *African Rhythm and African Sensibility: Aesthetics and Social Action in African Musical Idioms*. Chicago, IL: University of Chicago Press.

Daniel, Y. (1995) *Rhumba: Dance and Social Change in Contemporary Cuba*. Bloomington, IN: Indiana University Press.

Drewal, M. (1992) *Yoruba Ritual: Performers, Play, Agency*. Bloomington, IN: Indiana University Press.

Dreyfus, Hubert L. (1991) *Being-in-the-World: A Commentary on Heidegger's* Being and Time, Division I. Cambridge, MA: MIT Press.

Evans-Pritchard, E.E. (1928) "The Dance," *Africa* 1: 446–64.

Friedson, S. (1996) *Dancing Prophets: Musical Experience in Tumbuka Healing*. Chicago, IL: University of Chicago Press.

Goodridge, J. (1999) *Rhythm and Timing of Movement in Performance: Drama, Dance and Ceremony*. London: Jessica Kingsley Publishers.

Jablonko, A. (1968) "Dance and Daily Activities among the Maring People of New Guinea: A Cinematographic Analysis of Body Movement Style," PhD dissertation, Columbia University, New York.

Jackson, M. (1989) *Paths Toward a Clearing*. Bloomington, IN: Indiana University Press.

Katz, R. (1982) *Boiling Energy: Community Healing Among the Kalahari Kung*. Cambridge, MA: Harvard University Press.

Kurath, G. (1986) *Half a Century of Dance Research: Essays by Gertrude Prokosch Kurath*. Ann Arbor, MI: Cushing-Malloy.

Kurath, G. and Garcia, A. (1970) *Music and Dance of the Tewa Pueblos*. Santa Fe, NM: Museum of New Mexico.

Laderman, C. (1994) "The Embodiment of Symbols and the Acculturation of the Anthropologist," in T. Csordas (ed.), *Embodiment and Experience: The Existential Ground of Culture and Self*. Cambridge: Cambridge University Press, pp. 183–97.

Lamb, W. (undated) "Movement Observation," unpublished typescript.

Lewis, J.L. (1992) *Ring of Liberation*: *Deceptive Discourse in Brazilian Capoeira*. Chicago, IL: University of Chicago Press.

Limon, J. (1994) *Dancing with the Devil: Society and Cultural Poetics in Mexican-American South Texas*. Madison, WI: University of Wisconsin Press.

Meduri, A. (1988) "Bharatha Natyam – What Are You?" *Asian Theatre Journal* 5, 1: 1–22.

Mooney, J. (1965) *The Ghost-Dance Religion and the Sioux Outbreak of 1890*, ed. A. Wallace. Chicago, IL: University of Chicago Press (first published 1896, Washington, DC: Government Printing Office).

Ness, S. (1992) *Body, Movement, and Culture: Kinesthetic and Visual Symbolism in a Philippine Community*. Philadelphia, PA: University of Pennsylvania Press.

Ness, S. (1997) "Originality in the Postcolony: Choreographing the Neo-Ethnic Body in Philippine Concert Dance," *Cultural Anthropology* 12, 1: 64–108.

Novack, C. (1990) *Sharing the Dance: Contact Improvisation and American Culture.* Madison, WI: University of Wisconsin Press.

Radcliffe-Brown, A.R. (1948) *The Andaman Islanders* (first published 1922). Glencoe, IL: Free Press.

Rappaport, R. (1979) *Ecology, Meaning, and Religion.* Berkeley, CA: North Atlantic Books.

Schieffelin, E. (1976) *The Sorrow of the Lonely and the Burning of the Dancers.* New York: St. Martin's Press.

Sheets-Johnstone, M. (1979) "On Movement and Objects in Motion: The Phenomenology of the Visible in Dance," *Journal of Aesthetic Education* 13, 2: 33–46.

Sklar, D. (2000) "Reprise: On Dance Ethnography," *Dance Research Journal* 32, 1: 70–7.

Sklar, D. (2001) *Dancing with the Virgin: Body and Faith in the Fiesta of Tortugas, New Mexico.* Berkeley, CA: University of California Press.

Spencer, P. (ed.) (1985) *Society and the Dance: The Social Anthropology of Process and Performance.* Cambridge: Cambridge University Press.

Stoller, P. (1995) *Embodying Colonial Memories: Spirit Possession, Power and the Hauka in West Africa.* New York: Routledge.

Sweet, J. (1985) *Dances of the Tewa Pubos Indians.* Santa Fe, NM: School of American Research Press.

Zarrilli, P. (1998) *When the Body Becomes All Eyes: Paradigms, Discourses and Practices of Power in Kalarippayattu, a South Indian Martial Art.* Delhi: Oxford University Press.

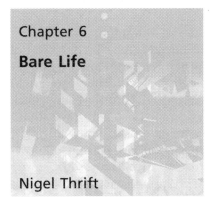

Chapter 6

Bare Life

Nigel Thrift

The rush of our thought forward through its fringes is the everlasting peculiarity of its life. We realise this life as something always off its balance, something in transition, something that shoots out of darkness through a dawn into a brightness that we feel to be the dawn fulfilled . . . in every crescendo of sensation, in every effort to recall, in every progress towards the satisfaction of desire, this succession of an emptiness and a fullness that have reference to each other and are one flesh is the essence of the phenomenon.

James (1912: 283)

What is it that, being itself invisible, is responsible for all that is visible?

(Katz 1999: 7)

Vast organizations exist to get our attention. They make cunning plans. They bite us with their ten second bites. Our consciousness is their staple; they live on it. Think of consciousness as a territory just opening to settlement and exploitation, something like an Oklahoma land rush. Put it in color, set it to music, frame it in images – but even this fails to do justice to the vision. Obviously consciousness is infinitely bigger than Oklahoma.

(Bellow 1991: ix)

Introduction: Detailing "Real" Experience

This chapter is concerned with disclosing some of the processes by which very small spaces and times have become intelligible. These very small spaces and times are hardly trivial, for out of them the key institutions of modern life are carving increasingly large projects of dominion. By mastering various knowledges of detail, these institutions are able to set off on courses of action whose endpoints are often unknown even to them but whose effects are already becoming clear: new kinds of "bodies" (understood as patterns of affective association and capacity cutting across "individual" biological bodies), which have quite different characteristic forces from those found before (Gatens and Lloyd 1999).

We are talking, then, about new kinds of "human nature," bodies that are able to be actively prefigured through the manipulation of very small spaces and times. These new natures are of intense interest currently for two reasons. One is the rise of academic interest in nonrepresentational approaches to the question of human being which conceive of timespace as having no determined actuality (and therefore challenge "the unhappy necessity for us not to know ahead of time – a necessity which would disappear once we acquire knowledge," Deleuze 1990: 54). Such approaches dwell more fully in the "now" and are therefore intent on articulating spaces of time that were heretofore thought to be inarticulable (Thrift 1996, 2000a, 2002; May and Thrift 2001). The second reason is the more general renewal of interest in the natural. Much recent work on nature has consisted of attempts to produce a redemptive understanding of the natural, an understanding which has some similarities with the nonrepresentational turn in that it depends upon a performative refiguring of time as knotted but also held open (e.g. Abram 1997; Kerridge and Sammells 1998).

In actual fact, I think there are clear cultural reasons for these expressions of interest in new human natures and the characteristic forces they make possible (though I am not, I should add, a fully signed-up cultural constructivist). One reason, which I do not have the space to take up here, is the rise of a therapeutic ethos, an ethos based upon the growth of an emancipated self, an emotivist stance, the psychologization of everyday life, and a commitment to "good" communication (Cameron 2000; Nolan 1998). In turn, this ethos has led to the formation of a series of therapeutic knowledges which take in nature as their own capacities. The other reason, which I will take up now, is the much greater emphasis on the effectivity of interaction taking place in very short periods of time that can allow us to expect that "our" nature, and life more generally, will show up in more concentrated form, so to speak, as flashes of intrinsically worthwhile experience.

In an attempt to find a means to understand the wherefore of this cultural shift, I will take up a leitmotiv, namely "bare life" (*zoé*). This little phrase has a long and complex genealogy. It was originally used by Aristotle as part of what might be called his "third personal" approach to life (Lawson-Tancred 1986). In Aristotle's work, bare life stands for a kind of primary experience, "simple natural sweetness," the "simple" fact of living itself, which stands outside the realm of politics, both because it is outside the activities of the *polis* and because it can be opposed to *bios*, the qualified way of life particular to a group – all the laws, customs, and conventions which both aggregate and differentiate humanity.[1] Yet, as Foucault (1998: 188) made clear, iron-ically it is this simple natural life which has become the main target of modern biopolitics. Bare life is now heavily politicized. "For millennia man remained what he was for Aristotle: a living animal with the additional capacity for practical existence: modern man is an animal whose politics call his existence as a living being into question." Indeed it is possible to argue that simple natural life is now the most active zone of politics. Much of the work on nature yearns for free-dom from this politicization and yet also actively tries to forge its own politics of this zone, one based around magic words like experience, the senses and embodiment.

But what is the simple fact of living itself? For perhaps the chief exponent of the interrogation of the politics of bare life, Giorgio Agamben, it is, I think several things. To begin with, calling on Agamben's past as the Italian editor of Benjamin's complete works, it is something like pure, "real" experience.[2] Agamben is well aware of the problems and contradictions inherent in such a term (see Agamben 1993: 31–43) but he clearly believes that there is a kind of mute infancy of experience, "something anterior both to subjectivity and to an alleged psychological reality" (ibid.: 37). Human being is always beyond and before the human.[3] Then, I think that, as a realm of potentiality, bare life for Agamben is also concerned with "every-dayness" as a common "place" and as an excess. Bare life emerges from "a spatio-temporal suppression of sorts: where effective differ-ence and transformative potential are not achieved in the apparent distance between departure and destruction, but through travelling along the cusp of inseparable points of flow, as a trajectory or line in continual variation with itself" (Seigworth 2000: 230). In other words, a kind of constant shimmer of the poiesis of praxis (Agamben 1999a). And, finally, bare life also I think signifies for Agamben the Benjaminian valorization of the "seemingly ephemeral, transient, incorporeal, and inorganic aspects of everyday life," which are granted equal status with "the presumably much harder and faster world of materiality and corporeality" (Seigworth 2000: 257).

So bare life becomes an impossible possibility focused by the contours of the simple living body. And what those contours are becomes what is at stake in modern society. But what counts as a simple living body? What is its address? This is the issue that I want to address in the subsequent two parts of this chapter.

In the first part of the chapter, I will argue that the "simple living body" should be identified with that small space of time – what is often called the half-second delay – between action and consciousness which has increasingly become attended to because of our enhanced ability to capture movement. And this small space of time has until recently been a largely undiscovered continent "made of rhythms, muffled pulses and fluxes traversing the corporeal machine (producing nervous discharges, reactions, in short the automatic writing of nature itself)" (Dagognet 1992a: 132). In the second part of the chapter, I will then show how, as this segment of time has become visible, so it has become available to be worked upon. Drawing my examples from new developments in capitalist business, I will show how a whole new zone of biopolitics has therefore gleefully been opened up, which should at the same time initiate a debate over what we can and should count as politics: at the very least, the half-second pause should give us pause.

The stakes are high. As Agamben points out, our biopolitical culture has separated out *zoé* from *bios* in ways that are deeply problematic because they give us little means of grasping what bare life is and yet prescribe what counts as its politics: "there is politics because man is the living being who, in language, separates and opposes himself to his own bare life and, at the same time, maintains himself in relation to that bare life in an inclusive exclusion" (Agamben 1998: 8). Caught outside the utterable, bare life languishes, and yet, as Foucault and Agamben make clear, it also becomes the object of all kinds of insidious body politics – included certainly, but as an exclusion. Thus "the possibility of differentiating between our biological body, and our political body – between what is incommunicable and mute and what is communicable and sayable – [is] taken from us forever" (Agamben 1998: 188). For Agamben the upshot is clear: "a law that seeks to transform itself wholly into life is more and more confronted with a life that has been deadened and mortified into juridical rule" (ibid.: 187). Victory is achieved by law, but at a terrible price.

Bare Life

If we are to ever attain in some form the "beautiful day" of bare life, some sense of sweetness of life, then the first thing we need to do is to understand what bare life might be. And what seems clear to me is that modern civilizations make that task easier – by providing various empirical means of sensing bare life which are historically novel because they allow us to attend *to much smaller spaces of time*: "the imperceptible, the fleeting, the tumultuous and the flashing" (Dagognet 1992a: 15). I will note just four of these revolutions in the means of perception. First, there is the ability to sense the small spaces of the body. This has become much greater (Amato 2000; Stafford 1996, 1998). Through the texts and instruments of science we can now think of the body as a set of micro-geographies. For example, "in the past, the microscope exposed the thickness of experience, the depth of the level" (Stafford 1991: 202). Today, the subvisible body is tracked in other ways too. For example, modern computerized tomography has, through magnetic resonance imaging, been able to map the emergent landscape of neuronal firing. (Carter 1998; Damasio 1999; Le Doux 1998).

Second, the ability to sense and freeze minute "transitional" bodily movements has become greater. Beginning with Darwin's use of photography to capture facial expression (Darwin 1872/1998; Prodger 1998), and continuing with the work of Edward Muybridge and Etienne-Jules Marey, new senses of visual procession-precision were invented which, in turn, created new conditions of visibility (Braun 1992; Dagognet 1992b; Snyder 1998). This mechanical imagination has become a key element of the age of media overload in which the camera can impose its own politics of time and space (Shapiro 1999); we can now think of space as minutely segmented frames of time, able to be speeded up, slowed down, even frozen for a while.[4] Thus nature can be transposed (Dagognet 1992a, 1992b; Gumbrecht 1998). Third, numerous body practices have come into existence which rely on and manage such knowledge of small times and spaces – most especially those connected with the performing arts, including the "under-performing" of film acting, much modern dance, the insistent cross-hatched tempo of much modern music, and so on (Thrift 2000b). And special performance notations, like Labanotation and other "choreo-graphics" (Hutchinson-Guest 1989), allow minute movement to be recorded, analyzed, and recomposed. Then, finally, a series of discourses concerning the slightest gesture and utterance of the body has been developed, from the elaborate turn-taking of conversational analysis to the intimate spaces of proxemics, from the analysis of gesture to the mapping of "body language," which, suitably packaged up, have made their way out into the world (e.g. McNeill 1995).[5]

In other words, what we can see is what was formerly invisible or imperceptible becoming constituted as visible and perceptible through a new structure of attention which is more and more likely to pay lip-service to those actions which go on in small spaces and times, actions which involve qualities like anticipation, improvisation, and intuition – all those things which, by drawing on the second-to-second resource-fulness of the body, make for artful conduct. Indeed, nowadays,

> One minute of social life looks like an affair so burdensome as to give a headache not only to the reader of its transcription, but to the subjects of its execution in the first place [but] that's not life. It is artfulness that keeps such exquisite interaction sensitivity do-able. The saving virtue of art is pragmatic; it lies in the weightlessness that gives grace to action. (Katz 1999: 344)

And in a sense the connection between science and art has become closer as the relation between science and art, the real and the figurative, has been retooled by the new imaginations produced by all the above developments strange and charmed (see Ede 2000; Jones and Galison 1998). We might say in summary that our structure of attention now involves the inhabitation of much smaller spaces and times than before, spaces and times which proceed out of the general assumption that perception can no longer "be thought of in terms of immediacy, presence, punctuality" (Crary 1999: 4).[6] Perception is both stretched and intensified, widened and condensed.

In turn, this new structure of attention, through the empirical construction of speed, has allowed us to slow up/speed down, so gaining a much greater understanding of "bare life." We can now see an undiscovered country hoving into view, the country of the "half-second delay." The discovery of this period of bodily anticipation arose out of work on the speed of the nerve impulse. The difficulties of the measurement of this impulse, and especially the time that a stimulus took to travel to the brain and back, eventually led to the production of a new world. Measuring the time differences involved was one of the major early contributions of the pioneering psychophysicist, Hermann von Helmholtz (Cahan 1993; Olesko and Holmes 1993). While it was formerly thought to be immeasurable, his experimental apparatus showed that the propagation velocity of the nerve impulse was both finite and measurable. That mid-nineteenth century discovery galvanized much of the scientific world (impressing, for example, Alexander von Humboldt), not least because of the comparatively *slow* speed of this propagation. Perception was not immediate: it took place in time. Pointing at an absence had produced a presence (Latour 1998). The process of discovery was continued by one of von Helmholtz's former assistants, Wilhelm Wundt.[7] In his later work, he distinguished between what he called perception and apperception (Bringmann and Tweney 1980; Rieher 2001). Perception was the term reserved for early-forming pre-aware responses to the world, the responses that allow us to hit a tennis ball or drive a car. Then, after perception, comes the fuller, more reflective consciousness of apperception. The investigation of perception blossomed, with the result that the time structure of the body began to be explored in much greater detail, often using the new technologies of movement. For example, it was shown that the brain anticipates and interpolates properties like motion and color in advance of the actual event (the famous "phi effect"). Consciousness, in other words, takes time to construct; we are "late for consciousness" (Damasio 1999: 127). In the 1960s, this insight was formalized by Libet, using the new body recording technologies. He showed decisively that an action is set in motion before we decide to perform it: our "average readiness potential" is about 0.8 seconds, although cases as long as 1.5 seconds have been recorded. In other words, "consciousness takes a relatively long time to build, and any experience of it being instantaneous must be a backdated illusion" (McCrone 1999: 131). Or rather a forecast. Thus,

[M]uch of our mental lives are lived in a twilight world of not properly conscious impulses, inklings, automatisms, and reflexive actions. The standard example of an intelligent, yet heavily automated, mental process is driving a car . . . this automation of quite dangerous decision-making and skilled action is not the exception, but the norm. Our brains seem designed to handle as much as possible at a subconscious level of awareness, leaving focal consciousness to deal with tasks which are either particularly difficult or novel.   (McCrone 1999: 35)

Of course, none of this is meant to suggest that conscious awareness is just along for the ride. Rather, we can say that the preconscious comes to be more highly valued and, at the same time, conscious awareness is repositioned as a means of focusing and sanctioning action. Put another way, what has been found is that the body has a number of ways of coping with time, each of which works through structures of anticipation, the something to be known which is very often the body's own movements, which "leave some aspect of the moment standing proud" (McCrone 1999: 158).

Thus, what we are able to see is that the space of embodiment is expanded by a fleeting but crucial moment, a constantly moving preconscious frontier of attention (Lowe and Schaffer 1999), a vibration in space and time.[8] And this small space of time, equally clearly, is linked to what and how we are. But there is more to say than this.

First, this fleeting space of the moment is utterly wrapped up with its context, and most especially the object world. "It is almost impossible to imagine a moment without a context. There is always something about what has just happened that predicts what is likely to happen – or not to happen – next. Even sitting in homes, lounging in a comfy chair and apparently not thinking about or doing anything in particular, we would still be deeply embedded in a set of expectations" (McCrone 1999: 148). Through the object world, "we" are orientated to our surroundings, and the body–object combination produces a carefully graded sense of the possibilities of any situation.

Second, this fleeting space is heavily political. The by now familiar work of Bourdieu and others on bodily hexis, drawing especially on the writings of Heidegger, Wittgenstein, and Merleau-Ponty, shows the ways in which the structure of expectation of the world (the background) – which is a huge part of the world – is set up by body practices which have complex and often explicitly political genealogies. The smallest gesture or facial expression can have the largest political compass (Ekman 1992). More recent work has added to this understanding by emphasizing the degree to which these body practices rely on the emotions, which are a vital element of the body's apprehension of the world; emotions are a vital part of the body's anticipation of the moment. Thus, we can now understand emotions as a kind of thinking (Damasio 1999; Le Doux 1998), but the reflection of emotions is corporeal rather than a matter of discursive reasoning. "Through our emotion, we reach back sensually to grasp the tacit, embodied foundations of ourselves" (Katz 1999: 7). Emotions quite literally shape the mo(ve)ment.

So, we now have a space of time which is increasingly able to be sensed, the space of time which shapes the moment and which I equate with bare life. Of course, once such a space is opened up it can also be operated upon and harvested. As Foucault and Agamben make clear, biopolitics is at the center of western modes of power; it is through the production and ordering of bodies that power is experienced. As a new biological domain becomes visible and so available to be worked upon, what we can see is the potential for new entities and new institutions. In other words, this domain, which has been implicitly political, through the mechanics of the various body positions which are a part of its multiple abilities to anticipate, becomes explicitly political through practices which are aimed at it specifically. This is a politics that arises out of the enormous efforts that are currently being made by numerous institutions across a range of different and intersecting arenas to foreground the background of bare life – to make it comprehensible and therefore able to be apprehended and so made more of. Of these interests and arenas the most powerful, and in certain ways the most astute, is capitalist business. In the second part of this chapter, therefore, I turn to a survey of the increasingly less hesitant incursions being made by business into bare life.

The Business of Bare Life

How has business been able to build a direct presence in the domain of bare life? It has been able to do this through mobilizing a series of practical and theoretical knowledges which operate on the structures of anticipation of bare life. These knowledges have four main characteristics. First, they operate in the presentational rather than the discursive register. Their chief interest is in how, not why. Second, they all actively use space in order to obtain effects. Third, they are chiefly concerned with providing new times in which new things can be constructed and attended to. And, fourth, they are all caught up in different ways with Benjamin's cinematically composed and expanded "time of the now." Gradually, such knowledges have been filled out by a growing archive based on a number of practical and, increasingly, theoretical sources, all of which stress knowledge-as-action (Pfeffer and Sutton 2000).

Four practical sources have been particularly important. To begin with, there has been tourism. Since the 1960s a new kind of tourism has emerged, which is based upon the theming of spaces in order to produce and manage anticipation and engage attention. Gleaned from experiences like running museums, theme parks, and certain kinds of themed retailing, a body of knowledge has been constructed of how to produce spaces which grip the senses. In recent times, the kinesthetic element of tourism has been amplified, relying on the construction of carefully nurtured peak experiences, on the engineering of extreme moments which grasp the body's attention, as in the various post-colonial forms of adventure, from hot-air ballooning to battle re-enactments and from helicopter hiking to white-water rafting. Then there is a second source: sport and exercise (Brailsford 1991; Shapiro 1999). Sport and exercise is not only a key element in the turnover of modern economies but it is also a key influence on modern bodily comportment, the result of careful micro-manipulations of specialized bodily spaces and times, involving a number of precision knowledges, and the slowed-down/speeded-up demands of media framings of sport spaces and times which many sports now actively play to or are even constituted by. A third source has been communicative interaction with customers. Increasingly, the smallest space of time is being sculpted. For example, small strips of conversation are increasingly acted out in venues as different as restaurants, shops, and call centers (Cameron 2000). Further, the idea is clearly to go beyond this. Through teaching employees styles of interaction, the aim is to produce impressions before the event: "the 'styled' communicator uses language less to do things (negotiate, argue, solve problems) than to be, or appear to be things (warm, friendly, enthusiastic, soothing). Expressiveness is valued over instrumentality" (Cameron 2000: 87). One more source has been performance. Since the 1960s the extensive knowledge of performance produced by the performing arts has moved out from the stage to fill all manner of venues, from corporate presentations to the streets. The arts of performance are fast becoming general (Abercrombie and Longhurst 1998). These four sources of micro-kinetic knowledge have been reflected, refined, amplified, and re-presented by two other more theoretical sources of such knowledge. To begin with there is, of course, the mass media, which have been the crucial means by which bare life has become visible. The slow-motion shot, the freeze frame, and all the other possible "time shifts" (Cubitt 1991), have become means of reconstructing the moment, and have increasingly become sensory standards which the general population plays into. Most recently, for example, advertising agencies (which have often stressed the "subliminal") and other such media institutions have been attempting to transfer more and more of bare life onto the screen, making claims that they can produce "high tech/high touch" through their knowledge of the potentialities of the screen. And then there are all the institutions of business knowledge – management consultancies, business schools, market research companies, and so on – which have reflected, refined, and synthesized so much knowledge of bare life, not least by importing practices from academic disciplines like psychology.

In what follows, I will consider just three of the incursions by business into the realm of bare life, namely the brand-new forms of commodity and management education orientated toward boosting creativity, as examples of how business is actively attempting to produce, through the mobilization of a series of knowledges of very small spaces and times, what Davenport and Beck (2001) call, more than aptly given the discussion above, an "attention economy." Based on the premise that the world is full of distractions (or as they put it, citing William James, "bloomin' buzzin' confusion"), the business of the attention economy is to fight for every bit of space and time by producing new comportments that are automatically engaged with those aspects of the world that favor particular commercial imperatives. Business therefore becomes a kind of second nature.

1 The Brand

Brands are an important element of modern business, but, until recently, even given the increasing value being placed on nonphysical assets, there was little understanding of how or why brands worked. In some senses, this lack of understanding is rather strange. For, in the guise of little badges and other emblems, they have a long history. In particular, they were, of course, one of the foundations of totalitarian modes of socialization, an "external proof that despite appearances to the contrary, [people] were always and already fundamentally and exclusively the same" (Gilroy 2000: 161). "Placed on or close to the body, 'such momentary iconic associations' expressed more than assent to the revolutionary transformation of social life. They were all the more potent when they were wordless and could . . . extend martial imperatives, habits, and disciplines beyond the bounds of the uniform-wearing minority" (ibid.). As Gilroy argues, part of the power of these little flashes of belonging seems to have come from the increasing ability of the population to register these cues, as a result of technologies like cinema.

Certainly such skills are a crucial element of the current power of brands, for it has become increasingly clear that brands work by establishing visual addresses in bare life, lines, steps, stops, and volumes in motion, which call attention to the time of seeing and the seeing of time-schematic attitudes. Establishing such minimal addresses involves three steps. First, brands must track their wearers' bodies in time and space, tracing out the contours of the human body in movement. Brands quite literally locate. Second, they must establish a particular timing of space, the repetitive space of the frame, the structure of attention of film taken into the space of the body: "the time of the brand is neither simply cut up by the clock nor caught up in a narrative; it is barely a sequence. Time takes place in a repetition of sound, in a loop of videos" (Lury 1999: 6). Third, they must act as "phatic images," "symbols which maintain discourse or dialogue and have little or no intrinsic meaning, for example, 'How are you?' In graphic media such as comics, phatic communication refers to panels, framing devices such as lines, balloons, rules and margins, and motifs such as special lines or arrows" (ibid.: 22–3). They are pure operators, in other words. Thus we can see that brands are way-finding devices in an informational age which, because of their parsimonious nature, are able to act in many different contexts as here–there connections, as marks of minimal association and maximum connectivity which, precisely because of their fragility, can endure. They are signs understood as immediate response, as in Wundt's notion of perception discussed above.

Brands, then, form a particular new kind of property – of a still difficult to determine value – able to exist only because of the automation of perception. But there are other means that business has found of gaining a grip on bare life. These appeal more directly to bare life by producing an engaging and compelling ethnology of the senses which can animate – "turn on" – the body. It is to these kinds of effects that I turn next.

2 The Experience Economy

In recent years commentators like Pine and Gilmore (1999) have argued that a new category of output is arising – what they call the experience economy – which through the constitution of object-experiences (the dividing line is either thin or nonexistent) can produce added value. It goes without saying (quite literally in a sense) that much of the force of this experience economy comes out of and is aimed at the domain of bare life. I will mention just four of the different object-experiences that have now become possible.

The first is objects that arise out of and engage with the automation of perception in a direct way, by emphasizing kinesthesia. What is fascinating is the speed with which knowledge of movement is becoming engrained into industries as different as film, animation, and special effects; into computer games and virtual reality games; into stadium presentations complete with music and light; into new forms of extreme sports; and into theme-park rides. Increasingly, in particular, this knowledge is projected through objects that are based on particular sequences of movement which engage the visceral sense as well as the proprioceptive and fine-touch senses in order to produce pure affect/effect.

The second object-experience is the growth of goods that provide rapid feedback to the senses and that engage them in attractive ways. The explicit sensorializing of goods has only just started but it is a boom industry:

> Doing so requires awareness of which senses most affect customers, focuses on those senses and the sensations they experience, and the corporate redesign of the good to make it more appealing. Auto makers, for example, now spend millions of dollars on every model to make sure that car doors sound just so when they close. Publishers greatly enhance the covers and interiors of books and magazines with a number of tactile innovations (embossed lettering, scratching, bumpy or ultrasmooth surfaces) and sigh sensations (translucent covers, funky fonts, clear photographs, three-dimensional graphics). Even presentation markers aren't just coloured any more; Sanford scents them as well (liquorice for black, cherry for red, etc). (Pine and Gilmore 1999: 18)

Then, the third object-experience is the explicit design of packaged experiences which build and manage anticipation. This packaging can range all the way from the increasing outsourcing of children's parties from the home to companies, to the most elaborate virtual environments, which are virtually self-contained ethologies:

> Companies that want to stage compelling capacities should . . . determine the theme of the experience as well as the impressions that will convey the theme to guests. Many times, experience stagers develop a list of

impressions they wish guests to store away and then think creatively about different themes and storylines that will bring the impressions together in the cohesive narrative. Then they winnow the impressions down to a manageable number – only and exactly those which truly denote the chosen theme. Next they focus on the animate and inanimate cues that could connote each impression, following the simple guidelines of accentuating the positive and eliminating the negative. They then must meticulously map out the effect each cue will have on the five senses – sight, sound, taste, touch and smell – taking care not to overwhelm guests with too much sensory input. Finally, they add memorabilia to the total mix, extending the experience in the customer's mind over time. Of course, embracing these principles remains, for now, an art form. But those companies which figure out how to design experiences that are compelling, engaging, memorable – and rich – will be the ones leading the way into the emerging experience economy.   (Pine and Gilmore 1999: 61)

Then there is a fourth kind of object-experience. This fourth kind of experience is the use of nonconscious cues to add ambience to retail environments so as to produce impulse purchases (what, in the trade, are called significantly "experiential" purchases). These cues can be of various kinds. They can consist of lighting, or smell, or sound (Walker Art Center 2000). Take the use of music. At its most general, music can be used as a way of reinforcing "visual materials in 'branding' products and their implicit consumers, serving as 'welcome mats' and 'keep out' notices, depending on how they are received" (De Nora and Belcher 2000: 93). Music outlines the retail space. But, more specifically, music can be used to set up what are hoped to be pliable moods. Music acts to cue a mood which can stimulate a purchase. But this cannot be construed in simple reflex terms. Rather, "music draws upon conventions (and perceived conventions) to place on offer what actors may perceive as frameworks of and for agency. These need not be perceived consciously, they may simply be 'felt.' The point, however, is that music is something to which its hearers respond . . ." (ibid.: 99).

These kinds of enhanced commodities and enhancements of commodities, which reach into bare life, are paralleled by attempts by businesses to reach into bare life to change the content and business itself, to redefine what business is about. This is the final incursion.

3 The Conduct of Business

Finally, bare life figures in attempts to provide new conduits for the conduct of business, conduits which are aimed at producing maximum creativity so as to produce a continuous stream of innovations, and so emphasize previously overlooked anticipatory qualities like intuition and improvisation, and which can provide an answer to heightened pressures of competition and ever more rapid turnaround and product development times.

In particular, we can see business taking a leaf out of the book of the performance arts, since these are the domain of human life which have most valued practices of creativity and are most attuned to them: such techniques especially depend upon the building of small, tightly formed groups, which can, then, through "serious play" (Schrage 2000), ignite creativity, "make sparks fly" (Leonard and Swap 2000). They must therefore not only have instrumental aspects but must also engage the passions, generate excitement and surprise, "stimulate to innovate." What is being produced, in other words, is an "art of business" experiment.

To enable such a process of customized surprise to happen, the managerial body must be made visible so that it can be worked upon. But this cannot be forced to happen in an unduly prescriptive way, as in, for example, the various form of drill often applied to workers. Instead, it must be of a participative nature, using interaction of a relatively open-ended kind:

> If we believe that people in organizations achieve goals by participating inventively in practices that can never be fully captured by institution-alized processes, then we will minimize prescription, suspecting that too much of it discourages the very inventiveness that makes practices effect-ive. We will have to make sure that our organizations are contexts within which the communities that develop these practices may prosper. We will have to value the work of community-building and make sure that participants have access to the resources necessary to learn what they need to learn in order to take actions and make decisions that fully engage their own knowledge ability.   (Wenger 1999: 10)

If this process of community-building is successful, then what will be produced will be a body-organization which will be committed to innovation and creativity:

> A whole variety of techniques from the performing arts are currently in use in business, all of which aim to stimulate creativity by fostering community. Companies are beginning to wake up to the advantages of a more creative approach to team-building – one that is altogether less

threatening and more enjoyable. No more ropes, no more freezing mud. All, then, to the arts which is producing the new source of inspiration when it comes to bringing out the best in your employees.

Marks and Spencer, Sainsbury's and Allied Domecq are using the UK companies to embrace this new approach to management training. Oxford Stage Company, based in Warwick, ran a workshop for Sainsbury's showing how much can be communicated through body language alone. Trade Secrets, another touring company, ran a series of communication workshops in Sainsbury's stores to accompany a national tour of *Twelfth Night*. The staff's thrill at undertaking Shakespeare for the first time (no mean feat in itself) was matched by their enthusiasm for the games and exercises.

Body and Soul, based in Gloucestershire, has workers dancing along in harmony – by teaching them Rio carnival-style salsa percussion. Employees without a musical bone in their body are eventually transformed into rhythmic pulsating beasts. It helps to increase their self-confidence and teaches them to work together.

Clients include city merchant banks, along with companies such as Pfizer and Virgin, Our Price. Mr Brotherton says: "It's very good for self-confidence and teamwork. The barriers come down, people take their shoes and socks off and start dancing. They find out an awful lot about each other."   (McKee 1999: 26)

In turn, many of these new techniques drawing on the performing arts are also explicitly stimulating creativity through operating on bare life. Such techniques explicitly ask: "What is the mind prepared to perceive? And in what form does chance, or surprise, make its appearance?" (Schrage 2000: 125). The answer seems to be: through a disciplined craft of play, of the kind found in forms of improvisatory acting, dance, and music, which involves working up a specific corporate "rehearsal style" in which participants learn to discover the properties of an interpersonal situation and to reflect-in-action on their intuitive responses to it (Schön 1991).

But it is with the arts that management theory is really coming into its own. . . . Living Arts, based in London, gets participants to stage their own performances with the help of performers and technical staff drawn from opera, theatre, circus and film. One group of UK business consultants on a "bonding" trip to Lisbon were given a week in which to create an entire opera – a refreshing variation on the usual team-building games. The effect was exhilarating. One participant said, "You forget most conferences within two days. We will remember this retreat in detail until we are 85."

Tim Stocki, ABSA's (Association for Business Sponsorship of the Arts) director of programmes, reports steadily rising demand for this approach to training. "This is a growth area," he says. "After years being taught to think logically and focus on the bottom line, employees are now being encouraged to think laterally and creatively. This is where artists are ideal." (McKee 1999: 27)

In other words, through group work, the anticipatory skills of intuition and improvisation can be worked on so that as circumstances change it is possible to react swiftly to them. Such a process of continual stimulation quite clearly depends upon making some of the processes of bare life visible – anticipation, improvisation, gesture, reaction – in order to be able to mobilize them to best effect.

Conclusions

What I have tried to demonstrate in this paper is the extraordinary investments currently being made in showing up and working on the domain of bare life, all aimed at the abstraction of perception, understood in Wundt's terms. The land of the half-second delay is being both constructed and explored simultaneously.

And this is a fiercely biopolitical process. Our perceptions are increasingly becoming instrumentalized. The half-second interval is being trained up. The dark side of this process is patently clear. Our room to play and dream is being cut down. There is a more and more habitual look to precocity. Our anticipation is being anticipated.

We can put this account of the narrowing of experience another way. For Agamben (1993) the colonization of bare life has led to a loss of the sacred. In particular, the capacity for the good life is being mechanized by the state or mass consumerism, and so is becoming a "senseless" shadow of its former self. Even in an age when some commentators (e.g. Kunde 2000) are proposing to construct corporate religions, this is too pessimistic. Surely "living exceeds, always exceeds" (Seigworth 2000: 257)? There are still a number of ways in which the essential multiplicity and virtuality of bare life can be restated; what has been transposed can be recomposed. What we need, I think, is a politics of the half-second delay. To some degree we already have it – in some of the modern performative techniques arising out of the various performance arts and other body disciplines (see Thrift 2000a, 2000b; Thrift and Dewsbury 2000). But there are other possibilities too. For example, the new electronic world now coming into existence does not offer only landscapes of consumption. It can also offer, through new conditions of visibility premised on software design of the kind offered by Winograd and collaborators (see for example, Winograd 1996), a means of constituting new forms of bare life by showing up new "half-second" worlds in new ways. As the aptly named Bill Joy (2000: 11) puts it (in *Fortune*, of all places):

> [A] century ago, the world was remade. We synchronised the clocks for the sake of railroad schedules, we discovered, through art and literature, new ways to perceive time; the automobile reshaped our notions of distance and adjacency. Now our world is being reshaped again, as a result of computing and communications technology. It is for this new digital world, and for its new landscapes, that we need digital design. These will be electronic places with manifold possibilities for designers and explorers, places where we can express and experience all the beauty we can.

It may seem strange to write of a politics of protest centered around the world of the half-second delay. But I think that its (little) time is coming. Bare life must be retaken. This will not be an easy task since it will involve the evolution of disciplines and skillful means of proceeding which, on the whole, we still currently lack (Irigaray 2001). But, unlike most forms of politics, I do not think it will be based on empty promises. Rather it will be founded on something akin to Varela's recent (1999: 75) call for "a re-enchantment of wisdom, understood as non-intentional action," which can prise open the openness of the moment (Thrift 2002). Summon life, summon it now.

Acknowledgments

Helen Thomas and Jamilah Ahmed helped enormously in honing the original manuscript.

Notes

1 This is somewhat akin to the distinction between *phusis* – simple life/ nature – and *nomos* – way of life. But note that simple life stands for something more than just survival (see Agamben 1999c).

2   As Deleuze (1994: 231) puts it, the Kantian conditions of experience are always surrounded by "subjacent conditions of real experience."

3   In fact, Agamben is somewhat elusive on what this state is (see Fitzpatrick 2001). Clearly he is suspicious of the entire "philosophy of life" represented by the *erlebnis* of Dilthey, the pure duration of Bergson, and others which "set out to capture . . . lived experience as retrospectively revealed in its preconceptual immediacy" (Agamben 1993: 35). In part, this is because he believes it either refuses to go into the realms of the mute or tries to make the mute speak, whereas he wants to ask, "does a mute experience exist, does an infancy (in-fancy) of experience exist? And if it does, what is its relationship to language?" (Agamben 1993: 37). Interestingly, he then describes a series of twilight states (drowsing, falling asleep, coming round from being knocked unconscious, etc.) that seem to approximate to this infancy of experience, which chimes rather well with Deleuze's (2001: 28) account of the "impersonalization" that is felt in the interval between life and death, as found in a cameo from Dickens's *Our Mutual Friend*:

> A disreputable man, a rogue, held in contempt by everyone, is found as he lies dying. Suddenly, those taking care of him manifest an eagerness, respect, even love, for his slightest sign of life. Everybody bustles about to save him, to the point where, in his deepest coma, this wicked man himself senses something soft and sweet penetrating him. But to the degree that he comes back to life, his saviours turn colder, and he becomes once again mean and crude. Between his life and his death, there is a moment that is only that of *a* life playing with death. The life of the individual gives way to an impersonal and yet singular life that releases a pure event freed from the accidents of internal and external life, that is, from the subjectivity and objectivity of what happens . . .

4   I could also have noted the web of fine-grained measurement of time and space that has grown up which is an important actor in itself (see Bowker and Star 1999). Milliseconds and microns constitute their own worlds.

5   Take the case of the hand (see Wilson 1998). The hand is a complex intermediary (in the Latourian sense). Our understanding of its particular corporealities has exploded because of recent research. The hand provides one of our key means of contact with the world; indeed, its characteristics are born out of negotiating context. Similarly, the development of the hand has produced parallel development in the brain. And, although we understand what is meant conventionally by the simple anatomical term, we can no longer say with certainty where the hand itself, or its control or influence, begins or ends in the body (McNeill 1999: 9). In turn, this kind

of understanding allows us to move away from the scholastic hegemony of sight, spectacle, and image toward other ways in which the world can be apprehended. For example, instead of cities of screens, cities of hands and pencils (Petroski 1992), cities of hands and keyboards, cities where large consequences are designed to follow from minute pushes and pulls (Amin and Thrift 2002).

6 Thus, as Crary points out, the critique of presence which has preoccupied so many philosophers is rendered (literally) pointless:

> Narrative explanations of attentiveness arose directly out of the understanding that a full grasp of self-identical reality was not possible and that human perception, conditioned by physical and psychological temporalities and processes, provided at most a provisional, shifting approximation of its objects. (1999: 4)

7 For a time, at the turn of the nineteenth century into the twentieth, such German psychophysical discoveries were the backbone of much philosophical thought:

> Prior to mid century, it was generally assumed that the time it took a stimulus to travel along nerves to the brain was so small as to be unmeasurable and, more importantly, it was believed that the onset of a stimulus and a subject's experience of it were effectively simultaneous. Helmholtz's calculation of how long it took electricity to move along the human nervous system astonished people by showing how *slow* it was, about ninety feet per second. It was a statistic that heightened a sense of a disjunction between perception and object, as well as suggesting startling possibilities of intervening between stimulus and response and of redefining a subject in terms of a new experiential domain of "reaction time." (Crary 1999: 311)

This influence showed up in France, for example, in Bergson's ruminations on "pure perception" in *Matter and Memory*. Thus:

> [P]ure perception, for Bergson, is an ideal that "exists in theory rather than in fact and would be possessed by a being placed where I am, living as I live, but absorbed in the present and capable, by giving up every form of memory, of obtaining a vision of matters both immediate and instantaneous". It is the dream of an inhuman immediacy, of an externality, the idea of a primordial and fundamental act of perception "whereby we place ourselves at the very heart of things", a perception, "confined to the present and absorbed, to the exclusion of all else, in moulding itself upon the external object. For Bergson, this dream is useful only as a hypothesis. He argues that

every perception, no matter how apparently instantaneous, constitutes a duration that prolongs the past into the present, inescapably contaminating its "purity" by giving it a composite status. . . . writing in the late 1890s, he cites available research data indicating that "the smallest interval of empty time which we can detect . . . equals .002 seconds". Likewise Bergson dismisses the notion of a pure memory or recollection and identifies the main problems that will occupy him: the various ways in which memory and perception interpenetrate each other. One of the places he begins is the assumption behind the general concept of a stimulus–response circuit. Bergson focuses on what is ignored in such a model: the complexity of what happens *between* awareness of stimulation and reaction to it. For him, this in-between is equivalent to lived experience, and is where attention performs a pivotal role. How the attentive body and mind process sensation decides not only the nature of one's perception but the degree of freedom of one's existence. When an action follows a stimulus "without the self interfering in it", one becomes, "a conscious automaton" and Bergson contends that the majority of our daily acts "have many points of resemblance with reflex acts". The richest and most creative forms of living occur in what he evocatively calls "a zone of indetermination".   (Crary 1999: 316–17)

Again, this influence is felt in thinking in the United States. William James's (1890/1967) classic *The Principles of Psychology* spends considerable time describing Wundt's key notion of apperception, a reaction that antedates the signal, as a "ripening" of the mind. Similarly, George Herbert Mead, who studied in Wundt's philosophy class in Leipzig in 1888/89, worked on attention at the beginning of his career (Joas 1985), and gave the topic considerable space in his subsequent writings on mind (Redding 1999; Strauss 1977). In particular, Mead took up Darwin and Wundt's emphasis on gesture in his analysis of the coproduction of space by eye and hand. The "ripening" was conceived as the beginnings of a social act in that it consisted of culturally pre-programmed responses, conversations before the event, so to speak (Gumbrecht 1998). The multitude of micro-gestures that prefigure an event are a psychosocial phenomenon that shape what interaction is possible.

8   Nowadays, research on these matters is back in fashion, chiefly built on the information-processing models of memory first put forward in the 1970s by authors like Craik and Walford, which continue to add further dimensions to the empirical construction of the space and time of attention (see Pashler 1998). However, I cannot help feeling that, in being captured by this one model form and by a commitment to quite narrow scientific protocols, this research has lost some of the richness of the earlier work.

References

Abercrombie, N. and Longhurst, B. (1998) *Audiences*. London: Sage.

Abram, D. (1997) *The Spell of the Sensuous*. New York: Vintage Books.

Agamben, G. (1993) *Infancy and History: Essays on the Destruction of Experience*. London: Verso.

Agamben, G. (1998) *Homo Sacer: Sovereign Power and Bare Life*. Stanford, CA: Stanford University Press.

Agamben, G. (1999a) *Potentialities*. Stanford, CA: Stanford University Press.

Agamben, G. (1999b) *The Man without Content*. Stanford, CA: Stanford University Press.

Agamben, G. (1999c) *Remnants of Auschwitz: The Witness and the Archive*. New York: Zone Books.

Amato, J.A. (2000) *Dust: A History of the Small and the Invisible*. Berkeley, CA: University of California Press.

Amin, A. and Thrift, N.J. (2002) *Cities: Re-imagining Urban Theory*. Cambridge: Polity Press.

Aristotle (1995) *Politics*. Oxford: Oxford University Press.

Bellow, S. (1991) *Something to Remember Me By: Three Tales*. New York: Viking.

Bergson, H. (1991) *Matter and Memory*. New York: Zone Books.

Bowker, G. and Star, S.L. (1999) *Sorting Things Out*. Cambridge, MA: MIT Press.

Brailsford, D. (1991) *Sport, Time and Society*. New York: Routledge.

Braun, M. (1992) *Picturing Time*. Chicago, IL: University of Chicago Press.

Bringmann, R. and Tweney, R. (eds.) (1980) *Wundt Studies: A Centennial Collection*. Toronto: Hogrefe.

Cahan, D. (ed.) (1993) *Hermann von Helmholtz and the Foundations of Nineteenth Century Science*. Berkeley, CA: University of California Press.

Cameron, D. (2000) *Good to Talk? Living and Working in a Communication Culture*. London: Sage.

Carter, R. (1998) *Mapping the Mind*. London: Weidenfeld and Nicolson.

Caygill, H. (1998) *Walter Benjamin: The Colour of Experience*. London: Routledge.

Crary, J. (1999) *Suspensions of Perception: Attention, Spectacle and Modern Culture*. Cambridge, MA: MIT Press.

Cubitt, S. (1991) *Timeshift*. London: Routledge.

Dagognet, F. (1992a) "Toward a Biopsychiatry," in J. Crary and S. Kwinter (eds.), *Incorporations: Zone 6*. New York: Zone Books.

Dagognet, F. (1992b) *Etienne-Jules Marey: A Passion for the Trace*. New York: Zone Books.

Damasio, A. (1999) *The Feeling of What Happens: Body, Emotion and the Making of Consciousness*. London: Heinemann.

Darwin, C. (1872/1998) *The Expression of the Emotions in Man and Animals*. London: HarperCollins.

Davenport, T.H. and Beck, J.C. (2001) *The Attention Economy: Understanding the New Currency of Business*. Boston, MA: Harvard Business School Press.

Deleuze, G. (1990) *The Logic of Sense*. New York: Columbia University Press.

Deleuze, G. (1994) *Difference and Repetition*. New York: Columbia University Press.

Deleuze, G. (2001) *Pure Immanence: Essays on Life*. New York: Zone Books.

De Nora, T. and Belcher, S. (2000) " 'When you're trying something on you picture yourself in a place where they are playing this kind of music': Musically Sponsored Agency in the British Clothing Retail Sector," *Sociological Review* 28: 80–101.

Ede, S. (ed.) (2000) *Strange and Charmed: Science and the Contemporary Visual Arts*. London: Calouste Gulbenkian Foundation.

Ekman, P. (1992) *Telling Lies*. New York: Norton.

Fitzpatrick, P. (2001) "These Mad Abandon'd Times," *Economy and Society* 30: 255–70.

Foucault, M. (1998) *The Final Foucault*. London: Sage.

Gatens, M. and Lloyd, G. (1999) *Collective Imaginings: Spinoza, Past and Present*. London: Routledge.

Gilroy, P. (2000) *Between Camps: Nations, Cultures and the Allure of Race*. London: Allen Lane.

Goldstein, K. (1995) *The Organism*. New York: Zone Books.

Gumbrecht, H. (1998) "Perception versus Experience: Moving Pictures and their Resistance to Interpretation," in T. Lenoir (ed.), *Inscribing Science: Scientific Texts and the Materiality of Communication*. Stanford, CA: Stanford University Press.

Hutchinson-Guest, A. (1989) *Choreo-graphics*. London: G and B Arts International.

Irigaray, L. (2001) *Between East and West*. New York: Columbia University Press.

James, W. (1912) *Essays on Psychology*. Boston, MA: Houghton Osgood.

James, W. (1890/1967) *The Principles of Psychology* (2 vols). New York: Dover Press.

Joas, H. (1985) *G. H. Mead: A Contemporary Re-examination of His Thought*. Cambridge, MA: MIT Press.

Jones, C.A. and Galison, P. (eds.) (1998) *Picturing Science, Producing Art*. New York: Routledge.

Joy, W. (2000) "The Future," *Fortune* V, 63: 11.

Katz, J. (1999) *How Emotions Work*. Chicago, IL: University of Chicago Press.

Kerridge, R. and Sammells, N. (eds.) (1998) *Writing the Environment*. London: Zed Books.

Kunde, J. (2000) *Corporate Religion*. London: Financial Times Books.

Latour, B. (1998) "How to be Iconophilic in Art, Science and Religion," in C.A. Jones and P. Galison (eds.), *Picturing Science, Producing Art*. New York: Routledge, pp. 418–40.

Lawson-Tancred, H. (1986) "Introduction," in Aristotle, *De Anima: On the Soul*. Harmondsworth: Penguin, pp. 11–115.

Le Doux, J. (1998) *The Emotional Brain*. London: Weidenfeld and Nicolson.

Lenoir, T. (1982) *The Strategy of Life*. Chicago, IL: University of Chicago Press.

Leonard, P. and Swap, W. (2000) *When Sparks Fly: Igniting Creativity in Groups*. Boston, MA: Harvard Business School Press.

Lowe, A. and Schaffer, S. (eds.) (1999) *Noise*. Cambridge: Kettles Yard.

Lury, C. (1999) "Marking Time with Nike: The Illusion of the Durable," *Public Culture*, 11: 499–526.

McCrone, J. (1999) *Going Inside: A Tour Round a Single Moment of Consciousness*. London: Faber and Faber.

McKee, V. (1999) "Dramatic Challenge to the Art of Team-building," *The Times*, February 6, pp. 26–7.

McNeill, D. (1999) *The Face*. London: Hamish Hamilton.

McNeill, W.H. (1995) *Keeping Together in Time: Dance and Drill in Human History*. Cambridge, MA: Harvard University Press.

May, J. and Thrift, N.J. (2001) (eds.) *TimeSpace*. London: Routledge.

Nolan, J.L. (1998) *The Therapeutic State: Justifying Government at the Century's End*. New York: New York University Press.

Olesko, K.M. and Holmes, F.L. (1993) "Experiment, Quantification and Discovery: Helmholtz's Early Physiological Researches, 1843–50," in D. Cahan (ed.), *Hermann von Helmholtz and the Foundations of Nineteenth Century Science*. Berkeley, CA: University of California Press, pp. 50–108.

Pashler, H.E. (1998) *The Psychology of Attention*. Cambridge, MA: MIT Press.

Petroski, H. (1992) *The Pencil*. New York: Alfred A. Knopf.

Pfeffer, J. and Sutton, R.I. (2000) *The Knowing–Doing Gap. How Smart Companies Put Knowledge into Action*. Boston, MA: Harvard Business School Press.

Pine, J.B. and Gilmore, J.H. (1999) *The Experience Economy: Work is Theatre and Every Business a Stage*. Boston, MA: Harvard Business School Press.

Prodger, P. (1998) "Illustration as Strategy in Charles Darwin's 'The Expression of Emotions in Man and Animals,'" in T. Lenoir (ed.), *Inscribing Science: Scientific Texts and the Materiality of Communication*. Stanford, CA: Stanford University Press, pp. 140–81.

Raffel, S. (1999) "If Goffman Had Read Levinas," *Edinburgh Working Papers in Sociology* No. 17.

Redding, P. (1999) *The Logic of Affect*. Ithaca, NY: Cornell University Press.

Rieher, R. (ed.) (2001) *Wilhelm Wundt in History*. New York: Plenum.

Schön, D.A. (1991) *Educating the Reflective Practitioner*. San Francisco, CA: Jossey Bass.

Schrage, D. (2000) *Serious Play*. Boston, MA: Harvard Business School Press.

Seigworth, G.J. (2000) "Banality for Cultural Studies," *Cultural Studies* 14: 227–68.

Shapiro, M.J. (1999) *Cinematic Political Thought: Narrating Race, Nation and Gender*. New York: New York University Press.

Snyder, J. (1998) "Visualization and Visibility," in C.A. Jones and P. Galison (eds.), *Picturing Science, Producing Art*. New York: Routledge, pp. 379–99.

Stafford, B.M. (1991) *Body Criticism*. Cambridge, MA: MIT Press.

Stafford, B.M. (1996) *Artful Science*. Cambridge, MA: MIT Press.

Stafford, B.M. (1998) *Good Looking: Essays on the Virtue of Images*. Cambridge, MA: MIT Press.

Strauss, A. (ed.) (1977) *George Herbert Mead on Social Psychology*. Chicago, IL: University of Chicago Press.

Thrift, N.J. (1996) *Spatial Formations*. London: Sage.

Thrift, N.J. (2000a) "Afterwords," *Environment and Planning D: Society and Space* 18: 213–55.

Thrift, N.J. (2000b) "Still Life in Nearly Present Time: The Object of Nature," *Body and Society* 6: 4–57.

Thrift, N.J. (2002) "Summoning Life," in P. Cloke, P. Crang, and M. Goodwin (eds.), *Envisioning Geography*. London: Edward Arnold.

Thrift, N.J. and Dewsbury, J.D. (2000) "Dead Geographies and How to Make Them Live Again," *Environment and Planning D: Society and Space* 18: 411–32.

Varela, F.J. (1999) *Ethical Know-how: Action, Wisdom and Cognition*. Stanford, CA: Stanford University Press.

von Helmholtz, H. (1995) *Science and Culture*. Chicago, IL: University of Chicago Press.

Walker Art Center (ed.) (2000) *Let's Entertain: Life's Guilty Pleasures*. Minneapolis, MN: Walker Art Center.

Wenger, E. (1999) *Communities of Practice*. Cambridge: Cambridge University Press.

Wilson, F.R. (1998) *The Hand*. New York: Pantheon.

Winograd, T. (ed.) (1996) *Bringing Design to Software*. Reading, MA: Addison-Wesley.

Chapter 7

Lolo's Breasts, Cyborgism, and a Wooden Christ

Simon Shepherd

This essay is interested in performance practices that take the body into domains which are beyond the daily, denatured, cyborged. In these practices there is a negotiation between body and non-body, but the terms of that negotiation change in different cultures. Performance, then, has something to do with the relationship between organism and object.

Body Gurus

Let us begin with things people will do to their bodies in the interests of being a better performer. This section will look at two examples of bodies trained and manipulated.

One of the performer-training regimes that is currently influential has been developed by the Japanese theater-maker Suzuki Tadashi. Suzuki's work came to preeminence in the late 1970s. Its roots lie in the Japanese classical tradition of *noh* and *kabuki,* mingled with a response to Japanese postwar reconstruction and western existentialism (Allain 2002). Suzuki wants to find a physical language that transcends cultural difference. The way toward that language is through training regimes. These consist of exercises that develop the physical concentration and control of the performer by setting physical targets which are very difficult to achieve. "At best, ideals of performance should be developed into a practical system; and even if that level cannot be reached, there is certainly no reason to give up trying, and so reveal a total lack of any critical spirit whatsoever" (Suzuki 1986: 63). The spiritual authenticity of the work is established, somewhat penitentially, in the struggle with the body's physical recalcitrance.

In his most famous theoretical text, "The Grammar of the Feet," Suzuki describes an exercise in which the performers pound their feet on the ground in time with rhythmic music. It requires "an even, unremitting strength without loosening the upper part of the body." Loss of concentration means an actor cannot continue to the end "with a unified, settled energy." That debilitating moment comes about when the actor "misses the sense of being toughened or tempered" (ibid.: 9).

A sense of physicality is acquired through consciousness of the feet. Whereas in daily life the relationship of the feet to the ground is taken for granted, "in stamping, we come to understand that the body establishes its relation to the ground through the feet, that the ground and the body are not two separate entities" (ibid.: 9). As a consequence of the training, then, the actor has a very different sense of her existence on stage from what she has in daily life. The achievement of this difference from the daily in its turn has value within a philosophical position which views modern life, negatively, as sterile and mechanized. The body trained to be outside the daily puts us in touch with "fundamentals." The drive is away from the localized, the specific, the culturally diverse, the individual, toward the abstracted and universal. This, for Suzuki, is the importance of *noh* performance, although he recognizes that modern practitioners such as Grotowski are on the same journey. When *noh* actors appear to inhabit sacred space, it is because of the relationship between their body and space. The traditional fixed arrangements of the *noh* stage have been "internalized into their very bodies . . . The actor's body and the space reveal a mutual connection. I call a space which is thus connected to the actor's body a *sacred space*" (ibid.: 91). The effect of this sacred space is to make a break in the flow of worldly time, reaching to fundamentals.

Those fundamentals can also be found through the stamping exercises. For although they seem to require an actor's excessive concentration on her own body, the stamping also works to call forth the energy of an object that is worshiped and to take that energy into oneself. What gets imaged, especially through the sound of the stamping (which on the *noh* stage creates echoes), is "a mutual response between actor and spirit" (ibid.: 14). The actor's body is penetrated, then, by that which is usually outside the body – the "spirit," the space of the *noh* stage, the ground. So that within the *noh* tradition actors "create gestures of true dignity and majesty, just as though they had no individual sense of their corporeal being" (ibid.: 46). And in being free of the corporeal they entertain the sacred.

The assimilation of body to non-body is a project to rediscover fundamental values in a world which is mechanized, culturally diverse, individualized. Or, to come at it another way, the exercise which compels awareness of the limitations of the body leads to a fixation on that which marks the limit and lies beyond it. A number of Suzuki's exercises have their rhythm set by the beating of sticks. In her account of participating in workshops, delivered at Performance Studies International 7 (unpublished), Julia Whitworth described the participant's body in direct relationship with normative demands on it. Crucial in this process is the sound of the stick cracking against the floor and cutting through the air. The exercise is undeniably led from outside. The participant is "at the mercy of the leader" with regard to how long difficult positions are held within a regime which sets "you against your body, your breath . . . the floor." The effect, as Whitworth described it, is "Pavlovian." But what could also be observed, as Whitworth herself realized, is that the effect was not confined to the duration of the workshop. Regularly in her account she returned to the beating of the stick – "which I keep emphasizing." There, at an academic conference an ocean away, the power of the stick was still inside her body. And that power seemed to speak a master discourse – where Suzuki's "tyranny" coexists with the participant's learned understanding of the physical and mental "purity" of the form.

Purity is an interesting word here. The training seems pure because of the totally focused concentration. But that concentration is produced in exercises, and theories, which promote the assimilation of body and non-body – ground, space, spirit; a mingling rather than a purifying. But a loss of individuality promoted by a loss of physical integrity is not always ideologically marked as "pure." Take for example the performances of the late Lolo Ferrari.

Known to most television viewers through Channel 4's *Eurotrash*, Lolo eventually had her own spot on the program, "Look at Lolo." In this she would demonstrate some simple leisure activity, such as inflating an airbed, throwing Frisbees, doing the hula hoop. In the latter sequence she and her constant pair of male companions showed their complete inability to produce the bodily dexterity required to keep the hoop anywhere near the hips. Performing with tanned bodies in swimwear, the three enacted bodily ineptitude. Sequences often ended with the men giggling at each other's efforts while Lolo stolidly presented herself to camera.

That presentation to camera generically fixed Lolo. She had come to fame in the world of media soft porn, where her artificially enlarged breasts were much photographed. With its surgically reorganized face and breasts, Lolo's body was produced as sex object within a heterosexual economy. And it is within that context that the arrangements of "Look at Lolo" seem deviant – for the men show no desire for her, and her own objecthood is foregrounded through her physical incapacity. Meanwhile elsewhere on the show female fashion models might appear live with the presenter, Antoine de Caunes, in routines in which he played clown to their sexiness, produced as elegance and charisma. Against these figures Lolo was one of the stream of physical eccentrics, the trash of *Eurotrash*.

Or she herself was a clown. That conspicuously modified body, the assimilation of flesh and silicon, somewhat disrupted the familiar and daily production of female body as sex object. It enacted unnaturalness. But that was an act of which Lolo didn't seem to be fully in control. For as the biographical film *Look at Lolo* revealed, Lolo did herself desire fame, and her husband helped her to that fame by suggesting, planning, and overseeing the modifications to her body. Those breasts were objects of his invention and pleasure. In the size of those breasts we see the body assimilated to more than silicon: we see perhaps the "mutual response between actor and" – well, not quite "spirit" – but a form of masculine desire.

The borrowing of Suzuki's phrase is intended not simply to provoke an exploration of Lolo's penetrated body but to reflect back on the terms of the exploration. For just as the master's tyranny, with its pounding rhythm and its stick, teaches the body to assimilate to that which is non-body – ground, space, spirit – so the husband's desire, and the promise of being extraordinary, transcendent even, may have taught the body to assimilate to non-body in the form of silicon. Lolo's body could be said to be inhabited by the project of her own guru. And that guru also had his drive toward abstraction. Lolo's body was designed to become the perfect female sex object. Or, put more precisely, it was designed to imitate an ideal of body that was in circulation, but which was never real, in any individual, localized way. In a similar way the Suzuki performer reaches for an ideal, losing a sense of individuality to make contact with fundamentals which, again, don't exist in any culturally specific, local form. Each body – in its relations with non-body – may be said to be a copy of that which doesn't exist, a simulacrum perhaps.

A difference between them is that one is "trash" and the other is serious. That distinction partly derives from the cultural frames around each. But those frames articulate a set of value judgments. Suzuki training is practiced in workshops that foreground effort, liveness that can't be mediated; Lolo is photographed, an identity always mediated, while the pain of the surgery – its liveness – has no discursive presence. The Suzuki performer trains to reach something "authentic," a set of values more fundamental than today's mechanized, localized, culture. Lolo's project to become an ideal female sex object is debased precisely to the extent that it moves away from the individual to the generalized. Values that oppose the mechanized seem to have more seriousness than values that affirm the sexualized body: one is a caricature, the other is not. Lolo's performance practice apparently shows her subjugation to the will of a characteristically masculine power; the Suzuki performer, on the other hand . . .

Finally, Lolo's silicon implants are really in there – in there in a way which the ground is not in the performer. For all Suzuki's insistence that the ground and the body are not two separate entities, the only way in which they can reach the effect of penetration is through sound and energy. Or, to use another of Suzuki's words, spirit. For the distinction of seriousness between Suzuki's dream of a body penetrated by non-body and Lolo's breasts is a distinction of value between spirit and matter.

Posthuman Body

The mingling of body and non-body has its own familiar contemporary name – cyborg. But neither the Suzuki performer nor Lolo Ferrari fit very closely with popular notions of cyborg. For those notions tend to be based on experience of science fiction movies, comics, and novels – Robocop's human face in a machine body, William Gibson's humans with a range of implants. In turn these fictional encrustations differ from cyborg's linguistic (if not cultural) point of origin. The article "Cyborgs and Space," written by Clynes and Kline, originally appeared in *Astronautics* in September 1960. It was a consideration of how the human body would need to adapt to space travel. And 35 years later Clynes still rejected the science fictionalization of the term, as a "monsterification of something that is a human enlargement of function" (in Gray, Figueroa-Sarriera, and Mentor 1995: 47).

But Clynes was fighting a losing battle against the deluge of cyborg-speak. For there is now a large number of entities regarded as cyborg. Indeed, from a point of view that regards cyborgness as a functional dependency of body on machine and the imbrication of body with information systems, then everyone in the developed world is a cyborg. In critical commentary as in popular imagination, however, it is not so much Clynes's human enlargement of function as the body–machine interface which is the object of focus. There is about cyborgs an air of scientificity, where the science feels new. Indeed it is this newness which for Gray and his coeditors marks the break with previous examples of body–machine interface. If we can look back and see earlier examples of humans using objects as cyborgian, that is because of our own mindset. This mindset has been produced in a world where "information disciplines, fantasies and practices" have "transgressed the machinic–organic border," so that there is no longer the clear break between machines and organisms (Gray, Figueroa-Sarriera, and Mentor 1995: 5).

Presumably it would be possible to trace a similar conceptual and physiological shift marking the invention of the wheel. But that "cyborg" needs to be delimited in its application to the present moment indicates its rhetorical productivity. That is to say, we know we have encountered the epistemological break into postmodernity because we can think cyborg. Commentators have noted this metaphoric and ideological potential (King 1989; Lupton 1995; Lury 1998; Penley and Ross 1991; Sobchack 1994; Wilson 1995). Analyses of movies and prose fiction show the cyborg as a place where, for instance, ideas about nature and gender are foregrounded, if not tested (Balsamo 1995; Holland 1995; Springer 1991, 1994). In Gabilondo's essay, "Postcolonial Cyborgs" (1995), the cyborg functions as part of a new ideological apparatus, together with consumer culture, in relation to modern capitalism. But when it is treated as rhetorical device, with whatever subtlety, a sense of the involvement of real body within cyborg begins to vanish. However imaginatively engaging they are, however kinesthetically activated the spectator, filmed bodies, computer-generated images, are not physically present to, inhabiting the same space as, spectators. And where we do encounter a cyborg, in real space and time, we tend not to notice – the person with contact lenses or heart pacemaker, the woman in the wheelchair or (as Clynes would say) the man on a bicycle (Hogle 1995; Wilson 1995). The rhetorical force of the word cyborg insists on it as a marker of a break. An achieved and naturalized assimilation of body and machine remains merely human – cyborg has, necessarily, to describe the posthuman.

A physical attempt to produce and inhabit the posthuman body has been undertaken by performance artist Stelarc. In a series of experiments/shows he has exteriorized the interior of his body by inserting a camera, and he has decentered control over his own organism by having his body electronically wired so that operators at remote terminals can initiate the impulses which activate his muscles (Farnell 2000; Stelarc 1998, 2000; http://www.stelarc.va.com.au). The poststructuralist body with no psychic interior, the body decentered across information systems – these are literally imaged. Yet at the same time, as a performer, Stelarc also initiates and organizes the experiments in which he risks his own body. He retains his managerial agency, and indeed his star status. Unlike the body kept alive by the pacemaker or the "dead" donor body with equipment and chemicals plugged into it, Stelarc's posthuman body is the product of a set of stunts which foreground their own scientificity. It is a dramatization of modernness, with Stelarc as both author and performer.

A way of avoiding the agency that comes with such adventuring is in the performed installation, using the body "in such a way as to reduce it to the status of a mere component in an economy of artifacts and environment." Using Roger Caillois's notion of psychasthenia, David Tomas argues that in this art the body's own representational space incorporates object-like attributes and thus "promotes a simultaneous *generalization of* [physical/artifactual] *space* at the expense of the individual' body's subjective autonomy." Later Tomas takes this beyond art practice to argue that in "technologically-intensive performed installations machine systems become . . . the determining factor in the definition of the body's physical installation." He goes on: "A modern fighter plane is a technological breeding ground for a new kind of site-specific 'self' " (Tomas 1995: 257, 259–60; see also Virilio 1991: 96 on the technician as a "victim of the movement he's produced"). I'd guess that the fighter pilot herself had a self-image that was to do with control, accuracy, quickness – agency. But the image of such a pilot, helmeted, within the controls, like the appearance of the performed installation, suggests an interrelation of body and objects. Once that's said, a problem arises.

For the production of apparent relationship between body and objects has been part of the work of performance for a number of centuries

(Garrick's Hamlet expressed shock by knocking over a chair; Lady Audley's vengeance travels from her candle to a flaming environment). These are clearly "apparent" relationships – not authentically felt as the installed performer might feel them. But there is another set of sensors in the room, those of the audience. Within certain modes of performance that audience is encouraged to – what? – lose itself, suspend disbelief, get caught up in the action. Or let's put it another way: "the imaginary of the word and the imaginary of the film or video image" can be taken, says Mark Poster, one step further by "placing the individual 'inside' alternative worlds." This one step further is "virtual reality" (Poster 1995: 86). Now although it's not what I think Poster means by "virtual reality," it is worth asking what sort of reality was being inhabited by the nineteenth-century audience that shouted – and threw things – at the villain. That audience could be said to be having its physiological mechanisms controlled by the discourses working upon it, finding itself physically caught up into an information system, cyborgized.

The point of that dip into the nineteenth century is not to suggest that there is no new thing on the face of the earth, but instead to suggest that much of the discussion of cyborg is an engagement with the mechanisms of performance and, particularly, spectatorship. Stelarc describes an experiment whereby analyses of JPEG files "provide data that is mapped to the body via the muscle stimulation system . . . The images that you see are the images that move you" (Stelarc 2000: 123). Alphonso Lingis suggests that this is always the case: "The apprehension of an exterior objective, as something soliciting the synergic hold of the sensibility, dynamically orients the postural schema" (Lingis 1994: 14). What Stelarc has done is to set up an experiment/performance which concretizes a basic, but hidden, neural–physiological process. The effect of the performance is to suggest that this is happening for the first time, and that it happens only as a result of the interface of body and technology – that a cyborg has been born.

The impact of that birth upstages the discussion and staging of body/non-body and virtuality which have occupied phenomenology and performance practice. It is able to upstage because, as we have seen, the cyborg is a marker of the new and its rhetoric is cathected. And this oddly dis-bodied cyborg – with its obliviousness to ordinary bodily processes – is the thing Manfred Clynes was critical of. He thought it traduced his project of "human enlargement of function." That project, adapting the body for space travel, depended on self-regulating "man-machine" systems. These would function "without the benefit of consciousness in order to cooperate with the body's own homeostatic controls." Such capabilities, at their minimal, are "demonstrated under control conditions such as yoga or hypnosis. The imagination is stretched by the muscular control of which even the undergraduate at a Yoga College is capable" (Clynes and Kline 1995: 30–1). That control of individual body may be taken further, as de Landa notes, through the widely available historical practice of military drilling, where individuals are taken up into a machinic system, becoming a body of men (de Landa 1991: 58ff.).

The bodily discipline that Clynes and Kline had in mind, for "human enlargement" – and certainly that of the drilled body – seem to be more akin to the training program of Suzuki than to the techno-acrobatics of Stelarc. But at this point the modern image of the cyborg intervenes, keeping apart the "modern" work of Stelarc and the performer-training system. Performer training may have everything to do with "human enlargement" but nothing to do with the production of cyborgs.

So Suzuki would attest, with his attacks on the loss of spirit in the modern world. But, in the widest sense of its application, these two rather unlike performance modes both could come under the word "cyborg." The limits of body and the possibilities of its enlargement – hollowed, united with the ground, decentered – are explored by placing the body within an external mechanical, and discursive, framework that takes it over (Haraway 1991). The stick, and its psychic spasm an ocean away, are as much an effect of the remote operator as the electronic spasm. That these things are regarded as separate has more to do with ideas about kinesthetics than with kinesthetic experience. The division of terms here is taken from Hillel Schwartz, who mobilizes it as part of an attempt to describe the new kinesthetic of the twentieth century, in which movement expresses bodily wholeness. Kinestructs, or kinesthetic ideals, differ from kinecepts, or "central kinaesthetic experiences" (Schwartz 1992: 105).

The kinestructs of Suzuki and Stelarc – and indeed Lolo Ferrari – are separated by ideas about spiritual purpose and modernity. But they are not so clearly distinguished as kinecepts. For it might be that we are now looking at the emergence of a new kinesthetic. That kinesthetic can be found in gym culture, in dieting, in "building" the body – but also in "personalizing" and inhabiting the accessory, the manner of using the mobile phone, the car that is driven and decorated as enhancement of the person. This new kinesthetic has to do with the experience not so much of alienated mechanization of the body but instead of the body as something that can be extended beyond "natural" limits – where that nature is sterile, humanist, not sexy enough.

The cyborg, then, rather than marking an epistemological break, is itself operated by rather older mechanisms. These mechanisms have to do with the activity of performance.

Cyborgisms

In November 1995 Stelarc conducted a performance experiment called "Ping Body/Proto-Parasite" experiment. His musculature, in Luxemburg, was wired so that it could be viewed, accessed, and activated from terminals in Paris, Helsinki, and Amsterdam. The body's movements were involuntary but it could trigger the upload of images to a website. Thus the body was moving "not to the promptings of another body in another place, but rather to Internet activity itself . . . stimulated not by its internal nervous system but by the external ebb and flow of data" (http://www.stelarc.va.com.au). The Internet activity comes from operators working at distance – like puppeteers, perhaps. The rods or strings have been replaced by electronic impulses but the model is similar. And for all the "postmodernity" of Stelarc's work the relationship of the puppet body to the human performer is quite old.

In that relationship the puppet body reveals human limit, offers an ideal of completeness beyond individual human capability. Kleist, in 1810, reported a dancer saying that the puppet exceeds the capacity of a human dancer. For the puppet will never show affectation, which appears when the soul "is found at any point other than the movement's center of gravity." And the puppet is "antigravitational," having nothing of "the inertia of matter." None of this can be equalled by man: "Only a god could compete with matter in this field" (Kleist 1989: 417–18). The puppet's activity embodies mechanical order, efficiency, control. From these qualities human performers have to learn, as Gordon Craig was later to say, if the art of the theater is to be saved from the decay caused by the attempt to imitate nature. No actor has yet reached "such a state of mechanical perfection that his body was *absolutely* the slave of his mind" (Craig 1980: 67). The aim, in Craig's famous formulation of 1907, is to become an "Ubermarionette."

Craig's views on the actor as a – so to speak – performing machine can be taken to be symptomatic of his cultural moment. The Italian futurists were also specifically interested in puppets, but in general modernist engagements with the body tended to focus on its capacity either to be machine-like or to learn from the machine – the word "robot," as Reichardt tells us, was coined by Capek in 1917, from a Czech word meaning "obligatory work or servitude" (Reichardt 1978: 31; see also Gropius 1961; Segel 1995; Wollen 1993). Meyerhold's explorations in biomechanics (1922) apply the "constant laws of mechanics" to muscular movement (Braun 1969). In Dziga Vertov's film *Enthusiasm* (1930) such mechanical efficacy is shown to derive from the activity and rhythm of productive work, where the body, by means of an object, transforms nature. These cultural interests, however, already had their industrial predecessors. Meyerhold wanted to maximize the productivity of the actor in the same way as Taylorism promoted a "scientific" organization of time and motion, and thus profit, on the factory floor. This seems to have produced its own aestheticization in the mechanical orderliness and predictable patterning of the female bodies in dance troupes such as the Tiller Girls and then the movies of Busby Berkeley (Kracauer 1995; Theweleit 1992; Wollen 1993: 54ff.).

That mechanical orderliness was critiqued by New York's socialist Yiddish theater troupe, the Prolet Buehne. Their show *Tempo Tempo* (1930) used verse rhythms to image the effects of capitalist factory speed-up on the workforce – and then used the same rhythms to celebrate the effects of the new Soviet Five-Year Plan. The mechanized body, whether of decorative Taylorism or productive biomechanics, is foregrounded as both an ideological proposition and an ideological naturalization, depending on your interest. It is this ideological foregrounding, rather than the mere conjunction of body and machine, which would seem to be characteristic of the modernist moment. Under the smiles of the Berkeley girls they work to balance on the movie set's scenic devices. They adjust their performances against the concealed machinery, which is working to produce an image of perfection, which in turn aestheticizes the notion of machine.

That concealed engine of perfection has a history in performance that extends well beyond the temporary ideological concerns of modernism. The tragic actor of ancient Athens learned physical techniques for performing in a face mask and buskins – those boots that gave elevation to the body. The worn objects produce in and on the body particular modes of walking and of looking: looking with the neck and shoulders, balancing, high-stepping. The outcome of these muscular disciplines is the effect of something more than human – the dignity and gravitas of tragedy. Differently positioned objects – say, a neck-ruff and a corset – will produce different muscular disciplines, accentuating the verticality of the body, holding stiff the length of its spine, producing a high center of gravity, a decorous stillness, and stability even while dancing. The outcomes of these particular techniques are the poise and decorum of the courtly body of the European late sixteenth/early seventeenth centuries (Franko 1993; Howard 1998; McClary 1998; Vigarello 1989). Later still there was a more famous – and indeed still current – attempt to elevate the body further, to raise it literally off the ground. With wooden wedges in her shoes the classical ballet dancer of the mid-nineteenth century minimized her contact with the stage to that of a single point (Foster 1996; Hammond and Hammond 1979). Through a training that developed her leg muscles to the edges of "womanly" delicacy and threatened permanently to distort her feet, she achieved an effect of disembodied female perfection, or female-ness extended beyond the body and hence perfect – the nymph that is more (or less) than human, woman as non-body.

And the ballerina in this sense comes to be almost like Kleist's puppet, transcending the earth-bound limits of human physicality. The effect is further enhanced by her appearance as one of a group, where each duplicates the others' movements, in an art form that not only inhibits individualization through speech but that also insists on similarities of coiffure and costume. The ballerina, barely an independent subject, is – hence – graceful. For in Kleist's terms grace is "purest" in a body that has either no consciousness or infinite consciousness: a puppet – or a god. Now, the image of a ballerina *en pointe* is not readily categorized as a cyborg. She is, however, an instance of the relationship with that which is non-body, her wedges, which modifies the organization of body. It seems even less appropriate to associate regimes of performer training with cyborg. But some of these regimes are also not too distant from the automaton as ideal. Barry King suggests that in general actor training is designed to re-duced physical behaviors to "a state of automaticity" (King 1985: 29). But there is a more specific link. One of the leading figures of modern mime, Etienne Decroux, looked toward "la naissance de cet acteur de bois" (Decroux 1963: 24). He was alluding to Craig's Ubermarionette, who in turn derived from Kleist's discussion of the puppet. But the genealogy comes forward as well. Craig, polemicist for the mechanical actor, was guest of honor at a mime show in 1945 done by Decroux and Jean-Louis Barrault; in 1972 Barrault met, and inspired, Suzuki, who went on to promote a training regime in which "the actor moves like a puppet to the rhythm of the music" (Suzuki 1986: 11).

The echoes and parallels I have been trying to generate here are intended to suggest that, far from being higher or more developed, the cyborg is a phenomenon that takes its place in a domain familiar from histories of performed practices. It is one instance of ongoing cultural formulations of the relationship of body and non-body (Gonzalez 1995; Hess 1995). Each of these formulations assumes specific terms and practices defining body and non-body. In turn the deployment of these terms and practices has the potential to articulate the specific values operating in a culture. The cultural cathexis of the neck ruff is a more insistent use of the carriage of the head as a marker of class than that of the neck-tie. So what cultural value might we observe in the accounts of cyborgs? Some suggest that the image of cyborg presents the body as a site of debate (about, for example, gender). But arguably this is the case for all imaging and discussion of bodies (early modern dance regimes articulated class values). The point is what the debate is about. In the case of cyborgs the focus seems to fall not so much on the limits of the human body – a more modernist concern, perhaps – but on the possibilities of human perception and definition.

While that may need arguing, the central point for my purposes here is that the cyborg presents for analysis what all performed practices present – namely particular conjunctions of body and non-body, where the specific selection of object and body part may be taken to be a form of cultural and ideological cathexis.

God and Puppet

It is the closing days of Easter Week, Granada, 2001. In a shopping precinct that is deserted in the quiet time of siesta there is a whiff of baroque music. Coming around the corner you see a still figure on a small podium. She wears a blue robe, her head veiled in white. The body tilts forward, leaning toward the flowers that stand in front of it. The only sound is the music.

On its own it is enigmatic – not even drawing much of a crowd. But for anyone who has recently visited the Ramblas of Barcelona, or London's Covent Garden, this performance slots into place. It is one of those living statues, a public art form in which the performer remains as still as possible. Those statues that make movement do so as if automata, repetitively and mechanically. And, to encourage the suggestion of statuary, any exposed flesh is painted in the same colors as the costume – total whiteness or a metallic sheen are the preferred effects. It is a form of busking by doing nothing, meticulously. But unlike the singing busker, the statue works to generate a sense of enigma, of not properly belonging to the public space it inhabits. For human occupation of public city space tends to involve activity and sound – reading the paper, chatting, crossing the square, looking in shops, making a speech. Statues are part of the environment of the activity – except when it's a human being behaving like a statue. And then, because it's clearly human, it becomes a performance of control, of sustaining – against the effects of time on the body – the condition of statueness, the willed choice to be as if non-body.

Here, at long last, I need to pause over the word "non-body." My use of it is intended to go beyond, or even go round, the word that might seem more obvious – "object." The relations between object and body in performance have already been dealt with eloquently by performance phenomenologists, in particular Stanton Garner Jr. That work draws on concerns that cluster around another binary, that between object and subject. In Merleau-Ponty's formulation that binary is firmly oppositional: "[e]very object can affirm its existence only by depriving me of mine" (in Garner 1994: 106). For Garner this tense relationship between object and subject is the new thing that comes to be staged by modern realism, with – in his account – Pinter's *Caretaker* (1960) picturing the subject's discovery of its own contingency and decenteredness in a setting full of defunctionalized and randomly assembled objects (Garner 1994: 110–19). So in their relationship to the body the objects have an effect on the subject: body and subject assimilate to one another on one side of the binary, kept there by antagonistic objects.

This model doesn't fully allow for the sense of body extended through, or invested into, objects. Within the phenomenological account these are objects which retain their functionality, being simply equipment for the subject. But that account has also provided the basis for Garner's thumbnail sketch of the development of performance from a time when stage props were properties, belonging to the person, to a time when they become defunctionalized and unsettling. It's an evolutionary history taking us to modern alienation. What that history occludes is the recurrence of various, but always cathected, body–object relations. For the cyborg is also modern. Indeed it is first formulated in the year of Pinter's *Caretaker*. And, while in itself I'd suggest it is simply another instance of the performed cathexis of body and object relations, as a concept cyborg offers us a way of modeling those relations that does not come with all the accumulated phenomenological baggage. This focus on body–object cathexes might give us a different sort of history of performance, which I have sketched bits of in the previous section. It also extends beyond mere object the concept of that which is outside but shaping the body. Cyborgism has given us the information system as bodily environment, something which carries the idea of extension and investment in a way which Foucauldian disciplinary discourses do not. So, by this argument, when Decroux famously says, "The more he holds, the less an actor is required to hold himself well," the first part evokes the (alienating) tension between subject and objects. It is the second part of the statement that envisages taking something into the body, discursively incorporating, in order specifically to make a new body. With Craig behind him, Decroux might be said to be envisaging actor as cyborg.

In front of the shop windows, holding herself well, the statue was much more enigmatic, more exotic, than those objects imitating bodies in the windows themselves. By the next day she had relocated, into the Cathedral precinct. Midday on Easter Sunday: the baroque tune drifted around the monumental stonework. The statue stood, people walked by. But there, so close to the Cathedral, a different context to the performance insisted itself. For all week still figures had been moving around the streets of the city. These figures were all explicitly religious. And all of them had converged at some point on the Cathedral precinct. In that space, now once again emptied of all the concentration and bustle that surrounded those religious figures, the statue stands. By contrast to that earlier activity the statue's customary enigma looks marginal, fading into something small and thin, individualized, laconic, arty – human.

For those other still figures were made out of wood. Painted and garbed, surrounded by candles and flowers, the figures are mounted on platforms which are carried on the shoulders of 32 bearers, hidden, but for their feet, under the wooden structure. One such, the day before, had come up the tree-lined street into the Plaza del Carmen. Preceded by hooded penitents bearing crucifixes and candles, followed by a band which features wailing brass and woodwind, the figure of Christ is bent under the burden of his cross. Caught by the wind the purple drapery on Christ flutters. As the platform rounds the corner, the bearers change the rhythm of their walk. Turning corners underneath the several tons of their load is a work of art, and to display their skill they change rhythm with the band into a *paso doble*. There, moving but not going forward, seized – informed even – by the rhythm of 32 bodies in unison, the platform sways. And with it, swaying too, "in the rhythm of the music," its drapery fluttering, the wooden Christ seems to move.

The total effect requires careful organization and hierarchies of effort. The progress of the procession is facilitated by its administrative minders, with dark suits, shades, and mobile phones. The front of the procession consists of penitents in the pointed hoods and robes of their order, adults and children, some barefoot. On a warm day the robes make it hotter. Behind the platform is the band, in uniforms with caps, with the heaviest instruments, the drums, doing most work. Most hidden, but working hardest, are the bearers. Their movement is constrained by the necessity to maintain complete unity among themselves, to liaise rhythmically with the band and, above all, to sustain and manipulate – and to display their capacity to manipulate – that object they inhabit. Weighing on their shoulders is the non-body which is god. We are in a culture of icons. As Baudinet says, "Transfiguration, *metamorphosis*, this is the name that designates both the glory of the resurrected body and the work of the spectator's gaze on the icon" (Baudinet 1989: 151). The statue is touched reverently as it passes. Yet the non-body's movement depends, as does a puppet, on its bearers. But the bearers' bodies are disciplined by the object, and its non-body, which contains them.

When they have departed from the Cathedral precinct, what is left on Easter Sunday is a woman performing her body as if it were non-body, a statue. The relationship between her and the processions is probably entirely fortuitous, produced by this essay. And that relationship could be mapped in various frames: independent performer or organized religio-economic brotherhood; secular versus religious; new art or invented tradition (some processions started as recently as the 1980s); individual woman or patriarchal community; solo effort versus group discipline. The mode of embodiment in each case makes meaning or, to use Donna Haraway's phrase, "Embodiment is significant prosthesis" (Haraway 1991: 195).

She uses the phrase in an essay about feminism and the production of knowledge. Inspecting the claims of impassive objectivity and decoding, she argues for a deliberate partiality, for "situated" knowledges. "Accounts of a 'real' world do not, then, depend on a logic of 'discovery', but on a power-charged social relation of 'conversation'. The world neither speaks itself nor disappears in favour of a master decoder" Haraway 1991: 198). She offers her survey of explanatory trends in biology as an "allegory" applicable to the project of feminist objectivity, and adds: "The boundary between animal and human is one of the stakes in this allegory, as well as that between machine and organism" (ibid.: 200). In another essay she then returns to this boundary. Her particular focus here is the discourse(s) of immunology, but her observations about the delineation of boundary have bearing, I think, on those performance practices in Granada – as indeed elsewhere: "Organisms are made; they are constructs of a world-changing kind. The constructions of an organism's boundaries, the job of the discourses of immunology, are particularly potent mediators of the experiences of sickness and death . . ." (ibid.: 208). Similarly, " 'objects' like bodies do not pre-exist as such. Scientific objectivity (the siting/sighting of objects) is not about dis-engaged discovery, but about mutual and usually unequal structuring" (ibid.). Insisting on the historical specificity of bodies, she suggests that the object of knowledge is "an active part of the apparatus of bodily production." Hence "[b]odies as objects of knowledge are material-semiotic generative nodes. Their boundaries materialize in social interaction" (ibid.). And, we might now add, these social interactions have to include performance practices.

The history of performance practices shows changing relationships between body and non-body. The particular point of physical contact, and the conceptual terms of the relationship, change historically. The cathexes in a particular culture's performance of body/non-body may tell us something about that culture. But from this point we can now take a further step. If Haraway's account of the delineation of boundaries is correct, it would seem that performance is one of those sites that enable this delineation to take place. Casting our minds back to those performances in Granada, we can see that they draw differing boundaries between object and organism, and that these boundaries pertain to such things as tradition and novelty, individuality and community, secularity and religion. As Haraway says, "what counts as an object is precisely what world history turns out to be about" (ibid.: 195). Or, in the more local case of that Spanish Easter Week, the relations of god and man.

References

Allain, P. (2002) *The Art of Stillness: The Theatre Practice of Tadashi Suzuki*. London: Methuen.
Balsamo, A. (1995) "Forms of Technological Embodiment: Reading the Body in Contemporary Culture," in M. Featherstone and R. Burrows (eds.), *Cyberspace/Cyberbodies/Cyberpunk*. London: Sage.

Baudinet, M.-J. (1989) "The Face of Christ, the Form of the Church," in M. Feher, R. Naddaff, and N. Tazi (eds.), *Fragments for a History of the Human Body: Part One*. New York: Zone.

Braun, E. (ed.) (1969) *Meyerhold on Theatre*. London: Eyre Methuen.

Clynes, M.E. and Kline, N.S. (1995) "Cyborgs and Space," in Gray, Figueroa-Sarriera, and Mentor.

Craig, E.G. (1980) *On the Art of the Theatre*. London: Heinemann.

Decroux, E. (1963) *Paroles sur le mime*. Paris: Gallimard.

Farnell, R. (2000) "In Dialogue with 'Posthuman' Bodies: Interview with Stelarc," in M. Featherstone (ed.), *Body Modification*. London: Sage.

Featherstone, M. and Burrows, R. (eds.) (1995) *Cyberspace/Cyberbodies/Cyberpunk*. London: Sage.

Figueroa-Sarriera, H.J. (1995) "Cyborgology: Constructing the Knowledge of Cybernetic Organisms," in C.H. Gray, H.J. Figueroa-Sarriera, and S. Mentor (eds.), *The Cyborg Handbook*. London: Routledge.

Foster, S.L. (1996) "The Ballerina's Phallic Pointe," in S.L. Foster (ed.), *Corporealities: Dancing Knowledge, Culture and Power*. London: Routledge.

Franko, M. (1993) *Dance as Text: Ideologies of the Baroque Body*. Cambridge: Cambridge University Press.

Gabilondo, J. (1995) "Postcolonial Cyborgs: Subjectivity in the Age of Cybernetic Reproduction," in C.H. Gray, H.J. Figueroa-Sarriera, and S. Mentor (eds.), *The Cyborg Handbook*. London: Routledge.

Garner, S.B. Jr. (1994) *Bodied Spaces: Phenomenology and Performance in Contemporary Drama*. Ithaca, NY: Cornell University Press.

Gonzalez, J. (1995) "Envisioning Cyborg Bodies: Notes from Current Research," in C.H. Gray, H.J. Figueroa-Sarriera, and S. Mentor (eds.), *The Cyborg Handbook*. London: Routledge.

Gray, C.H. (1995) "An Interview with Manfred Clynes," in C.H. Gray, H.J. Figueroa-Sarriera, and S. Mentor (eds.), *The Cyborg Handbook*. London: Routledge.

Gray, C.H., Figueroa-Sarriera, H.J., and Mentor, S. (eds.) (1995) *The Cyborg Handbook*. London: Routledge.

Gropius, W. (ed.) (1961) *The Theater of the Bauhaus*. Middletown, CN: Wesleyan University Press.

Hammond, P.E. and Hammond, S.N. (1979) "The Internal Logic of Dance: a Weberian Perspective on the History of Ballet," *Journal of Social History* 12: 591–608.

Haraway, D. (1991) *Simians, Cyborgs, and Women: The Reinvention of Nature*. London: Free Association Books.

Hess, D.J. (1995) "On Low-Tech Cyborgs," in C.H. Gray, H.J. Figueroa-Sarriera, and S. Mentor (eds.), *The Cyborg Handbook*. London: Routledge.

Hogle, L.F. (1995) "Tales for the Cryptic: Technology Meets Organism in the Living Cadaver," in C.H. Gray, H.J. Figueroa-Sarriera, and S. Mentor (eds.), *The Cyborg Handbook*. London: Routledge.

Holland, S. (1995) "Descartes Goes to Hollywood: Mind, Body and Gender in Contemporary Cyborg Cinema," in M. Featherstone and R. Burrows (eds.), *Cyberspace/Cyberbodies/Cyberpunk*. London: Sage.

Howard, S. (1998) *The Politics of Courtly Dancing in Early Modern England*. Amherst, MA: University of Massachusetts Press.

http://www.stelarc.va.com.au

King, B. (1985) "Articulating Stardom," *Screen* 26, 5: 27–50.

King, B. (1989) "The Burden of Headroom," *Screen* 30, 1–2: 122–38.

Kleist, H. von (1989) "On the Marionette Theater," in M. Feher, R. Naddaff, and N. Tazi (eds.), *Fragments for a History of the Human Body: Part One*. New York: Zone.

Kracauer, S. (1995) *The Mass Ornament* (trans. T.Y. Levin). Cambridge, MA.: Harvard University Press.

de Landa, M. (1991) *War in the Age of Intelligent Machines*. New York: Zone.

Lingis, A. (1994) *Foreign Bodies*. London: Routledge.

Look at Lolo, written and produced by Peter Stuart, Planet Rapido, for Channel 4.

Lupton, D. (1995) "The Embodied Computer/User," in M. Featherstone and R. Burrows (eds.), *Cyberspace/Cyberbodies/Cyberpunk*. London: Sage.

Lury, C. (1998) *Prosthetic Culture: Photography, Memory and Identity*. London: Routledge.

McClary, S. (1998) "Unruly Passions and Courtly Dances: Technologies of the Body in Baroque Music," in S.E. Melzer and K. Norberg (eds.), *From the Royal to the Republican Body*. Berkeley, CA: University of California Press.

Penley, C. and Ross, A. (1991) "Cyborgs at Large: Interview with Donna Haraway," *Social Text* 25/26.

Poster, M. (1995) "Postmodern Virtualities," in M. Featherstone and R. Burrows (eds.), *Cyberspace/Cyberbodies/Cyberpunk*. London: Sage.

Prolet, Buehne (1980) *Tempo Tempo*, in D. Bradby, L. James, and B. Sharratt (eds.), *Performance and Politics in Popular Drama*. Cambridge: Cambridge University Press.

Reichardt, J. (1978) *Robots: Fact, Fiction & Prediction*. London: Thames and Hudson.

Schwartz, H. (1992) "Torque: The New Kinaesthetic of the Twentieth Century," in J. Crary and S. Kwinter (eds.), *Incorporations*. New York: Zone.

Segel, H.B. (1995) *Pinocchio's Progeny: Puppets, Marionettes, Automatons, and Robots in Modernist and Avant-Garde Drama*. Baltimore, MD: Johns Hopkins University Press.

Sobchack, V. (1994) "New Age Mutant Ninja Hackers: Reading *Mondo 2000*," in M. Dery (ed.), *Flame Wars: The Discourse of Cyber Culture*. Durham, NC: Duke University Press.

Springer, C. (1991) "The Pleasure of the Interface," *Screen* 32, 3: 303–23.

Springer, C. (1994) "Sex, Memories, and Angry Women," in M. Dery (ed.), *Flame Wars: The Discourse of Cyber Culture*. Durham, NC: Duke University Press.

Stelarc (1998) "From Psych-Body to Cyber-Systems: Images as Post-Human Entities," in J. Broadhurst Dixon and E.J. Cassidy (eds.), *Virtual Futures: Cyberotics, Technology and Post-Human Pragmatism*. London: Routledge.

Stelarc (2000) "Parasite Visions: Alternate, Intimate and Involuntary Experiences," in M. Featherstone (ed.), *Body Modification*. London: Sage.

Suzuki, T. (1986) *The Way of Acting* (trans. J. Thomas Rimer). New York: Theater Communications Group.

Theweleit, K. (1992) "Circles, Lines and Bits," in J. Crary and S. Kwinter (eds.), *Incorporations*. New York: Zone.

Tomas, D. (1995) "Art, Psychasthenic Assimilation and the Cybernetic Automaton," in C.H. Gray, H.J. Figueroa-Sarriera, and S. Mentor, *The Cyborg Handbook*. London: Routledge.

Vigarello, G. (1989) "The Upward Training of the Body from the Age of Chivalry to Courtly Civility," in M. Feher, R. Naddaff, and N. Tazi (eds.), *Fragments for a History of the Human Body: Part Two*. New York: Zone.

Virilio, P. (1991) *The Aesthetics of Disappearance* (trans. P. Beitchman). New York: Semiotext(e).

Wilson, R.R. (1995) "Cyber(body)parts: Prosthetic Consciousness," in M. Featherstone and R. Burrows (eds.), *Cyberspace/Cyberbodies/Cyberpunk*. London: Sage.

Wollen, P. (1993) *Raiding the Icebox: Reflections on Twentieth-Century Culture*. Bloomington, IN: Indiana University Press.

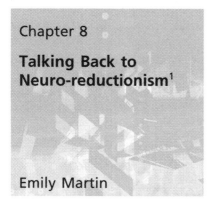

Chapter 8

Talking Back to Neuro-reductionism[1]

Emily Martin

So even though our stories are
Intangible, ethereal,
Our mental composition is
Essentially material;
And though we don't experience
This transubstantiation,
To know ourselves requires
Its detailed elucidation.

And not just to design some
More effective medications,
But also to define a view
With wider implications,
Since understanding molecules
That drive us to insanity
Provides a giant window on
The nature of humanity.

Barondes, *Molecules and Mental Illness*, p. 208

Introduction

A variety of contemporary modes of thought about the human mind are bent on reducing "mind" to "body" by interpreting psychological processes as neuronal ones. In what follows I will discuss two cases of contemporary "neuro-reductionism," their differences, and why their differences matter. I am interested in the work such new scientific accounts are able to do, what their effect might be on cultural concepts of mind, mental illness, and health, and the self, and how these potential effects are received or rejected in particular social contexts.

Neuro-reductionism in Biological Psychiatry

Nikolas Rose has discussed one example of a science that locates mental events in the neurons of the brain. He delineates the main tenets of a style of thought known as biological psychiatry:

> This style of thought shapes what there is to be explained . . . what is to be explained by biological psychiatry is a brain kind of a thing. Depression is a brain thing. We may not know what kind of a brain thing. But depression is one of the things a brain does. . . . It's the brain thing that has to be explained – even when the explanation refers to outside events, biography, substance abuse, child abuse or whatever, the brain has become the obligatory passage point for the explanation.   (2000: 8–9)

In this world view, the brain does not act as an undifferentiated organ. It acts through its constituents, understood at the molecular level:

> Some central philosophical questions are being re-posed. . . . In terms of the shaping, maintenance, modulation, and multidirectional pathways between the capacities, wills and passions of persons – mood, affect, urges, impulsivity, stress, thought itself – and events at the molecular level – largely the secretion, destruction, uptake, re-uptake, and mode of action of neurotransmitters and their relations to other synaptic events involving receptors and the like.   (ibid.: 10)

In biological psychiatry, genes manifest themselves in brains of various kinds, which in turn lead to behavioral patterns. The causal links between gene and brain, brain and behavior, are usually measured statistically.

Research by anthropologists and others in science studies has shown that these obligatory passage points in the brain have a far broader place than the labs of research scientists in biological psychiatry (Dumit 1997; Star 1989). In my own ongoing research project, I have found that the very elements Rose describes are frequently depicted in mass market advertisements and other materials for psychotropic drugs. For example, simple, schematic diagrams of two nerve endings, with neurotransmitters circulating between them, are at the center of a ubiquitous ad for Zoloft, an antidepressant, and the circulation of the neurotransmitters is often animated when the ad is shown on television.

One of the key interlocutors in my fieldwork, an artist funded by NIH (National Institutes of Health) to make films in collaboration with neuroscientists, produces videos directed at teenagers that draw directly on the science of neural processes:

> In the work I keep bringing up issues about the brain, neuroscience, and so forth. It's sort of what God was to Renaissance people, the brain is to at least this video artist. . . . When we talk about natural pathways to euphoria, the message is very simple and natural. Through one's art, through one's exercise, there are ways to get the neurotransmitters in your brain to give you euphoria. You very much set out that this is a chemical process. You have those chemicals already available in your body. There are ways to trigger that. . . . And I really wanted to let people feel that they have the potential, that everybody has the potential with what's inside their own mind. (Lee Boot, interview on *Media Matters*, WJHU, 2001)

Lee Boot's vision of teaching people to trigger happiness by learning to tap chemical processes in their brains marks a significant turning point in the history of efforts to understand disorders of the mind.

One must look a long way back in time to find another turning point in psychiatry of similar magnitude. Michael MacDonald has enabled us to understand such an earlier turning point through his research on the English "Magi," Richard Napier. From 1597 to 1641, Napier took notes on his thousands of patients, providing a concise astrological chart for each, and linking physical, mental, social, and cosmological features:

> The purpose of this astral cartography was to situate the patient in the cosmos, placing him at the vortex of the natural forces that impelled the universe, discovering the correspondences that linked microcosm and macrocosm. Astrological medicine presumed that the perturbations of the mind and body were mirrored in the motions of the stars, and the horoscope was an aid to discovering their nature and origins. If the correspondence was to be exact, the patient's symptoms had to be observed as precisely as the heavens, and below this horoscope of each client Napier carefully listed the sufferer's description of his malady or the signs reported by his representative. Now the astrological circumstances and the disease's manifestations could be compared; and remedies possessing the appropriate celestial and medical virtues selected. (MacDonald 1981: 26)

At around the same time, in a similar manner, Robert Burton's *An Anatomy of Melancholy* (1651) regarded melancholy as embedded in a wide range of circumstances, including faulty education, stress, childhood events, heredity, supernatural elements, the stars, God, and the devil (Grob 1994: 9).

As MacDonald demonstrates, after the English Revolution, and over the course of the seventeenth and eighteenth centuries, secular and medical explanations of mental disorders steadily gained ground (1981: 9–11; 230). There was set in motion a growing shift away from the cosmological view of mental disorder that characterized the early modern period, a shift that constituted a fundamental change.

The story of how medical theories of the origin and treatment of mental illness developed is far too complex to be summarized here, but Rose's summary statement about medical psychiatry is a useful guide: up until the mid-twentieth century, psychiatry could only gain access to the interior of the mind through looking at the surfaces of the body and listening to and interpreting the voice of the patient (2000: 11). This means that developments in the second half of the twentieth century, which gave biological psychiatry access to the "depths of the living brain," including information about the structure of neurons and their chemical interactions, constituted another fundamental change (ibid.).

Neuro-reductionism in Cognitive Science

In order to both broaden and deepen our understanding of how biological psychiatry works in contemporary culture, I would like to set alongside it recent styles of thought in an area of cognitive science known as computational neuroscience. This is another area of brain-related research, one not so directly tied to medicine, psychiatry, and drugs, which works by simulating neuronal activity with computer networks. In this domain, rather than focusing on statistical links between genes, brains, and behavior (as in biological psychiatry), researchers build computer models based on what neurons in the brain do. Then, if the model can perform cognitive operations describable as "remembering," "deciding," or "choosing," the argument is that it must be because the brain works in a similar, computer-like way.[2]

The significance of these cognitive models for biological psychiatry is this: biological psychiatry snares chemical processes in the brain as obligatory passage points for accounts of irrational or disordered behavior, as Rose shows. But it leaves untouched and still open for interpretive accounts what patients say about their condition and what the criteria for "irrational or disordered behavior" are. In fact, for generating a diagnosis, biological psychiatry remains completely dependent on interpreting the meaning of the patient's (together with friends', relatives', and witnesses') words about what he or she does, feels, and thinks. It is precisely the meaning of language and the criteria of rationality that are in turn apparently snared and made biological by computational neuroscience. These developments in biological psychiatry and neuroscience, considered together, raise the possibility of a more total neuro-reductionism than is imaginable by means of biological psychiatry alone.

My interest in the topic of cognitive science models of the mind began with scholars George Lakoff and Mark Johnson (1980), whose work on mind and body in relation to language in their book, *Metaphors We Live By*, inspired the focus on metaphor in my earlier work, and allowed me to relate the metaphorical structure of language to changing social and cultural contexts.[3] I had once thought the odd bits of Lakoff and Johnson's book that attached metaphors to "natural" kinds of experience (ibid.: 118) could be ignored because the bulk of the account looked at metaphors as they function in relation to other metaphors and in relation to the social context. For example, their final chapter looks at how the metaphor "labor is a resource" functions in both capitalist and socialist systems to allow labor to be treated as a single, homogenous category whose cost should be kept down, concealing the difference among kinds of labor, some of which are exploitative and demeaning (ibid.: 236–7).

The experience of reading Lakoff and Johnson's latest work, *Philosophy in the Flesh: The Embodied Mind and its Challenge to Western Thought* (1999), was for me a massive shock. In place of the play of metaphors with and against each other, they now provide an account of consciousness as consisting of neural structures in the brain. Here are some of the main tenets of Lakoff and Johnson's new position.

"Conceptual structures are neural structures in the brain" (1999: 20). Neural structures in the brain, what they call the "cognitive unconscious" constitute a large and essential part of our "conceptual systems, meaning, inference, and language" (12). The claim is not that neural structures are necessary for our cognitive operations; the claim is that neural structures *are the same thing as* our cognitive operations.

"Metaphors are realized in our brains physically as a consequence of the nature of our brains, our bodies and the world we inhabit" (59). By definition, metaphor consists in two physically separate parts of the brain, two domains, that are neurally linked in response to experience. When the metaphor "prices hit bottom" is activated, "prices" activates the quantity-domain network in the brain and sends activation to the connected verticality-domain network. "Hit bottom" activates an inference mechanism in the verticality-domain which computes: "as far down as it can go." "Activation then flows back to the quantity-domain network indicating Maximum Negative Change" (55). "This correspondence between quantity and verticality arises from a correlation in our normal everyday experiences, like pouring more water into the glass and seeing the level go up" (47).

"Neural structures are learned, not innate, but they are limited in number to several 100's, and are widespread around the globe" (56–7). "We acquire a large system of primary metaphors automatically and unconsciously simply by functioning in the most ordinary of ways in the everyday world from our earliest years. We have no choice in this. Because of the way neural connections are formed during [childhood], we all naturally think using hundreds of primary metaphors" (47). "We have a system of primary metaphors simply because we have the bodies and brains we have and because we live in the world we live in, where intimacy does tend to correlate significantly with proximity, affection with warmth, and achieving purposes with reaching destinations" (59). "If you are a normal human being, you inevitably acquire an enormous range of primary metaphors just by going about the world constantly moving and perceiving" (57). "It is not just that our bodies and brains determine *that* we will categorize; they also determine what kinds of categories we will have and what their structure will be . . . the peculiar nature of our bodies [mostly shared by all humans] shapes our very possibilities for conceptualization and categorization" (18–19).

Given the physical instantiation of categories and metaphors in our brains, they cannot easily be changed. "Though we learn new categories regularly, we cannot make massive changes in our category systems through conscious acts of recategorization (though, through experience in the world, our categories are subject to unconscious reshaping and partial change)" (18–19).

The neural structures that reason is made up of are a product of evolutionary processes. "Reason is evolutionary, in that abstract reason builds on and makes use of forms of perceptual and motor inference present in 'lower' animals. The result is a Darwinism of reason, a rational Darwinism: Reason, even in its most abstract form, makes use of, rather than transcends our animal nature" (4).

The area of cognitive science concerned with models of the brain is far broader than the path that led me out from Lakoff and Johnson's work, but for reasons of space and coherence, I will restrict my discussion here to their immediate interlocutors. The elimination of society and culture, not to mention history, from Lakoff and Johnson's account of language, followed the publication of Pat Churchland's *Neurophilosophy* in 1996, a book that opened the door to claims of direct causal linkages between the structures of neural networks in the brain and the phenomena studied by linguists and philosophers of language.[4]

Pat Churchland (and her colleagues Paul Churchland and Terry Sejnowski, among others), working in a field called computational neuroscience, hold that the brain represents the world by means of networks of neurons. Neural networks can be modeled in computers using "Parallel Distributed Processing" (PDP) or "Connectionist" units. This approach has stirred up a lot of enthusiasm in many quarters. Some have claimed it amounts to a "scientific revolution" (Smith and DeCoster 1998: 111), "a major paradigm shift" (Read and Miller 1998: vii), that it has made meetings of the Cognitive Science Society into "connectionist pep rallies" (Smolensky 1988: 1), and that it is going to require major changes in how we think about ourselves (Smith and DeCoster 1998: 111).

What is a connectionist unit? It is a computer into which we could enter data in the form of numbers, patterns, sounds, or images. Inside the computer, there is a dense network of simple computing units, often compared to neurons. Each unit receives input signals and sends output signals over connections that have a numerical weight indicating their importance. Each unit "decides" the strength of its output signal by a calculation based on the strength of all the incoming signals. The units together "learn" by checking their output against correct outputs we would provide. For example, the input could be a written phonetic transcript of a story a 5-year-old American child told about visiting his grandmother. The neural net would have the correct output when it had learned to read the transcript out loud (using a voice synthesizer) in understandable English. As it learns, the network reweights the inputs and "grows neurons" as needed to produce the correct outcome:

The hardware mechanisms are networks consisting of large numbers of densely interconnected units, which correspond to concepts. These units have activation levels and they transmit signals (graded or 1–0) to one another along weighted connections. Units "compute" their output signals through a process of weighting each of their input signals by the strength of the connection along which the signal is coming in, summing the weighted input signals, and feeding the result into a nonlinear output function, usually a threshold. Learning consists of adjusting the strengths of connections and the threshold-values, usually in a direction that reduces the discrepancy between an actual output in response to some input and a "desired" output provided by an independent set of "teaching" inputs.   (Pinker n.d.: 2)

Paul Smolensky, a computer scientist, explains: "These networks *program themselves*, that is they have autonomous procedures for tuning their weights to eventually perform some specific computation" (Smolensky 1988: 1). "The network itself 'decides' what computations the hidden units will perform; because these units represent neither inputs nor outputs, they are never 'told' what their values should be, even during training" (ibid.: 1). Once "trained up," the neural net is not limited to the input–output combinations it matched during training: it can handle new inputs (read new stories) flexibly and intelligently, making only the kind of errors a human reader would also make, such as mispronouncing proper names.

In many ways, these learning neural nets are extremely appealing. Many of us might look forward to having them appear in our lives, which will be soon, judging from the success of early applications: neural nets are being used successfully in speech recognition, robot design, auto emission regulation, stock market analysis and prediction, and detecting buried ordnance, to name just a few. So stunning are these early successes that they inspire a great deal of confidence – and here is where my alarm bells sound: computational neuroscientists are wont to assert that building up from connectionist models, all human experiences and activities, including social behavior, can eventually be produced. In the Churchlands' vision:

Accounting for a creature's knowledge of the spatial location of a fly is difficult enough. Accounting for its knowledge of a loved one's embarrassment, a politician's character, or a bargaining opponent's hidden agenda, represents a much higher level of difficulty. And yet we already know that artificial neural networks, trained by examples, can come to recognize and respond to the most astonishingly subtle patterns and similarities in nature. If physical patterns, why not social patterns? We confront no problem in principle here. Only a major challenge. (Churchland and Churchland 1998: 77)

Even rationality could be understood as an evolutionary product of brain networks:

I am assuming that there is a real difference in what we may loosely call "life success" between agents whose behaviour is generally at the "in control" end of the spectrum – agents typified by the fictional Captain Kirk – and on the other hand, agents whose behaviour is often at the "out of control" end of the spectrum, typified by the obsessive-compulsive subject . . . the relevant behavioural differences . . . are almost certainly deeply related to properties to which natural selection is sensitive. (ibid.: 244)

And here is how moral values could arise out of the same processes:

On the whole, social groups work best when individuals are considered responsible agents, and hence, as a matter of practical policy, it is probably wisest to hold mature agents responsible for their behaviour and for their habits. That is, it is probably in everyone's interests if the default assumption in place is that agents have control over their actions and that, in general, agents are liable to punishment and praise for their actions. . . . Feeling those consequences is necessary for contouring the state-space landscape in the appropriate way, and that means feeling the approval and disapproval meted out. (ibid.: 251)

For rationality and morality, the social group becomes the "teaching network" that provides feedback to the learning human neuronal system (see Flanagan 1996: 193).

Although both Lakoff and Johnson and the Churchlands believe mind can be reduced to brain, so to speak, Lakoff and Johnson see mind right in the neuronal structures, while the Churchlands allow the possibility that cognition could be an "emergent" property at a higher level of the system (Churchland 1996: 282). But the levels in their system are all in the body. In the introduction to *The Computational Brain*, Pat Churchland and Terry Sejnowski argue repeatedly that knowledge of the molecular and cellular levels of the brain, though important, is insufficient to understand cognition, which would have to entail knowledge of networks at higher levels (Churchland and Sejnowski 1992: 4). But the levels in the illustration they provide of "neuron man," a figure frequently reproduced in other neuroscience texts as well, is telling. The illustration shows a human figure composed only of its nervous system alongside a vertical list of terms from smallest to largest: molecules, synapses, neurons, networks, maps, systems, and finally the CNS (central nervous system). No higher levels are depicted or named (Llinas and Churchland 1996: 283).

Churchland and Sejnowski also assert that we should eventually expect to be able to explain emergent properties, *reduce them*, to lower-level properties (1992: 2). Throughout, the emphasis of all these researchers is overwhelmingly on the ways all kinds of learning can be reduced to the operations of neural nets. When they think about the environment as a "teacher" of these neural networks in the brain, their purview is narrow: Lakoff and Johnson think about universal human bodily experience, Ramachandran about the experience of amputated limbs, the Churchlands about behavior adaptive by the lights of natural selection.

With their research expensively underwritten by foundations, corporations, and the government,[5] and their claim to provide reductive accounts of the social/cultural without taking much account of what social and cultural dimensions of existence are about, I see the neuro-reductive cognitive sciences as the most dangerous kind of vortex – one close by, and one whose power has the potential to suck up and pull disciplines like history and anthropology into itself, destroying them as it does so. Fortunately, there is some opposition to the reductive enterprise even within cognitive science. Here I want to briefly join forces with two of these opponents: Hilary Putnam and John Searle.

Hilary Putnam, who some years ago advocated the analogy – the brain is to the mind as the computer is to its software – has now rejected the implications of this view (1988: 73). He now argues that commonsense concepts involving intention have an integrity of their own and cannot be accounted for by reductive scientific stories. "Such things as believing that snow is white and feeling certain that the cat is on the mat – are not 'states' of the human brain and nervous system considered in isolation from the social and nonhuman environment" (ibid.). Putnam wants to argue that

> intentionality won't be reduced and won't go away. . . . I shall try to show that there is no scientifically describable property that all cases of any particular intentional phenomenon have in common. By this thesis I mean to deny that there is some scientifically describable "nature"

that all cases of "reference" in general, or of "meaning" in general, or of "intentionality" in general possess; I also mean to deny that there is any scientifically describable property (or "nature") that all cases of any one specific intentional phenomenon, say, "thinking that there are a lot of cats in the neighbourhood" have in common.   (1988: 1–3)

To rebut Putnam, the Churchlands argue he mistakenly relies on a model of folk psychology to account for intentionality. "Folk psychology" (FP) is "the prescientific, commonsense conceptual framework that all normally socialized humans deploy in order to comprehend, predict, explain, and manipulate the behaviour of humans and the higher animals" (1998: 3). There is something theory-like about folk psychology, because it "embodies generalized information, and . . . it permits explanation and prediction in the fashion of any theoretical framework" (ibid.). But it is a theory that is soon to be eclipsed by a better one, neuro-reductionism, which explains much more, is rapidly developing, and integral with an emerging consensus in numerous physical and life sciences (8). Folk psychology will inevitably be eliminated, like other outmoded notions – phlogiston, caloric fluids, or the crystal spheres of ancient astronomy. "FP's emerging wallflower status bodes ill for its future" (ibid.).

How could Putnam's critique be strengthened? The Churchlands are right that there is a common cultural view among Euro-Americans that a person is made up of inner mental states (Crapanzano 1992, among others, has shown this definitively). Their mistake is to think that such a cultural world view is a theory of a scientific kind. World views do not seek to prove or disprove, they do not seek to explain by means of general laws: instead they are part of what people use to build up a view of the world, of possible worlds. Therefore, the anthropologist might argue, the Churchlands have made a category mistake. Americans' folk psychology won't necessarily be replaced by the view that inner states are neural structures, any more than a habitual gambler's view that a score of 21 wins a hand of blackjack would be replaced by the view that habitual gambling is caused by the form of a particular set of genes. If a more reductionistic, brain-based picture of human action did displace our current everyday mental concepts, it would not be because the neural net theory had won in the court of scientific opinion. It would be because the environment we live in (and that scientific theories are produced in) had shifted so that a brain-centered view of a person began to make cultural sense.

We might also observe that by relegating Putnam's ideas to the realm of the "folk," which is then given "wallflower" status, they neatly place themselves on the side of the male, rational, mature, and reliable, and Putnam on the side of the female, irrational, immature, and unreliable.

John Searle is another critic of neuro-reductionism. Although Searle accepts that "Conscious processes are *caused by* lower-level neuronal processes in the brain" (1998: 53, emphasis added), he argues that consciousness cannot be *reduced to* micro-physical causes without leaving out subjectivity. Such experiences as pains, tickles, itches, thoughts, and feelings "exist only as they are experienced by some human or animal subject" (ibid.: 44). "Although consciousness is a biological phenomenon like any other, its subjective, first-person ontology makes it impossible to reduce it to objective third-person phenomena in the way that we can reduce third-person phenomena such as digestion or solidity" (57):

> Consciousness only exists when it is experienced as such. For other features, such as growth, digestion, or photosynthesis, you can make a distinction between our experience of the feature and the feature itself. This possibility makes reduction of these other features possible. But you cannot make that reduction for consciousness without losing the point of having the concept in the first place. Consciousness and the experience of consciousness are the same thing.   (Searle 1997: 213–14)

The Churchlands' reply to Searle tries the same feminizing tactic they used on Putnam: they accuse Searle of having a "Betty Crocker Theory of Consciousness." They are referring to an explanation of microwave cooking in a Betty Crocker cookbook from the early days of microwave cooking, which says the microwaves agitate the molecules in food, which vibrate and create friction, which in turn creates heat. The Churchlands' point is that this account, relying on folk understanding that friction causes heat, is "massively misleading" and reveals a "decisive failure of comprehension": in reality vibration of the molecules just *is* heat. The cookbook, and Searle, are perpetuating "commonsense, prescientific folk-psychological conceptions" (121–2). In other words, the Churchlands are with the "men" over there in the neurophysiology lab developing dynamic, powerful, explanatory, hard, rational truth; Searle and Putnam are over here with the "girls" in the kitchen, stuck in modes of thought that are rigid, inept, sloppy, soft, irrational, and false.[6]

I think most scholars interested in history and culture would join Putnam and Searle in opposition to a position in which the dyke between Nature and Culture has indeed been breached, but as a result nearly all of what anthropologists call "culture" has drained out through the hole and dissolved in the realm of neural networks. Transcendental reason, the prototype of masculine, abstract thinking, has indeed been dislodged from its eminent position, and the body, prototype of feminine concrete existence, has risen to take its place. But this "body" is universal, unhistorical, unconscious of its own production, and possesses many of the characteristics of modernist scientific accounts: its core operations (in the cognitive unconscious) are (to point to the metaphors informing Lakoff and Johnson's account – metaphors they themselves do not attend to) hidden in the depths, rooted deep below the surface, and can apparently generate causally almost everything humans do (Lakoff and Johnson 1999: 12–13).

Even before Lakoff and Johnson's most recent book, Naomi Quinn already made perhaps the most important response an anthropologist could make to their argument: "Where is culture in this picture?" (Quinn 1991). Do all cultures even have concepts of "intimacy" or "affection," or "journeying," let alone give them meaning in the same way? We might want to raise extremely serious questions about the political effects of a theory that sees reason as a result of Darwinian evolution, yet posits experience directly affects the physical structure of the brain. Will "abnormal" individuals, who are not able to "go about the world constantly moving . . ." be unable to form the same cognitive structures as "normal" people, and hence be unable to participate in the "psychic unity of mankind"? Will Lakoff and Johnson be taken to be saying differences among bodies produce significantly different brains? Is there one kind of brain for males, another for females? Different brains for those with white skins, brown skins, black skins?

If we juxtapose biological psychiatric with neural net/connectionist accounts of the brain we do not find a seamless project with one unified effect. The business interests connected to biological psychiatry, for example, would be found in the pharmaceutical industry (Healy 1997; le Carré 2001) while the business interests of cognitive science are mostly in artificial intelligence and computer design. I think it is important to look at these developments side by side, however, because they do both have the effect of making it harder and harder to see what is lost when we adopt accounts of what humans do that reduce them roundly to what neurons do. Both could be joined under the rubric: neuro-reductionism.

The brain becomes "sovereign," and its "sovereignty" conceals what Geertz argued in 1962: that the human brain is a product of a *relation with culture*:

> The synchronic emergence in primates of an expanded forebrain, developed forms of social organization, and, at least after Australopithecenes got their hands on tools, institutionalized patterns of culture indicates that the standard procedure of treating biological, social, and cultural parameters serially – the first being taken as primary to the second, and the second to the third – is ill-advised. On the contrary, these so-called "levels" should be seen as reciprocally interrelated and considered conjointly. (Geertz 1962: 729)

More recent critiques of this work are plentiful and compelling. John Lucy (1998) and Dorothy Holland (Holland and Valsiner 1988: 264–5)[7] have stressed that cognitive theories focus far too much on the products of the brain and too little on how they work "in the life and functioning of actual people" (Lucy 1998: 105); they ignore how the meaning of metaphors, for example, is shaped by culture beyond the brain and body.[8]

Claudia Strauss and Naomi Quinn acknowledge in a recent work that connectionist models hold interesting potential for anthropologists because, unlike earlier linear models, they are "flexibly adaptive rather than rigidly repetitive. They can adapt to new or ambiguous situations with 'regulated improvisation' to use Bourdieu's term" (Strauss and Quinn 1997: 53). But they also insist that cognitive scientists "oversimplify the variety of ways in which cultural knowledge is transmitted" (ibid.: 76). Relying on simple models of "supervised" or "unsupervised" learning, they ignore the immense complexity of social learning, by turns guided, as Roy D'Andrade has shown (1981), taught, modeled, rewarded, ignored, or coerced (Strauss and Quinn 1997: 77–8). Maurice Bloch stresses how much of social learning happens outside of the circle of language use proper: Zafimaniry children learn kinship concepts as they breastfeed not only from the mother but from other women of the same moiety, and as they are carried on the back of an older child from the same moiety, and so literally become an "integral part of another body, 'connected' to another brain" (Bloch 1998: 50–1).

In anthropological linguistics, the very division between language and culture is being challenged. As Jane Hill and Bruce Mannheim recently put it: "there is no prima facie way to identify certain behaviours – or better, certain forms of social action – as linguistic and others as cultural. Even the most formal and minute aspect of phonetics – syllable timing – completely interpenetrates the most identifiably nonlinguistic, unconscious part of behaviour – the timing of body movements and gestures" (Hill and Mannheim 1992: 382). In computational neuroscience, the sense in which human acts are imbued with meaning through layers of intentionality and complexly interrelated contexts – and therefore the reason simple descriptions of behavior observed are inadequate to attribute meaning – is missing. Clifford Geertz called the kind of description that would be adequate "thick description," and turned to Ryle's account of how intricate human intentionality is to get the point across:

> The point is that between what Ryle calls the "thin description" of what the rehearser (parodist, winker, twitcher . . .) is doing ("rapidly contracting his right eyelid") and the "thick description" of what he is doing ("practicing a burlesque of a friend faking a wink to deceive an innocent into thinking a conspiracy is in motion") lies the object of ethnography: a stratified hierarchy of meaningful structures in terms of which twitches, winks, fake-winks, parodies, rehearsals of parodies are produced, perceived, and interpreted, and without which they would not . . . in fact exist, no matter what anyone did or didn't do with his eyelids. (Geertz 1973)

The intentions of the people involved determine what description the action should be given. One act is a wink and another is not, even though as recorded by video or audio means they might look and sound indistinguishable. This is *not* because the cultural meaning of behavior lies in a hidden domain within the mind or brain: the meaning of the behaviors lies in the context (what are the social norms governing communication in this place and time?). One could think of the acts, thoughts, utterances, explanations, facial expressions, clothing, etc. as interrelated elements of a linguistic system: the meaning of any one of them resides in how it is combined with all the others.

Talking Back to Neuro-reductionism

Our task as critics who wish to draw attention to what the reduction to neurons costs is in large part a rhetorical one: we need to produce accounts of what humans do that are so richly imbued with webs of significance and meaning attached to complex context, that any reduced account simply loses its appeal. If only for reasons of space, I cannot fulfill that objective here, but I would like to end this paper with a hint of how I would proceed.

I am engaged in a research project focused on cultural meanings now being attached to hyper mental conditions, including mania. One location of the research is Orange County, in southern California, where manic depression is almost considered a criterion for success in the entertainment industry, so common is it thought to be. One of the things I do is attend weekly support groups for people diagnosed with and medicated for manic depression. I have found it startling that enactments of manic behavior quite frequently occur during support group meetings. For example, on one occasion, a support group was watching a video called *Dark Glasses and Kaleidoscopes*, produced by Abbott Laboratories, the makers of one of the major psychotropic drugs used for manic depression, Depakote. The film screening was billed as a kind of holiday from the usual more serious business of hearing about people's lives during the week. Soda and snacks were served in a relaxed atmosphere in which people chatted and joked with each other before the film started.

Throughout the film, people were dismissive or hostile, criticizing and mocking its optimistic portrait of manic depression. Some of the comments were: "that's an ideal world"; "that's bull shit – that medications can be fixed to keep you 'just right'"; "yeah, you can work in a profession as long as you don't tell your employer'"; "go ahead and call the 1 800 number [for information about Depakote] as long as you can block a tracer on the call."

There was all-round scoffing when the video showed a person with manic depression saying, "Losing the ability to monitor my own behavior . . . is what having manic depression is." When the video ended, a male member of the group, who frequently expressed his opinions with considerable force, said, "You know what I always say, the whole world needs a dose of lithium." Someone else added, "Yeah, put it in the air . . .!"

After the film, a man who for many weeks had sat very quietly, saying nothing, head hanging down, with a gloomy expression and dejected appearance, said, "I usually don't say anything at all, I have been silent here for weeks and weeks, but tonight I realize I can't hold it all in, I have to let it out." Then he launched into a string of shockingly barbed and funny jokes. The whole group dissolved into a hilarious session of joke telling that took up the entire rest of the two hours. Every now and then someone would say plaintively, but obviously not really seriously, "What are we doing? What if someone wants to *share*?!?" Virtually every person there told more than one raunchy, gross, lewd, or ethnic joke, which managed to poke fun at Catholics, Jews, Poles, blondes, men, women, spouses, and seniors. Everyone shrieked with laughter as what could only be called manic energy built and built. Food and drink cascaded over tables, chairs and the floor; people draped themselves every which way over up-ended furniture.[9]

How might we understand this response? One description might be that it is a carnivalesque reversal of the established order. The group's behavior was a reversal of the usual decorum of the support group, and might be taken to signify a reversal of the can-do theme of the video: most group members are not working regularly, and subsist on disability payments. They have frequently experienced discrimination because of being mentally ill.

Another description might be that it is "mimetic." As Gebauer and Wulf explain, mimesis "isolates an object or an event from its usual context and produces a perspective of reception that differs from the one in which the prior world is perceived. . . . Mimetic action involves the intention of displaying a symbolically produced world in such a way that it will be perceived as a specific world" (1995: 17).

The key is the last phrase: *the intention of displaying* [in order that something can] . . . *be perceived as a* specific *world*. Bakhtin's concept of double-voicing helps us see how the *display* is brought about. "In . . . the double-voiced word, the sounding of a second voice is a part of the project of the utterance. In one way or another, for one reason or another, the author makes use 'of someone else's discourse for his own purposes by inserting a new semantic intention into a discourse which already has and which retains, an intention of its own'" (Morson and Emerson 1990: 149).[10]

In my fieldwork example, the story of mania in the video becomes a tool in the hands of the group as they enact another story of mania. The Abbott Laboratories story is thus *displayed* as a specific world produced in particular circumstances: one in which Depakote manages moods perfectly and everyone has a job. But more important, in the Abbott world, the condition "manic depression" means the person cannot monitor his own behavior (sound a second voice about his behavior) without the aid of a drug. Because it is at least somewhat self-conscious and purposeful, the manic meeting runs against the grain of the irrationality manic depressives are supposed to have.[11]

The support group could also be said to be made up of actors simulating mania, even though they embody mania (they are manic) from time to time in their ordinary lives. Their depiction de-instantiates the category mania, puts it in quotes, demonstrates and mocks it at the same time. The mimetic aspect of their actions might be toward rationality, which they achieve by being able to talk rationally *about* a condition they *have*, one that is understood to be irrational. The group's performance also introduces a note of expressive violence. Mimesis is not only a move to acquire the power of the represented, as Taussig argues, it is also to wrest something away from the represented, perhaps violently, perhaps in anger.[12] In mimesis, "the replication, the copy, acquires the power of the represented . . . the magical power of this embodying inhere(s) in the fact that in reading such examples we are thereby lifted out of ourselves into those images" (Taussig 1993: 16).

Concluding Remarks

Because neuro-reductionism has powerful effects on our subjectivity, making culture harder for us to see, the need for dissent becomes more acute. One answer is to show how rich and multilayered human speech acts are, even when performed by those with mental illness. This I have tried to sketch in a small way above. Another answer is that we are in a position to articulate how new facts about the mind and body generated in biological psychiatry and cognitive science are taken up by people and made part of cultural world views. Joe Dumit has explored how the ability to image mental illness as in the brain can reduce its stigma: "The diseased brain . . . becomes a part of a biological body that is experienced phenomenologically but is not the bearer of personhood. Rather, the patient who looks at his or her PET brain scan is an innocent sufferer rationally seeking help" (1997: 96). In other words, although neuro-reductionism appears to be invading the domain of culture and reducing it to electrical and chemical events, the penchant humans have to make cultural meaning out of everything that comes along, which means that even neuron man can become material for building worlds of meaning. Perhaps we have not lost altogether Richard Napier's desire to chart meaningful connections between the mind and every corner of the cosmos.

Notes

1 Support for this research was made possible by grants from the Spencer Foundation and the National Science Foundation (NSF) (grant BCS 9973154). The conclusions reached are solely the responsibility of the author.

2 See Stephen Jones (2001) on the modeling of neural nets on actual neurons.

3 The sections of this paper on Lakoff and Johnson and connectionism were published in another context in "Mind/Body Problems," *American Ethnologist* (2000), 27 (3): 569–90.

4 Commentators on this book remarked: "she is . . . a real reductionist. The title of her book is to be taken literally – no hyphen between the *neuro* and the *philosophy*; a unified science of the mind/brain is indeed the aim" (Marshall and Gurd 1996: 180).

5 NSF's 1999 budget, political science, provides $18,279,879 to the *four* subfields of the "Behavioral and Cognitive Sciences" (social psychology, linguistics, human cognition, and child learning) and $79,737,206 to the *nine* subfields of the "Social and Economic Sciences" – which include cultural anthropology, economics, sociology, law, physical anthropology, archaeology, geography, and decision and risk management (Stuart Plattner, personal communication; http://www.NSF.org).

6 As a small footnote, just out of curiosity, I asked a physicist how microwaves cook food. He read both Betty Crocker and the Churchlands on the subject and said:

> Betty Crocker is right! When microwaves are absorbed by the charged molecules of food, the molecules absorb the microwaves and oscillate. Just as Betty Crocker says, there is no heat yet. The molecules could simply re-radiate the microwave energy in its original form, as microwaves. Or, if they collided with other molecules (which they are likely to do if there is any moisture in the food), the energy would be converted into random molecular motion. Only at that point would we say the energy had been converted into heat.

7 Holland and Valsiner point out, contra Lakoff and Johnson, that metaphors may be affected by cultural models, as well as the reverse. "Highlighted by a new metaphor, a cultural model may be developed in different directions, and similarly the meaning of the 'new' metaphor itself may come to be elaborated in new ways" (1988: 264).

8 Suzanne Kirschner urges cognitive psychology to redirect its focus from the autonomous individual to the ways human existence is "fundamentally social" (Kirschner 2000).

9   Some examples: What are three things wrong with the penis? It has a ring around the collar, hangs out with nuts, and lives next to an ass hole. Why is the blonde's belly button black and blue after sex? Because her boyfriend's a blond too.

10 For Bakhtin's work on language, see Bakhtin (1968) and (1986).

11 The mimetic faculty "get[s] hold of something by means of its likeness. . . . [it copies] or imitates, and [seeks] a palpable, sensuous, connection between the very body of the perceiver and the perceived" (Taussig 1993: 21).

12 René Girard has built a theory of human action in general based on the claim that mimetic action begins "with one person's appropriation of goals that are deemed valuable and worth striving for solely because they are desired by an Other – who may have achieved the goal or may be seeking to achieve it" (Gebauer and Wulf 1995: 256).

References

Bakhtin, M. (1968) *Rabelais and His World*. Cambridge, MA: MIT Press.

Bakhtin, M. (1986) *Speech Genres and Other Late Essays*. Austin, TX: University of Texas Press.

Barondes, S.H. (1999) *Molecules and Mental Illness*. New York: Scientific American Library.

Bloch, M. (1998) *How We Think They Think: Anthropological Approaches to Cognition, Memory, and Literacy*. Boulder, CO: Westview Press.

Burton, R. (1968) *An Anatomy of Melancholy*. London (first published in 1651).

Churchland, P. (1996) *Neurophilosophy: Toward a Unified Science of the Mind/Brain*. Cambridge, MA: MIT Press.

Churchland, P.S. and Sejnowski, T.J. (1992) *The Computational Brain*. Cambridge, MA: MIT Press.

Churchland, P.M. and Churchland, P.S. (1998) *On the Contrary: Critical Essays, 1987–1997*. Cambridge, MA: MIT Press.

Crapanzano, V. (1992) *Hermes' Dilemma and Hamlet's Desire: On the Epistemology of Interpretation*. Cambridge, MA: Harvard University Press.

D'Andrade, R.G. (1981) "The Cultural Part of Cognition," *Cognitive Science* 5: 179–95.

Duesberg, P. (1994) "Infectious AIDS – Stretching the Germ Theory Beyond Its Limits," *International Archives of Allergy and Immunology* 103: 118–26.

Dumit, J. (1997) "A Digital Image of the Category of the Person: PET Scanning and Objective Self-fashioning," in G.L. Downey and J. Dumit (eds.), *Cyborgs and Citadels: Anthropological Interventions in Emerging Sciences and Technologies*. Santa Fe, NM: School of American Research.

Dumit, J. (n.d.) "Mind Matters: The Social, Material and Entrepreneurial Development of Functional Brain Imaging." Unpublished manuscript.

Flanagan, O. (1996) "The Moral Network," in McCauley, R.N. (ed.), *The Churchlands and Their Critics*. Cambridge, MA: Blackwell Publishers, 192–215.

Gebauer, G. and Wulf, C. (1995) *Mimesis: Culture, Art, Society*. Berkeley, CA: University of California Press.

Geertz, C. (1962) "The Growth of Culture and the Evolution of Mind," in J.M. Scher (ed.), *Theories of the Mind*. New York: Free Press, pp. 713–40.

Geertz, C. (1973) "Religion as a Cultural System," in *The Interpretation of Cultures: Selected Essays*. New York: Basic Books, pp. 87–125.

Grob, G.N. (1994) *The Mad Among Us: A History of the Care of America's Mentally Ill*. New York: Free Press.

Healy, D. (1997) *The Antidepressant Era*. Cambridge, MA: Harvard University Press.

Hill, J.H. and Mannheim, B. (1992) "Language and World View," *Annual Review of Anthropology* 221: 381–406.

Holland, D. and Valsiner, J. (1988) "Cognition, Symbols, and Vygotsky's Developmental Psychology," *Ethos* 16: 247–72.

Jones, S., "Neural Networks and the Computational Brain," web page (accessed April 9, 2001), available at http://www.culture.com.au/brain_proj/neur_net.htm

Kirschner, S.R. (2000) "Postmodern Psychology," in A.E. Kazdin (ed.), *Encyclopedia of Psychology*. Washington, DC: American Psychological Association.

Lakoff, G. and Johnson, M. (1980) *Metaphors We Live By*. Chicago, IL: University of Chicago Press.

Lakoff, G. and Johnson, M. (1999) *Philosophy in the Flesh: The Embodied Mind and Its Challenge to Western Thought*. New York: Basic Books.

le Carré, J. (2001) "In Place of Nations," *The Nation* 272, 14: 11–13.

Llinas, R. and Churchland, P.S. (1996) *The Mind–Brain Continuum: Sensory Processes*. Cambridge, MA: MIT Press.

Lucy, J.A. (1998) "Space in Language and Thought: Commentary and Discussion, *Ethos* 26, 1: 105–11.

MacDonald, M. (1981) *Mystical Bedlam: Madness, Anxiety, and Healing in Seventeenth-century England*. Cambridge: Cambridge University Press.

Marshall, J.C. and Gurd, J.M. (1996) "The Furniture of the Mind: a Yard of Hope, a Ton of Terror?," in R.N. McCauley (ed.), *The Churchlands and Their Critics*. Cambridge, MA: Blackwell Publishers, pp. 176–91.

Morson, G.S. and Emerson, C. (1990) *Mikhail Bakhtin: Creation of a Prosaics*. Stanford, CA: Stanford University Press.

Pinker, S. (n.d.) "On Language and Connectionism: Analysis of a Parallel Distributed Processing Model of Language Acquisition," web page (accessed March 5, 1999), available at http://cogsci.soton.ac.uk/~harnad/Papers/Py104/pinker.conn.html

Posner, M.I. and Raichle, M.E. (1994) *Images of Mind*. New York: Scientific American Library.

Putnam, H. (1988) *Representation and Reality*. Cambridge, MA: MIT Press.

Quinn, N. (1991) "The Cultural Basis of Metaphor," in J.W. Fernandez (ed.), *Beyond Metaphor: The Theory of Tropes in Anthropology*. Stanford, CA: Stanford University Press, pp. 56–93.

Read, S.J. and Miller, L.C. (eds.) (1998) *Connectionist Models of Social Reasoning and Social Behavior*. Mahwah, NJ: Lawrence Erlbaum Associates.

Rose, N. (2000) "Biological Psychiatry as a Style of Thought: Model Systems, Cases, and Exemplary Narratives," Princeton Workshops in the History of Science, 2000–2001.

Searle, J.R. (1997) *The Mystery of Consciousness*. New York: New York Review.

Searle, J.R. (1998) *Mind, Language and Society: Philosophy in the Real World*. New York: Basic Books.

Smith, E.R. and DeCoster, J. (1998) "Person Perception and Stereotyping: Simulation Using Distributed Representations in a Recurrent Connectionist Network," in S.J. Read and L.C. Miller (eds.), *Connectionist Models of Social Reasoning and Social Behavior*. Mahwah, NJ: Lawrence Erlbaum Associates, pp. 111–40.

Smolensky, P. (1988) "On the Proper Treatment of Connectionism," in *Behavioural and Brain Sciences* 11: 1–74.

Star, S.L. (1989) *Regions of the Mind: Brain Research and the Quest for Scientific Certainty*. Stanford, CA: Stanford University Press.

Strauss, C. and Quinn, N. (1997) *A Cognitive Theory of Cultural Meaning*. Cambridge: Cambridge University Press.

Taussig, M. (1993) *Mimesis and Alterity: A Particular History of the Senses*. New York: Routledge.

Part III
Theory and Ethnography

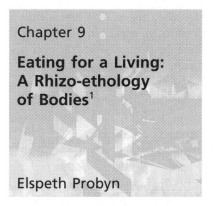

Chapter 9

**Eating for a Living:
A Rhizo-ethology
of Bodies**[1]

Elspeth Probyn

Roots and Shoots

How do you get into a body? How do you penetrate it? How would you capture the body's textures and movement? When and how do bodies open to another? How do you draw out lines that are coiled within? Where would they lead?

I've been writing around bodies for years, yet as an object of study they still mystify and beguile. As Jean-Michel Berthelot (1992) has argued, any sociology that wishes to study the body soon ends up somewhere else. You think you're on to the body yet it becomes apparent that what you're describing is symbolic systems, the structures and effects of class, race, or gender, practices of sport, or organizational principles of sociality. Recently, some feminist critics of science have chastised those of us who "do" theories of embodiment as merely studying "culture" or "semiotics."[2] It's a somewhat harsh and overly generalized critique. And truth be told, it's not that novel. Years ago, the reaction to discussions of body and discourse was that it missed "the flesh and blood" of bodies.

But what would it mean to *get at* the matter of bodies? Where is the flesh and blood and how would it affect accounts of the body? These questions take on an added edge when we specifically consider ethnographies of the body. How do we write of the ethnos of and through bodies?

In this chapter I attempt to trace several aspects of the body. The object of analysis is a doubled one. On one level, I will use this occasion to think through a research project that is in progress. This concerns the role of food writing in mediating taste, a three-year comparative project focused on elucidating not only what food writers do, but what they do to us, the eating public.[3] Thus far we have collected interviews and ethnographic material about a range of issues. On another level, I also want to rethink more traditional notions of ethnography, and to introduce other theoretical ideas about interaction and connection into discussions of ethnographic research.[4] In particular, I want to displace the normative, and oft-critiqued, pairing of ethnographer and object, with a rhizomatic view of the world. In broad terms, this would entail replacing one sort of mapping with another. In the stead of interpreting the meaning of structures from a detailed description of people's interaction, in a rhizomatic account one would trip over points of interaction. Or they would trip you up.

Botanically, rhizome is a term for an underground stem that bears both roots and shoots. Used theoretically and analytically, the term rhizome is a central motif in the work of Deleuze and Guattari. For those with only a passing acquaintance with their work it may seem filled with arcane jargon. Terms like BwO (Bodies without Organs), molar and molecular, de- and re-territorialization may be daunting and even annoying. However, they are merely different ways of trying to describe facets of social, human, and nonhuman interactions. Given how radically varied these are, it's perhaps not surprising that Deleuze and Guattari enlist a wide assortment of terms.

The rhizome is relatively straightforward. Like all their terms, it's not to be thought of as metaphor. It is, rather, a figuration, and a way of figuring and tracing movement and connection. These connections are called "agencements," or "enmeshments," or assemblages. They describe the way "an arrangement . . . exists only in connection with other arrangements." They continue: "We shall wonder with what it functions, in connections with what it transmits intensities or doesn't, into what multiplicities it introduces and metamorphoses its own" (Deleuze and Guattari 1983: 3–4).

This is a complex and yet obvious way of seeing interaction. It depends on an understanding of bodies as multiple and as always engaged with other bodies and entities. The body is a moving assemblage that finds itself enmeshed with other assemblages. Or, as Moira Gatens puts it, " 'the body' *in situ* [i]s always already implicated in its milieu" (1999: 14).[5] As we'll see later, it is not only how and where the body is implicated, but with what and whom that matters. Central here is the question of movement. Elsewhere Gatens describes how for Deleuze (and following Spinoza) "the human body is understood as a complex individual, made up of a number of other bodies . . . in constant interchange with its environment . . . the body as a nexus of variable interconnections, a multiplicity within a web of other multiplicities" (1996: 7).

While I will expand on the implications of this description, for the moment we can say that in this framework, the movement of bodies is as important as their placement. In other words, this perspective has the benefit of wrenching bodies from the stasis that much description, be it ethnographic or other, attributes to them. To be sure this movement may be nearly imperceptible, or at least occurring at a micro level in terms of practices. Yet it contrasts nicely with the static nature that much ethnographic description may have (inadvertently) fostered upon them. Think of how in traditional accounts the ethnographer goes back to his or her beloved tribe, and finds them unchanged, frozen, waiting the touch of a pen, the brush of observation to give them life.

Deleuze's assertion that he takes from Spinoza is informative. "We still do not know what a body can do." It is galvanizing that our very ignorance could send us off in search of unknown and untold connections that bodies enact. If the body is a "molecular mire" (Deleuze 1997: 124), a limitless and shifting composition of entities, this isn't to posit the body as without history. In Deleuze's framing of Spinoza, a body is both kinetic and dynamic. On the one hand, a body is composed of an infinite number of particles, and it is "the relations of motion and rest, of speeds and slownesses between particles that define a body." And on the other, in its dynamic mode, a body is defined in its interaction with other bodies: "it is this capacity for affecting and being affected that also defines a body in its individuality" (1992: 625). Movement is the principle of connection and contact. This perspective thus accepts randomness, and an open-ended view of connection, or indeed disconnection. Movement is inherent and what makes possible a politics of becoming. At the same time, the implied emphasis on spatiality shouldn't be seen as preempting the temporal nature of the possibility of connection. As Gatens reminds us, "what a body can do is, at least in part, a function of its history and of those assemblages in which it has been constructed" (1996: 10).

Brought together, these various aspects of bodies are the object of what Deleuze calls ethology. Simply put, ethology defines bodies, animals, or humans by the affects they are capable of (1992: 627). Strictly speaking, ethology began as an offshoot of zoology and evolution. One can see the connection between the study of plant and animal evolution and the definition that Deleuze takes from Spinoza: "ethology studies the compositions of relations or capacities between different things" (1992: 628). Both require that minute attention be paid to the possibility of change at a micro level. Concomitant with the figure of the rhizome, and conjoined with the injunction that we cannot know beforehand what a body is capable of, the point is to focus on the specificities of bodies in each given encounter, arrangement, or combination.

In terms of the objective of this chapter, the principles of ethology and rhizomatics guide my description of bodies that eat. Formally the object of analysis is bodies that eat for a living. Of course, we all eat for living but here the bodies in question are those professionally involved with food. I will be describing my encounters with them: encounters which are variously face-to-face interviews, in close proximity as I observe their encounters with other bodies that cook or produce food, and textually, as encounters with their writings of their encounters with food. Elsewhere I have been greatly influenced by Deleuze and Guattari's statement that "[w]hat regulates the obligatory, necessary, or permitted interminglings of bodies is above all an alimentary regime and a sexual regime" (Deleuze and Guattari 1988: 90; Probyn 2000). Here my exploration is more open-ended, and accordingly perhaps more attuned to the principles of ethnology. I may stumble across unexpected connections with assemblages not immediately apparent. But there is no overarching argument about the priority of any of these assemblages, be they organized in terms of sex or of gender. Let's just see what bodies do.

Cooking with Gas

From the ethereal heights of theory, we now turn to bodies in action.

> I should have seen this well-practiced ritual for what it was, understood the level of performance here in Marioland, appreciated the experience, the time served together which allowed these hulking giants to dance wordlessly around each other in the cramped, heavily manned space behind the line without ever colliding or wasting a movement. (Bourdain 2000: 32)

This quotation could have been excerpted from any number of ethnographies. It is indeed reminiscent of classical anthropological entry scenes into the culture of the other. For example, think of Raymond Firth's 1939 description of "crowds of naked chattering youngsters ... [who] darted about splashing like a shoal of fish, some of them falling bodily into pools in their excitement" (Firth, cited in Geertz 1988: 12). Everything is in movement, bodies dance and splash before the eyes of the observer.

The opening quote is not, however, from a traditional ethnographer. It is the voice of Anthony Bourdain, taken from his best-selling book, *Kitchen Confidential*. Subtitled "Adventures in the Culinary Underbelly," it is a "tell-all" account of the restaurant trade in New York. "Marioland" is the kitchen staffed by large ex-convicts in Maine where Bourdain began to learn his trade.

The book is sex, drugs, rock 'n roll, and food. It's an appealing combination with just enough spice to tantalize the jaded foodie. The noted American food writer A.A. Gill provides a cover blurb describing it as "Elizabeth David written by Quentin Tarantino."[6] While this is a bit rich, nonetheless it does forefront some of the challenges and delights of writing about bodies that cook. Bourdain captures well the movement of bodies in a kitchen:

> They turned from cutting board to stove-top with breathtaking economy of movement, they hefted 300-pound stockpots onto ranges, tossed legs of veal around like pullets, balanced hundreds of pounds of pasta. (2000: 32)

Later Bourdain expands on this movement, describing "Line cooking done well [a]s a beautiful thing to watch. A good line cook who has 'moves' – meaning economy of movement, nice technique and, most important, speed – can perform with Nijinsky-like grace" (55).

In terms of genre, Bourdain's book could be described as an example of the *Bildungsroman*, where the young hero/author learns about life. Bourdain gives up drugs and the wild life and becomes a somewhat moralistic and successful chef. It's also a good example of auto-ethnography, and carries much of the punch of that genre, as well as its tendency toward solipsism. Despite the annoying aspects of Bourdain's voice, again and again he conveys how bodies move in restaurant kitchens:

> David the Portuguese busboy is making expressos and cappuccinos behind me, but he moves pretty gracefully back there, not bumping me

or spilling. We're used to each other's movements in the narrow space we share, knowing when to move laterally, when to make way for incoming dishes, outgoing food, the fry guy returning from downstairs with another 100-pound load of freshly cut spuds. I feel only the occasional light tap on the shoulder as he squeezes through with another tray of coffee and petit-fours, maybe a whispered, "Behind you" or "Bajando" Fred and Ginger time. (203)

Bourdain gets the movement right. He also captures all too well what bastards chefs are. We are utterly within another universe, *un monde à part*. With bravura, Bourdain explains that he doesn't know "how a normal person acts. I don't know how to behave outside my kitchen. I don't know the rules" (248).

Bourdain certainly knows the rules of his world, and by the end of the book comes up with a professional code of 14 rules. Together these rules form a clear ethnographic description of Bourdain's world. Indeed seen as an elucidation of the symbolic system of another culture, Bourdain's elaboration is deeply anthropological in its vision. Some rules are clear-cut, as in "don't be late." Others veer to deeper connections. For instance, in New York kitchens it makes sense to speak Spanish if you want to communicate with the work force. As Bourdain puts it, "The very backbone of the industry, whether you like it or not, is inexpensive Mexican, Dominican, Salvadorian and Ecuadorian labor – most of whom could cook you under the table without breaking a sweat" (294). This is then followed by an injunction to also learn about their different cultures in order to understand how to manage the fact that a right-wing Cuban will not get on with a refugee El Salvadorian. Instructing aspiring cooks in basic politics, Bourdain instructs them to "Eat their food," and show them respect.

Bourdain comes off as a self-styled principled bastard. Beyond his obsession with himself, as a piece of auto-ethnography it works precisely because of its emphasis on the interaction of bodies – his own and others. In the compact space of the kitchen, bodies fall apart, are stoned or drunk, in the midst of copulating, throw up, get burned, and cut. They are in constant contact with other bodies, described as body parts: "All comments *must*, out of historical necessity, concern involuntary rectal penetration, penis size, physical flaws or annoying mannerisms or defects" (222). Speed moves bodies and connects them: "there is a near-telepathic relationship between chef and runner, requiring only a glance or a facial expression to communicate scads of information" (230). The entire universe is one where bodies are understood in terms of their different capacities to affect and be affected. So there is "a symbiotic relationship" between the chef and the bartender: "the kitchen wants booze, and the bartender wants food" (232). The bartender is "raconteur, showman and personality," the chef "wants to drink anything he desires, anytime he wants it." These capacities form specific connections, which are precisely described in terms of bits of bodies, shaped by space and motion, interacting with other bits of bodies.

Ethno-flashback

It's a peculiar and particular way of seeing things. Once instilled, it continues to guide how you perceive the world. I spent very formative years, from the age of 16 to about 25, working in restaurants and bars. At the time I hardly thought that I'd ever be grateful for the experience. But it instilled an appreciation of bodies – in movement, in fraught connection, in terms of eating, and behaving with and toward others – that preceded any theoretical comprehension of why these things matter. I suppose I might have gained a love for bodies in movement had I worked or trained in other milieus. But it is the specificities of this universe where bodies are moving in different directions, at different speeds, with different functions that I retain.

The restaurant kitchens and floors that I remember most clearly were Franco-Canadian. I'd moved to Montreal with the desire to become *québécoise*.[7] It was the recession of the early 1980s, and the only thing I was trained to do was wait tables. Unlike other cities where I'd worked, the staff at the *Poissonnerie* were lifers, not out-of-work actors or unemployable university graduates. They came from backwoods places way up north, sent off in search of work or to escape the confines of a small town – often because of their sexuality. Or they came from the poorest parts of Montreal, and spoke that particular mixture of working-class English and French. I learned to speak their *québécois*, and learned something of the historical and political culture. Much later when I got a job at a prestigious Francophone university, the former didn't help me at all. In terms of the latter, however, I had an appreciation of "the other" against which my middle-class colleagues and students defined themselves. While the waiters were white, the kitchen staff was Haitien and Vietnamese. Except, that is, for the chef who was doubly a bastard: by definition one because he was the chef, and equally so in the eyes of the floor staff because he was an Anglophone.

From the field notes inscribed in my memory, here's a brief description of the job.

In English it's waiting on tables, in French the waiter is *un serveur*. They are, of course, both correct. There is a lot of waiting around, and one serves. In general, the hours are pretty terrible, and the formal pay appalling. It's not uncommon to have split shifts, *faire un double*, which means coming in about 10 a.m. to set up for lunch, doing lunch, having an hour off and then starting again for dinner, which might mean getting out at midnight. We were paid less than minimum wage, $2.25 an hour, because we were "tipped employees." We were expected to pay taxes on tips, but the logic of that was patently dumb considering we had none of the benefits.

To spend 12 or 13 hours a day working with the same people sets the stage for an intensive experience. The day was clearly marked by rhythms of time and speed. Lunch service hits like a sledgehammer on tired and hung-over bodies. Dinner would start with the early-bird specials, and those who partook of such deals were despised. The worst ones were those who came every Monday night to scoff the crab specials. *Les mangeurs de crabe* were not a pretty sight. It was all the crab you could eat for under ten bucks – huge plates of steamed spindly crab and masses of melted butter. By the end of the night you were soaked in crab juices and smeared with butter. You could spend hours replenishing crab and get a measly dollar for your services – a 10 percent tip on a bill for hours of crab and tap water.

The restaurant was not fancy but it was popular. The name of the game was to turn tables as fast as possible. It was a good idea to be in the good books of the hostess, who might fill up your section first, and even guide apparently well-heeled types your way. Conversely if you had offended the hostess you could spend your time out the back next to the garbage smoking cigarettes as your section lay as cold and deserted as Siberia. Then just to catch you, she'd fill it all up at once.

You'd be in the juice. *"Chus dans l'jus,"* you'd cry in hopes that someone would help you out. Whether they did depended on moods, previous reciprocal help, or whether they too were in the juice. If you wanted to turn tables as fast as possible, there would always be moments of being in the juice. The point, however, was to be just on the verge. That's when everything flowed: your drink orders were ready, then the appetizers were quickly eaten, the plates cleared just as some inner clock told you the mains were up. On huge bus-trays, you could easily stack a couple of tables of grub. Then with a heft onto your shoulder, a kick to the kitchen door you'd be out, meals delivered and back again for the next. Along the way making eye contact and a promise to be back to the new tables, you'd direct the busboy to wipe down an empty table, while you deposited bread on another. On the verge of being in the juice was when everything interconnected in an array of movement and glances, when one hand garnished drinks, the other poured glasses of water, while you joked with the bartender and smiled at a table.

It is a particular economy of movement, one that is addictive. I still find it strange to only do one thing at once. The timing, however, was not your own. The bastard of a chef would throw out meals that stood under the heat lamps for longer than a minute. And you'd pay. Just as you would for any breakages. He also didn't feed the floor staff, which led to other arrangements. One of the things that goes unsaid is that waiters eat the leftovers from the plates of customers. It is a common practice, and in fact has links back to the tradition of passing on "les restes" in nineteenth-century France.[8] It's stunning what people don't eat even when they've ordered it in restaurants. It's not a very hygienic habit, and certainly doesn't provide you with all the required major food groups, but a seemingly untouched scallop or uneaten oyster didn't go to waste. Had any of us thought about the way in which we were viscerally connected to the mouths of our customers, we probably would have stopped. Especially fine left-over morsels would also be passed on as bribes to the busboys and bartender. In a reciprocal move, the bartender would keep your teacup filled with wine.

Bourdain is absolutely right in describing the kitchen as a world apart. The floor of a restaurant also operates by different rules.[9] It is equally oiled by drugs, and an acceptance of what might elsewhere be regarded as strange behavior. Many of us made good money, although part of it came not from tips but from scamming the management. We always had wads of cash, and the drug of choice was cocaine, which was then plentiful and cheap. You didn't last long if you weren't into speed (the motion), and coke gave an added edge to the perception of movement, control, and grace. Of course it took its toll on bodies, and it was a matter of honor to help out someone whose nerves and hands could hardly handle a tray of dirty dishes let alone precariously full cocktail glasses. After hours the front bar would fill with waiters doing deals, and then with pockets filled with tips it'd be off to one of the many late bars where the restaurant trade gathered.

It was a strange world but the rules, and knowledges shared, made it absolutely normal. I presume in its general outline it hasn't changed much. There were, however, specificities such as the mix of languages and linguistic politics, the fact that we did make good money, and the way that hatred of the chef made us want to be faster, better, and harder. Even during my stint many couldn't hack the insults, the pace, and the hours. And I'm sure many burned out since, or maybe settled down elsewhere.

I got out because I was awarded a postgraduate scholarship. The desire not to end up a waiter zealously drove me in my studies and after. However, that feeling for bodies in motion, for the ways in which corporeal movement is choreographed under pressure, hasn't left me. At a basic level, those memories are marked in my body, and the ways it reacts to others. It's also given me another angle through which to think about eating. Part of its legacy is that I still hate to waste food and I probably eat too fast – though not off the plates of others. I also think that the saddest sight is a couple eating who no longer have anything to say to each other.

Food Lines

In more academic terms, my experience in restaurants has given me an appreciation of the intricate nature of the food industry. So many lines are drawn out by food, and conversely food draws out so many vectors. To use a term from historical studies of food, "foodways" designates the travel of an item through space and time. In this way, one can trace the potato from South America through to Europe. In addition, one would examine the role the potato has played in terms of large cultural and economic transformations. Thus, for instance, one would consider the potato blight (*Phytophthora infestans*) in Europe in May of 1845. Leading to the Irish potato famine, it caused a million people to die of starvation and a million more to emigrate. It was caused by the fact that at the time all the potatoes in Europe were descended from two original introductions that had no resistance to blight (Cherfas 1996: 41). Without drawing causal conclusions, nonetheless the state of the world would be very different had the blight not hit, or had the potatoes not been so disastrously similar in stock. It is a small instance where the account of species coincides with an ethological analysis of the movement of bodies, where the vegetable has intersected with the human.[10]

In this sense, foodways or food lines can be an interesting optic through which to consider the imbrication of culture, history, and economics, all written on the bodies that eat. Food connects a bewildering array of specialized functions, and otherwise unconnected people. It can have unexpected and cataclysmic results, as in the mass migration of the Irish, or indeed the more recent impact that the migration of southern Europeans has had on many cultures.[11]

The fact that food is always connected to any number of areas, and that eating always connects us to others, tends to get forgotten in the celebratory mode of food writing. Food, at the moment, is treated in rarefied ways. It is cooed over in glossy books and television shows, which frame cooking in saccharine ways. In terms of restaurant reviews, we either get pomposity on the part of the critic, or the vaunting of the pomposity of the chef. As a random example, a review of a beach restaurant outside of Sydney talks about lamb with "tagine flavours, hints of Middle East spicing and some scattered chestnut mushrooms adding a touch more class." The reviewer, a young man with a diamond stud and a bad haircut, adds that "the subtle spicing is very wine friendly" and suggests a glass valued at $19 (Evans 2001: 6). The lamb is $31, although it is from Flinders Island and not any old pasture. In Australian parlance, this is pure wankerism.

To be fair, the critic in question, Matthew Evans, is actually not as bad as he sounds. He is certainly more down to earth than the reviewer he replaced. He is, however, placed and must be understood within the different forces and pressures of the job and the food milieu in Sydney. At the moment, Sydney is one of the more overheated foodie scenes in the world, with the concomitant emphasis on discovering "the new."

I want now to turn to two food writers who have been unusually self-reflective in terms of their practices. Over the last couple of years I have interviewed them, observed them in their professional milieus, and read their food writing closely. The topics we have broached have centered on their own food lines – how they got interested in food, and into food journalism; how they perceive and map the food scene, what is particular about writing about eating, and their perceptions of their own bodies in terms of food. Interestingly, it is this last topic that is the hardest to talk about.

In the time I've been researching food I've grown accustomed to the fact that discussions of eating can lead into quite intimate areas of people's lives. Talking about the evening meal may lead to

– sometimes painful – revelations of personal pasts or present affective relationships with family or partners. It's clear that beyond the public presentation of food as comfort, it is also a prime site for very personal memories, or where issues of control and power within intimate relationships are revealed.[12] However, questions about the body are almost never responded to in a direct manner. Just as I argued that the sociology of the body always leads somewhere else, so too does a discussion of food and bodies. The line meanders off into abstract topics such as health, or taste, or habits. However, if the argument about the fact that the body is always composed of various particles has any merit, it is precisely in allowing us to recompose a body that is made of many lines of flight. And certainly a discussion of food and eating encourages those lines.

From the Mouths of Food Writers

I first met John a couple of years ago at a food conference organized by the Centre for the Study of Food and Drink at the University of Adelaide, in Southern Australia. As the title makes clear, these academics are very serious about their object of study. Adelaide is the stately capital of South Australia, and it is positioned as a jewel between the foodie regions of, on the one side, the Barossa Valley, and on the other, the Clare. Both are superb wine-producing areas, and have built up a cuisine to match. Adelaide is the home of Maggie Beer, one of the most influential food writers in Australia: a cook, restaurateur, and now manufacturer of patés, jellies, and assorted food items such as verjuice (unfermented wine) – something that through her writing has become an essential ingredient in any foodie's kitchen. It is very good.

The conference met above her restaurant, Charlick's. I was a little nervous as it was my first foray into the academic world of food. The audience tended toward nonacademic foodies, who were evidently very knowledgeable and who all knew each other. I can't actually remember what my paper was about but I must have mentioned Foucault and Bourdieu. John's paper followed mine, and he started by saying that he "knew f-all about Foucault." Apart from that immortal line (which prompted others such as "bugger all about Bourdieu"), I don't remember much about John's talk. At the coffee break – only the best, with that expensive lumpy golden sugar and little friands – I sidled up to him. The conversation began with John giving me his ideas about academic life. I pointed out that they were about 20 years behind the reality. It wasn't a great start.

"Studying up" is an interesting sociological exercise and personal experience. It commonly refers to a research situation where the researcher and the researched share a similar level of cultural capital. This decreases the relations of power that may structure ethnographic situations where the academic is more obviously "in control." However, it raises other tensions. For instance, it is sobering to interview journalists who interview for a living. This is exacerbated when I am talking to food journalists who are more knowledgeable about the subject than I am. Conversely there can be a jostling around cultural capital, where my incorporation of titles and the other outward manifestations of cultural capital add to the complications of the interview situation. For instance, in Australia the title even of Associate Professor is taken quite seriously. Added to this is the fact that I teach at what is the oldest and debatably the most prestigious university in Australia. This can produce a tinge of defensiveness on the part of those interviewed, who may metonymically displace any prestige of the position onto my body.

In terms of our encounter, John immediately voiced a certain strain of Australian anti-intellectualism in his (dated) ideas about how easy my job was. In turn, I was awkward because he was a "real writer." We have, however, become friends over the course of our many encounters. This again reflects some of the particularities of "studying up." It may not be strictly scientific. However, the admission of becoming friends seems to me to be more honest than the enduring and strange anthropological habit of taking on kinship titles and ties. Certainly there is a sense of mutuality in our relationship that may be harder to attain in ethnographic situations characterized by unequal levels of cultural capital.

We have talked about everything, from food to families and relationships. We've tried talking about bodies straight on, but it hasn't worked. We end up talking about politics, sex, gender, advertising, Spain, and more food. John is in his late forties, and before he got into food writing he was in advertising. He says that he always wanted to be a journalist but his mother was a well-known figure in Sydney journalism, and in fact wrote the first serious restaurant reviews. She didn't want him following her. He got a break in terms of food writing when he wrote a column on affordable places to eat for the now defunct *Australian Gourmet*. These establishments were in fact the backbone of Sydney's now fabled, and more pricey, multicultural eating.

Since then his *Cheap Eats* guides have become a yearly feature of the food publications in Sydney. He is freelance, which he likes, although there are the inevitable pressures of placing stories. He writes regularly for the weekend edition of the *Sydney Morning Herald*, as well as for Melbourne's *The Age*. With the advent of electronic magazines he now writes reviews of Sydney restaurants for international sites such as *e-luxury*. He has written several books, including co-authorships with Stephano Manfredi, a well-known chef and co-owner of Bel Mondo, an upmarket Italian restaurant.[13] He also wrote *Wog Food* (Newton 1996), a serious examination of how that term went from epithet to celebration of southern European cooking. Envy-making for me is the fact that he has written several novels, one of which is a terrific send-up of the advertising milieu he left years ago.

I'll try to tease out some of the lines which might constitute one way of seeing bodies that eat. As I mentioned at the outset, I didn't set out to frame our encounters in terms of a particular theme. The connections that emerge are ones that we stumbled over in our rambling conversations.

John's invited me to accompany him on a review of a restaurant. The review is for a ritzy publication and we're going to Paramount. Now closed, Paramount was one of the more interesting of the trendy restaurants in Sydney. Owned by two lesbian lovers, Margie Harris is up front, and Christine Manfield is in the kitchen. It is a very mannered place, which served as the venue for different events in the Sydney Gay and Lesbian Mardi Gras. Manfield is noted for her innovative use of spices,[14] and beautifully prepared food. She's also a darling of the queer scene, and has appeared in glossy gay magazines complete with s/m gear and whipped cream.

We enter the restaurant and John gets a warm welcome from Margie. This obviously isn't going to be an incognito meal. I'm glad as I've never been privy to such treatment. Later when I remark on the manners of both sides, reviewer and reviewed, John replies that "Chris and Margie are both very stylish people. Margie decided that the best thing she could do was ignore me or us and Chris just came out and said G'day and talked about the food. Which is the best thing to do. The worst thing that can happen is fawning." This wasn't quite true but we had a great meal.

John orders for us, and in consideration of his figure (which looks perfectly fine) we have a series of entrées which the waiter will bring nicely divided onto separate plates. He goes walking at the crack of dawn each morning. That's as close to the body in the conventional sense that we get. He does tell me a joke about another noted food writer who used to proudly boast that people asked him how he ate so much and stayed slim. Now they just ask him how he eats so much.

As we drink wine, the sight of a well-laid out restaurant turns the conversation to John's mother:

> I remember going out with my mother who was perhaps the first sort of food critic in the 1960s who started writing negatively about places. I remember going to restaurants with her and sitting there, a little Scots College [a Sydney private school] boy with short pants and long socks and hair scrubbed back and being polite and shiny in the way I see my daughter being polite and shiny now, sitting down in restaurants with thick linen and heavy silver and watching my mother being fêted in much the same way that I am now, which is weird.

In terms of habitus, John stands as an exemplar of an early bodily incorporation of food, and ideas about food. As he describes his background there is a tinge of awe that remains for his mother. He tells of the way she "was always dragging me off to places. I went to Demitris' Golden Ox, I went to Princes; she had Indian friends who would cook for us, so it was all part of my childhood experience in cosmopolitan Sydney."

In this way, the idea of writing about food never struck John as strange:

> I've always thought that food is a good thing to write about. Eating and the social aspects of eating . . . because it seemed to me that as a boy and as a young man you did a lot of things and one of the most interesting things you did was to eat. People wrote about the films they went to and that was considered perfectly OK. I wrote about the meals I had. Those were the things we did.

For another encounter I cooked for John, a slightly risky thing to do for a professional eater. I tried out vitello tonnato, something I'd not cooked before. As a former vegetarian I still get thrown by cooking meat. I was lucky and it came out rosy pink as it should. The sauce is made of tinned tuna, capers, lemon juice and mayonnaise. A recipe from a Sydney-based food writer recommends horseradish, which I added. It was good. However, on his arrival John immediately wanted to know whether I'd taken the recipe from said writer. "No," I lied.

We sat and talked outside in the quiet of the inner-city night, with occasional squeaks from the flying foxes caught on the tape recorder. Lines of conversation went off in several directions. As John says, he "gets angry and worked up about things." We talked about the lack of interest in indigenous foods and white "Australia's deep dark hatred of Aboriginals."[15] He reminded me of the fact that the explorers "Burke and Wills would have died rather than eat what they were offered by perfectly healthy human beings (the Aboriginals)." We talked about the horrendous health issues for Aboriginal Australians living in the outback in terms of the poor food that is now available to them. We talked about the effects of globalization and the ludicrous idea of importing oranges to Australia from Brazil. He told me about his week, which included riding on "a large 1970s orange potato harvester called a Grimmer with a potato farmer ripping King Edward potatoes from the side of the hill with beautiful basalt soil."

As it got really late I asked John about what he wanted to do next in terms of writing. After his passionate tales of food, it was a bit of a surprise when he mentioned that he'd like to be able to push food into the background and write about other things. One of the last sentences I recorded was John's comment about food: "It's something that I love a lot but occasionally I feel like food is eating me."

From this brief description of our encounters, several points arise. In terms of the incorporation of class and social background, John's comments reveal the common sense of Bourdieu's description of habitus. We will recall that the gist of his argument is that "a class culture turned into nature, that is *embodied*, helps shape the class body" (Bourdieu 1984: 190). The little private-school boy in shorts dining on fine linen is incorporated into the body of the food critic. His early education in multiculturalism ingested through the food of his mother's friends lives on in the food writer who did much to render "cheap" foreign food acceptable. Less obvious yet still palpable are the ways in which a visceral connection to food, its preparation, production, and meanings, forges a line of understanding of Australia's history and deep racism against the original custodians of the land.

In clear ways we can see that a class habitus allows John to connect with food differently than could be the case for a *québécois* waiter from the poor rural backwoods. In one case, habitus contributes to the taste of a food writer, in the other a lifetime of serving food. The apprehension that eating was as worthy of writing about as film-going is a wonderful example of the ease that habitus bestows on certain bodies. In some ways the privilege of the middle-class body can be precisely seen in its openness, its ability to reach out, taste, and incorporate the world. Of course this is a specific body and there is no causal link between an early broad education of the palate and a resulting openness to politics and new ideas. Nonetheless, in the terms I discussed earlier, one can see this particular food writer's body as constantly engaged, and enmeshed with other practices. It may be as simple and as complex as the fact that if the body is trained early in tasting difference, it may later be open to the incorporation of different abstract and political issues. Certainly it leads to seeing issues in tangibly connected ways. Thus racism is discussed in terms of what whites still will not eat, and the continuing devastation on Aboriginal communities fostered by a dependence on bad white food (literally, white sugar and flour). The failings of a globalized system of food production is rendered patent in terms of why Australia imports orange concentrate from Brazil when we grow abundant crops of citrus here. King Edward potatoes are praised not because they are now trendy, but for the red soil from which they come, and the hard work of harvesting them.

There are of course no guarantees that such connections will be made. And professionally John is frustrated by the difficulty of placing "big issue" stories in a food media overwhelmingly structured by fashion, on the one hand, and product placement, on the other – food retailers bombard food writers with "goodies" in the hopes that they will be written about. Between the hype of Jamie Oliver and Nigella Lawson, and the hard sell of the food industry, there's not a lot of room to talk about eating and social equality.

But what of the food writer's body in the more obvious sense? What of the flesh and blood? To round off the discussion, I want to briefly introduce another corporeal line of connection. One would be hard pressed to speak of food without mentioning its feminine connections, and a very gendered politics of bodies and eating. To draw this out, I'll turn now to another food writer with whom I shared encounters over the last year.

Lyndey Milan is the Food Director of the *Australian Women's Weekly*. This is an incredibly important role in a magazine that has constantly introduced new ideas about food to the Australian public. Their recipe books also travel farther afield and are widely read in the UK. But it is in Australia that *Women's Weekly* has had the greatest impact. It can in fact be credited with introducing the ingredients and techniques of multicultural cooking long before multiculturalism was a recognized term. Its circulation figures are staggering: in a country with a population of some 18 million, it has a readership of 3.2 million a month. In Lyndey's calculation, per head of population it is the most read magazine in the world. Something like 828,000 men a month read it. If one wanted a popular medium through which to introduce alternative representations of gender, this would be it.

I first met Lyndey at a Dymock's Literary Luncheon in a downtown hotel in Sydney starring the ubiquitous Naked Chef, Jamie Oliver. For $35 a head, the room was packed with lots of young women but also a sizeable proportion of women "of a certain age," all manifestly in love with Jamie (there were several offers to adopt him in the question time). By chance I was seated at the *Women's Weekly* table. Lyndey and I bonded over our aversion to Oliver. The Essex lad was hung over, and even more shallow than he appears on television. When I asked if I could interview her later, she agreed and immediately launched into a discussion about girls' health, their lack of cooking skills, and the fact that they smoke. We met at several functions, including the Food Writers Media Club of which she is president. Watching her wend her way through the assembled writers, cajole the kitchen for more canapés, and preside over the discussion, there was no doubt that this is a formidable woman.

Lyndey is in her late forties; she is a large and attractive blonde elegantly dressed, and exudes a frightening amount of energy. Like John, she too had a background in advertising. She has owned a catering company, and as well as having done a stint as a high-school teacher, she was one of those wives that probably don't exist any more. She recalls being incredibly involved with her (then) husband's career. "The entertaining was extraordinary, absolutely extraordinary. So we used to have six-course dinner parties and I used to paint quail wishbones in gold leaf, and do hand calligraphy on the menus and the whole bit." She remembers that she started having dinner parties when she was 16 and her parents were overseas: "It is always a good way to impress boys."

When we met at her office – overflowing with "goodies," care of the food industry – she immediately raised the issue of how food changes us. This was framed first in terms of multiculturalism, and more particularly about the politics of Pauline Hanson, the right-wing leader of the xenophobic One Nation party. She wagers that Pauline Hanson's diet is "Anglo-Saxon." As she elaborated, "You see I believe that if you eat the food of another culture, how could you possibly hate the people that have brought that food to you." Her complaint is that "food is still not central to our culture in Australia, and until our culture becomes less Anglo-Saxon, and more Asian or Italian or French, then it won't be."

The other burning issue for Lyndey is girls' relationship to eating, and the necessary contradiction she walks in terms of being the food editor of a women's magazine that – like most, if not all – still publishes diets along with Lyndey's recipes. Her reaction to this is forceful: "Personally, if I had a magazine I would never run a diet ever again. I think that it is the most irresponsible thing you can do. I think we are breeding a generation, well we are, we are breeding a generation of kids with eating disorders." Her own very lived philosophy is "guilt-free enjoyment," and that basically eating is a matter of faith in your taste buds and common sense: "I think we have become too intellectual about food. I really do."

I broached the question of food writers' bodies with some hesitation. Given my (inherited) wiry body, on first reading not only might it appear that I don't know much about food, but also that I don't eat much. The vestiges of girl culture die hard in terms of women comparing their bodies with other women. I needn't have worried about her, although I wonder what life would be like as a statuesque blonde. In response to my question Lyndey gave me this anecdote:

> I had gone to Melbourne for a [cooking] Master class and there was this cheese dinner on the night before and I had been shopping, couldn't find any clothes to fit me and I thought I just have to change careers because putting on 5 kilos a year is no good and I decided I'd change careers. Oh well, I have changed careers twice before. Then I went into this cheese dinner and there was this waiter with a silver salver and the beautiful crisp white linen napkin and these little jolt balls of something. I popped one in my mouth, it was an explosion of duck liver mousse and sherry, and it was just like I'd come down from my second orgasm.

Now here, as if we needed it, is proof of the connection between bodies, pleasure, and food. But it is also a striking statement of particular gendered pressures on the body as well as a gendered response to them. Can one imagine Antonio Carluccio worrying about what he's going to wear? There's something so female about the practicality and confidence of "Oh well, I'll just change careers," which then meets the orgasmic explosion of taste.

In terms of the body that emerges from my encounters with Lyndey, once again the eating body is what connects different issues. In

Lyndey's case eating grounds concerns that are as political as those that John raised. They may not be as overtly elaborated upon as politics, but the force with which they are articulated is of note. Within progressive circles, there is a tendency to scoff at the idea that eating changes our values and beliefs. Indeed Ghassan Hage (1998) has a sustained argument against the idea that white cosmopolitan habits, including eating, have had any impact whatsoever on the racist structure of our societies. Hage's argument is a complex one that draws out the psychical and structural incorporation of the other in multicultural societies, and the violence it does in the name of tolerance. However, his political paradigm precludes a serious consideration of how eating does affect white middle-class bodies. This should not lead to easy celebration and congratulation on the part of the affluent, the conceits of which Hage effectively punctures. Nonetheless it does justify greater attention to connections that are routinely made between bodies, everyday ethics, and politics. It also requires that we look seriously at how ideas are ingested by food writers and then circulate in forums like *Women's Weekly*, with the potential to affect bodies on a scale that academics can only dream of.

"Food is Eating Me"

John's line clearly captures the intimacy between what he does for a living – his passion and preoccupation – and his body. Strangely enough, in interviews for another project, an ex-anorexic described how she "would eat the food before it ate her." What could possibly connect a young woman recovering from anorexia and a successful middle-aged male food writer? Who knows? It may be merely indicative of an intense connection with food.[16] While the clichés that abound about food, and the metaphorical slides it is sent on, can get in the way of thinking through some of the issues I'm interested in, it is hard to avoid the fact that eating is profoundly intimate. Moreover, those who reflect seriously on food (like some anorexics and certain food writers) tend to think about their bodies in different ways. The body is not an empty receptacle for food; there is a constant multiplicity of contact between what goes in, where it comes from, what it means, what it feels like, whether it makes you feel good or bad, etc. When Lyndey says she experiences an orgasm in her mouth, it is not just a passing quip. Her mouth has, after all, been trained through years of experience to distinguish, to taste, to reflect, to connect.

In terms of the framework with which I opened this chapter, it seems to me that, brought down into the world of eating, the idea of bodies as a nexus of multiplicities interconnecting with others makes perfect sense. As Noëlle Châtelet aptly puts it, we are "mouth machines." "To eat is to connect" (1977: 34). But some of us are more practiced mouth machines than others. The interest of food writers, or those who work within the food industry, is that they are constantly called upon to reflect on what this tastes like, and why. In certain cases, this strikingly reveals bodies that engage in different assemblages: the economic assemblage that is food production and distribution, the cultural one of food's meanings within a given place and time, the gender assemblage that forcefully assigns meanings to bodies and eating. Bodies demonstrate how these assemblages constantly cross-, and inter-connect.

In terms of an ethological approach to the body, I have barely scratched the surface here of the connections possible. At every twist of the rhizome, other connections and engagements could be pursued. Following Deleuze's definition of the body, I have first examined bodies in motion in terms of the choreographing of movements within a restaurant. Of course, much more could be done on tracking the differing speeds and slownesses between particles, which come to define a body. I have taken Deleuze at face value (which he encourages us to do). How do bodies move in combination with other bodies? I think there is a case for arguing that this level of analysis could in fact shed new light on the intricate processes of subjectification that have tended to take either the psyche or a generalized "culture" as their object. If we watch bodies carefully, analyze ethologically their kinetics, we may find interesting nodes of practice, past, present, caught in a simple bodily movement. A good osteopath can immediately tell the occupation from the body. He or she can also pinpoint imbrications in the body of what can no longer be distinguished as physical or emotional. A massage can bring forward the memory of a physical wound long healed. In these ways and others, we arrive at the fact that an ethological analysis of the body reveals capacities that we may have overlooked in more abstract analysis.

Secondly, I have attempted to analyze bodies in terms of what Deleuze calls their dynamic mode: "this capacity for affecting and being affected." The idea of rhizomatics or a rhizo-ethology can extend ethnological research. Again what is offered here is the barest tip of bodies in complex milieus opening or closing to others. At a methodological level, this involves a mapping that may not distinguish between the person, the book, the said, the gesture, the animate, and the nonanimate. "Food is eating me" is, after all, a clear statement about a different order of connections, one that displaces the human with the actual contact of mouth and thing, stomach and past. Without making a grand principle, it also means that the researcher herself is always positioned as a body: she must be attuned to her own capacities for affecting and being affected. This may not work in every encounter, but in terms of this specialized case in studying up, there is little point in making the case either for objective distance or for subjective partiality. In a way it becomes a matter of common sense. As Lyndey put it, you can be too intellectual about food. You can probably be too intellectual about how you go about trying to record and capture connections.

In conclusion, the point has been to explore some epistemological suggestions in terms of getting closer to bodies. I'm sure that I've again missed the flesh and blood of bodies, but at times I have felt the slight brushing, the passing of goose-bumps, as corporeal lines connect.

Notes

1 My thanks to John Newton and Lyndey Milan for their time. This research is funded by an Australian Research Council Large Grant.
2 At a meeting of the Australian Women's Studies Association (Macquarie University, February 2001) Elizabeth A. Wilson offered this as a challenge. My citing of her remark should be seen as part of an overture to bring together different disciplinary-based critiques in a more comprehensive study of bodies. See the Australian Feminist Studies issue on *Feminism, Bodies and Science* (1999), edited by Wilson, for an interesting collection of feminist writings on science.
3 As such it is inspired by Arjun Appadurai's (1981) early article, where he calls for comparative ethnographic studies of the role of food and eating in different cultures. The larger project involves a comparison of Canadian and Australian discourses on food and belonging, based in a recognition of the similarities and differences wrought by histories of white settler nationhood.
4 I am not an ethnographer in any conventional sense. Nonetheless I have been engaged by some of the discussions that followed the "textual turn" in anthropology. One of the worrying aspects of that debate (to which in a very small way I contributed: "Moving Selves and Stationary Others: Ethnography's Ontological Dilemma," Probyn 1993) is that it encouraged

some bad or misplaced literary criticism, and it discouraged people from doing fieldwork. On the positive side, it has considerably expanded on what "doing fieldwork" means. It remains to be seen if the definition is large enough to include this present offering.

5   One of my favorite essays of Deleuze's that brings out the importance of the milieu is "What Children Say" (1997). This is a reading of Freud's case, Little Hans, in terms of the boy becoming horse. Here Deleuze argues for a way of understanding the unconscious as a "map of intensity that distributes the affects, and it is their links and valences that constitute the image of the body in each case – an image that can always be modified or transformed depending on the affective constellations that determine it" (1997: 64). For a reading of this essay in terms of bodies and movement see my "Becoming-Horse: Transports in Desire" (1996).

6   It isn't, but a biography of Elizabeth David by Bourdain would be interesting. Certainly it would be an improvement on the "authorized biography" by Artemis Cooper (1999). *Writing at the Kitchen Table* starts off well, including this provocative description of David's writing: "behind those crisp sentences, one can feel the pressure of her loves and hates, her enthusiasm and her passion. The reader becomes acutely aware of these emotions, although they are never mentioned" (1999: xiii). However, the emphasis on David's writing soon shifts to a preoccupation with accounting all "the unsaid" about David's private life.

7   I detail some of what this might entail empirically and theoretically in "Love in a Cold Climate" (1996).

8   Jean-Paul Aron (1979) offers a fascinating account of how leftovers from the plates of the rich circulated in nineteenth-century Paris. They were called "les bijoux," "jewels passed from plate to plate" (1979: 102), and constituted a complex industry of stallholders and middlemen who passed a "little disinfectant over it all, a little decoration, and for 17 sous you can eat the feast of Luculus" (1979: 100). As Aron argues, in terms of *"mentalities,"* "leftovers are related to a specific frame of mind made up of the need to economise and a hankering for luxury" (1979: 103).

9   See Philip Crang's (1996) ethnographic study of waiters in which he too focuses on "a thickening of interconnections," although from a slightly different perspective.

10   I won't push the analysis too far by noting that the potato is a rhizome. However, in a poetic manner the idea of the roots and shoots of the potato plants spreading and irrupting all over the world in terms of the Irish migration is appealing.

11   In Australia one cannot escape the celebration of multiculturalism in terms of what migration did for the Australian diet. Before the mass migration of southern Europeans, especially Italians and Greeks, in the 1950s eating in Australia was pretty much defined and limited by the dominant British food culture of stodge. Now thanks are given for the

fact that the migrants brought their culinary traditions here and introduced olive oil and garlic. See Marion Halligan's ode to olive oil (1990). John Newton (1996) gives a more attentive account, which includes reminiscences by Italian and Greek Australians of the conditions they found here and the racism that greeted their arrival in Australia. The later arrival of people from the Asian region, along with the influence of the southern Europeans, has produced the style of cuisine now recognized as "Mod Oz," or Modern Australian.

12 It is in fact these affective issues that most interest me in terms of food. For instance, Wendy Walker-Birckhead (1985) gives a lovely ethnographic account of the strategies deployed by elderly women in an Australian country town in order to secure power through the contest for the best scones. In a different vein I have explored issues of power and taste in a ficto-critical essay (Probyn 1997). I have also discussed how shame and disgust operate in terms of the eating body ("Eating Shame, Feeding Disgust," Probyn 2000).

13 Stephano Manfredi and John Newton have produced a gorgeous coffee/ restaurant table book on different aspects of Bel Mondo and restaurants in general. Of course, they too highlight the beauty of restaurant rhythm, putting it this way: "It feels like driving a very fast car through a long, dark tunnel not knowing when it will finish, not able to see the light behind or in front" (Manfredi and Newton 2000: 125).

14 Manfield has written a stunningly beautiful, if daunting, book on spices and cooking, which is dedicated to the rhizomatic "traders for opening up the world, and in doing so, opening our every sense to the pleasure of spices" (1999: ix).

15 Elsewhere I've argued that the extent of ingrained and historical racism in Australia against Aboriginal Australians can be seen in the conceptions that whites have of what blacks eat ("Eating in Black and White," Probyn 2000). Tim Rowse (1998) gives an extensive description of the forms of regulation imposed on Aboriginals by white government. Rowse details the forms of punishment or of simple control that were enforced through practices such as forced communal feeding, and enforcing a dependence on flour and sugar at the expense of bush tucker. There were worse examples, such as the out-and-out murder committed through the poisoning of water and flour rations. The question of whether Aboriginals "tilled the land" is deeply integrated with the racist myth of Terra Nullius. The connection between whether or not land was cultivated also formed the basis of exchanges between whites and indigenous peoples of North America. In James Tully's (1995) argument, the influence of Locke's theories can be seen in where and whether treaties were signed, indicating acknowledgment on the part of whites that the land was used, and belonged to different indigenous peoples. Such is not the case in Australia, although Anna Haebich (1988) gives a clear account of the

role of Aboriginals in agriculture. A recent example of the horror that whites still have for the food traditionally eaten by Aboriginals could be seen in the television show *Survivor II: The Outback*, where the contestants had to eat such food as witijii grubs and sea snake as part of the competition. It was nearly comical to see this reenactment of white ignorance and starving in the face of plenty.

16   With hindsight I'd have to say that this is what has happened with my research. So perhaps it's not that strange that I have gone from early research on anorexia to a wider study of eating and its affects.

References

Appadurai, A. (1981) "Gastro-politics in Hindu South Asia," *American Ethnologist* 8, 495–511.

Aron, J-P. (1979) "The Art of Leftovers: Paris, 1850–1900," in R. Foster and O. Ranum (eds.), *Food and Drink in History: Selections from the Annales*. Baltimore, MD: Johns Hopkins University Press, pp. 99–104.

Australian Feminist Studies (1999) Special issue on Feminism and Science, 14: 29.

Berthelot, J-M. (1992) "Du Corps comme Opérateur Discursif ou les Apories d'une Sociologie du Corps," in E. Probyn (ed.), *Entre le corps et le soi: Une sociologie de la subjectivation, sociologie et sociétés* 24: 1, 1–18.

Bourdain, A. (2000) *Kitchen Confidential: Adventures in the Culinary Underbelly*. London: Bloomsbury.

Bourdieu, P. (1984) *Distinction: A Social Critique of the Judgement of Taste*. Cambridge, MA: Harvard University Press.

Châtelet, N. (1977) *Le corps à corps culinaire*. Paris: Seuil.

Cherfas, J. (1996) "Sustainable Food Systems," in B. Mephram (ed.), *Food Ethics*. London and New York: Routledge.

Cooper, A. (1999) *Writing at the Kitchen Table: The Authorized Biography of Elizabeth David*. Harmondsworth: Penguin.

Crang, P. (1996) "Displacement, Consumption and Identity," *Environment and Planning A*. 28: 47–67.

Deleuze, G. (1992) "Ethology: Spinoza and Us," in J. Crary and S. Kwinter (eds.), *Incorporations*. New York: Zone.

Deleuze, G. (1997) *Essays Critical and Clinical* (trans. D. Smith and M.A. Greco). Minneapolis, MN: Minnesota University Press.

Deleuze, G. and Guattari, F. (1983) "Rhizome," in *On the Line*. New York: Semiotext(e).

Deleuze, G. and Guattari, F. (1988) *A Thousand Plateaus* (trans. B. Massumi). London: Athlone Press.

Evans, M. (2001) "Having a Whale of a Time," in "Good Living" section, *The Sydney Morning Herald*, June 5–11, p. 6.

Gatens, M. (1996) "Sex, Gender, Sexuality: Can Ethologists Practice Genealogy?" *Southern Journal of Philosophy* XXXV: 1–17.

Gatens, M. (1999) "Privacy and the Body: The Publicity of Affect," in Mieke Bal et al. (eds.), *Brief Privacies*. Amsterdam: ASCA.

Geertz, C. (1988) *Works and Lives: The Anthropologist as Author*. Stanford, CA: Stanford University Press.

Haebich, A. (1988) *For Their Own Good: Aborigines and Government in Western Australia*. Nedlands, WA: The University of Western Australia Press.

Hage, G. (1998) *White Nation: Fantasies of White Supremacy in a Multicultural Society*. Sydney: Pluto Press.

Halligan, M. (1990) "From Castor to Olive Oil in One Generation: A Gastronomic Education," *Meanjin* 49, 2: 203–12.

Manfield, C. (1999) *Spice*. Victoria: Viking-Penguin.

Manfredi, S. and Newton, J. (2000) *Bel Mondo: Beautiful World*. Sydney: Hodder.

Newton, J. (1996) *Wog Food*. Sydney: Random House.

Probyn, E. (1993) *Sexing the Self: Gendered Positions in Cultural Studies*. London and New York: Routledge.

Probyn, E. (1996) *Outside Belongings*. London and New York: Routledge.

Probyn, E. (1997) "The Taste of Power," in J. Mead (ed.), *bodyjamming*. Sydney: Random House.

Probyn, E. (2000) *Carnal Appetites: FoodSexIdentities*. London and New York: Routledge.

Rowse, T. (1998) *White Flour, White Power: From Rations to Citizenship in Central Australia*. Cambridge and Melbourne: Cambridge University Press.

Tully, J. (1994) "Aboriginal Property and Western Theory: Recovering a Middle Ground," *Social Philosophy and Policy* 11, 2: 153–80.

Tully, J. (1995) *Strange Multiplicity: Constitutionalism in an Age of Diversity*. Cambridge: Cambridge University Press.

Walker-Birckhead, W. (1985) "The Best Scones in Town: Old Women in an Australian Country Town," in L. Manderson (ed.), *Australian Ways*. Sydney: George Allen & Unwin.

Wilson, E.A. (1999) "Somatic Compliance: Feminism, Biology and Science," *Australian Feminist Studies* 14 (29): 7–18.

Chapter 10

Health and the Holy in the Afro-Brazilian *Candomblé*

Thomas J. Csordas

The relation between medical and religious definitions of human experience is of critical importance for understanding embodiment, for the body is a principal point of intersection between them. Equally, the medical and the religious are of central concern for the cross-cultural study of illness and healing. The importance of this relation stems from the following empirical circumstances: (1) many forms of religion are essentially concerned with health and healing; (2) many religious phenomena, and at times religion as a generic entity, have been interpreted as pathological; (3) many forms of healing can simultaneously be interpreted as forms of religion (Bourguignon 1976; Csordas 1990; Frank and Frank 1991; LaBarre 1972). These circumstances raise a methodological dilemma: while it is possible to generate accounts of certain phenomena from the point of view either of comparative religion or of medical anthropology, the two accounts may not be of great relevance to one another, and may not necessarily even be mutually intelligible. Contributing to the resolution of this dilemma is the central concern of the present chapter.

Parts of this chapter were originally published as "Health and the Holy in African and Afro-American Spirit Possession," in *Social Science and Medicine* 24,1 (1987): 1–11. Reprinted with permission from Elsevier Science.

One of the most vivid ways in which the relation between the medical and the religious plays itself out on the field of embodiment is in spirit possession and possession trance. The classic monograph by Roger Bastide (1958) on the Afro-Brazilian *candomblé* emphasizes the relation between myth and ritual, examines the cosmological structure of the *candomblé* universe, and treats possession trance as a form of religious mysticism. Interestingly, in a retrospective some 15 years later, Bastide stated that this approach had been necessary to countervail the medicalization of his time, which saw possession trance as hysteria and neurosis, but that ultimately an approach more balanced between religious and medical meanings would be necessary:

> In the end, after having repudiated the psychiatrists' interpretation as a unilateral interpretation, it was necessary to incorporate from it that which could be of value to what I was calling the sociology of trance. For in Africa possession is, if not always, at least very often linked to therapeutics, not only of madness but of all illnesses of psychosomatic origin or nature. It was necessary to lay the foundations for a unified discourse, where the sociological and psychiatric were no longer identified, but on the contrary once again separated, complementary . . . (Bastide 1972: 56, 57, my translation)

In any case, what must be explored are the implications of *starting* from either a "medical-therapeutic" or a "comparative religion" orientation. What is the relation between statements like Young's that "it is these sickness episodes, together with the therapies and rituals they entail, that dominate the interest of many devotees" (Young 1975), and a statement like Bastide's that "The structure of ecstasy is the structure of myth" (Bastide 1958)? Admittedly these statements are taken out of context – Young is a student of the *zar* and Bastide of the *candomblé*. Beyond the issue of whether such statements are true for specific ethnographic instances, the problem is that they tend to be made as generalizations across the field of possession trance studies. Do they contradict one another, or can they be reconciled? The question is large. Here I will take only a first step by presenting some material on the Afro-Brazilian *candomblé*, with particular emphasis on the reflections of a remarkable man who was both a psychiatrist and an intimate patron of this religion.

Candomblé

Candomblé in Brazil is essentially Yoruba (in Brazil Yoruba = Nagô = Quetu) religion transplanted from West Africa. Participants honor the gods and goddesses, or *orixas*, of the traditional Yoruba pantheon (Guimares de Magalhaes 1974). In Afro-Brazilian culture as a whole the Angolan influence is strongest, due to its presence since the sixteenth century; however, in the domain of religion, the Yoruba pantheon, introduced in the nineteenth century, has largely displaced or assimilated other deities. At the same time, each *orixa* is paired with a Christian saint who is its counterpart with respect to shared attributes. *Candomblé* has an established liturgical calendar, the festivals of which only partially overlap with the feast days of Catholic saints. Within the spectrum of Afro-Brazilian possession cults, the Nagô *candomblé* of Bahia is said to be the most orthodox. Other cults with varying degrees of Yoruba influence include Xango of Recife and Rio de Janeiro, Angolan *candomblés*, Umbanda, Batuque, Macumba, Catimbo, and Caboclo (Monfouga-Nicolas 1972). These cults are prominent in different regions, and represent various syncretisms of *orixas*, Angolan deities, native Indian spirits, and spirits of the two found in Kardecist spiritism (Bastide 1978; Leacock 1972; Pressel 1973; Williams 1979).

The first Bahian congregation, or *terreiro*, was founded by a priestess from Africa in 1830, with former slaves as members (O'Gorman 1977). Periodically repressed by the predominantly Catholic authorities, it has only been since 1976 that Bahian *terreiros* have not been required to register with the police. *Terreiros* participate publicly in the carnival, and annually stage a public festival for Yemanja, the *orixa* patroness of the waters. Many Brazilians make use of the spiritual resources of the *candomblé*, and its members include people of European as well as African descent. The impact of this religion extends even to diet, with the publication of books on preparation of the ritual cuisine honoring the *orixas* – each deity having his or her favorite dish (Varella 1972).

In the summer of 1979, the African and Afro-American Studies Program at the University of North Carolina, Chapel Hill, was fortunate to have as a guest the Brazilian psychiatrist Dr. Alvaro Rubim de Pinho. A series of intensive interviews with Dr. Rubim, coordinated by the present author and historian Linda Guthrie, provided the data upon which the present chapter is based. In these interviews, Dr. Rubim offered a valuable key informant perspective, based on his unique dual position as chairman of the Department of Psychiatry in the Faculty of Medicine at the University of Bahia in Salvador, and initiated elder of the *candomblé terreiro* of Axé Opô Afonja. This participation is not as astounding as it may at first seem to non-Brazilians, for it continues a trend begun by liberal intellectuals in the 1930s and 1940s, who found in Afro-Brazilian culture a focus of populist concern with folk culture in response to discouragement of activist politics by an authoritarian right-wing government. Dr. Rubim attributes his personal interest in *candomblé* to three sources. First was his reading of works by an earlier generation of anthropologically concerned Brazilian psychiatrists, notably Nina Rodriguez (1935) and Arthur Ramos (1939); also influential were the works of Rene Ribeiro (1952; 1959) and Edison Carneiro (1940; 1961). (Few of these works are available in English translation.) Through this reading, Dr. Rubim was self-instructed about issues of ethnopsychiatry, and decided that it should be a responsibility of psychiatrists of his own generation to resume these studies. A second influence was the discovery that his patients frequently submitted themselves to religious treatments without being open about it to him. His chance discovery of these visits led him to explore their consequences for his patients at a private psychiatric hospital where he was employed. Third was the matter of curiosity, which led him to attend his first *candomblé* ceremony in 1968, along with a group of colleagues participating in the transcultural psychiatry symposium sponsored that year in Bahia by the World Association of Psychiatry. His initial encounter with the cult leader evolved into a longstanding involvement with the affairs of the *terreiro*.

Axé Opô Afonja is one of three daughter *terreiros* of the original Nagô *terreiro* of Bahia. It is organized around an *ialorixa* or *Mãe-de-Santo* (Mother of Saints), who is invariably a woman of African descent. Male cult heads (*babalorixa* or *Pai-de-Santo*) have been known, but are infrequent in the Nagô *candomblé*. Second in rank is the *iaquerere* or *Mãe Pequeno* (Little Mother), whose responsibilities include directing the music at ceremonies and who is the temporary replacement for a deceased *Mãe-de-Santo* until a successor is chosen. She also directs the initiation of the *yaôs* or *Filhas-de-Santo* (Daughters of the Saints) who constitute the remainder of female devotees who experience possession by the *orixas*. Males seldom experience possession; in Axé Opô Afonja the relation of male to female *yaôs* is 1 : 10. Finally, among female participants, the *ekeide is* a kind of general protectress. There are seldom more than three *ekeide* in a *terreiro*, and they are typically women of higher social status than the *yaôs*. They serve as auxiliaries in charge of coordinating decorative and aesthetic aspects of *terreiro* festivities, especially those of a more social and less sacred character.

Four ceremonial offices are available to male participants. There are eight *ogan de faca* (*ogans* of the knife), full-time officiants of the *terreiro* who must be present in all public and private rituals, and who are the only persons ritually consecrated to kill sacrificial animals. The *ogan de quarto* (*ogans* of the room) are a larger group that may vary in number; there are slightly more than 20 in Axé Opô Afonja. Aside from attending festivals of their guardian *orixa*, their primary responsibility is as patron to the *yaôs* consecrated to the same *orixa*. These *ogans* offer advice and support to the *yaôs* and in certain instances financial support as well: for example, they may help defray the cost of an *orixa's* expensive ritual costume. They also act as general supporters of the *terreiro*. They are typically both black and white men, and in Axé Opô Afonja a small but significant group of artists and intellectuals of European ancestry occupy this office, including Dr. Rubim. Above the *ogans* in rank, and serving the *Mãe-de-Santo* as direct advisors, are eight *obas*. All are consecrated to the *orixa* Xango, who is also the principal deity of the *terreiro*. The *obas* are organized hierarchically among themselves: first *oba* on the right of Xango, first on the left, second on the right, etc. This group is responsible for choosing a new *Mãe-de-Santo* on the death of one in office. Finally, the drummers or players of the *atabaque* are generally young men responsible for ceremonial music, producing the sacred rhythms that indicate the presence of particular *orixas*. None of these male cult participants experiences possession trance.

Whether or not a person experiences possession trance, each participant is consecrated to a single *orixa* that serves as his or her guardian. Dr. Rubim acquired his patron when, while attending his second *candomblé* ceremony in 1969, he was *levantado para ser ogan* (raised up to be *ogan*) by an entranced *Filha-de-Santo* who was possessed by the deity Oxala. During the following year he was required to attend all public ceremonies of the *terreiro*, and undergo a series of interviews with the *Mãe-de-Santo*, during which she instructed him about the structure of the religion, his ritual obligations, and how to comport himself during rituals. His initiation occurred at the end of this period, at the culmination of a three-week cycle of ceremonies that constitutes the festival of Oxala. The night before the initiation, he was dressed in white, the sacred color of Oxala, and required to keep vigil before Oxala's altar. The night was punctuated by rituals that included a sacred bath, animal sacrifices, and rites of purification and strengthening by means of the animals' blood and cooked meat. On the day of initiation he was given a necklace sacred to Oxala as a sign of his office, and a ritual name in the Yoruba language. From this time he was entitled to attend private as well as public rituals. Having achieved the status of *ogan*, Dr. Rubim anticipated access to valuable ethnopsychiatric data. As he states, in the course of 10 years this anticipation was disappointed:

> At the time of my initiation, it looked like the circumstances which led me to be an *ogan* would give me the opportunity to study what I wanted: the treatment of mental illnesses. In fact, experience did not bear this out, because in the Nagô *candomblé* few treatments of mental illnesses are applied. There are far more religious practices than there are treatments. The Nagô *Mãe-de-Santo* makes appointments in which she gives advice, which is either moral advice or advice about how to fulfill religious obligations. When one talks about authentic mental illnesses – psychoses – she generally recommends going to a doctor. I continued as an *ogan* to frequent the *terreiro* and attend the rituals, but for purposes of research I have preferred to take another route, using questionnaires [in general population surveys]. (Csordas interview with Rubim de Pinho, 1979: 72)

In general it is not, strictly speaking, an episode of illness that indicates initiation as a *yaô* capable of possession trance. On occasion an uninitiated individual attending a public ceremony will become possessed, and this is a possible indication that she is chosen by an *orixa*. The more usual process is through consultation with the *Mãe-de-Santo*, again not for an illness, but for some difficulty, problem, or conflict in life, and not with the advance intention of becoming a member of *candomblé*. In such a consultation, the *Mãe-de-Santo* seeks advice from Xango through the technique of Ifa divination (Bascom 1969). Xango indicates the cause of the problem and tenders advice. Becoming a *yaô* or *Filha-de-Santo* is only one of his possible recommendations. The person may need the ritual of *bori* (not to be confused with the Hausa *bori* cult), in which one is strengthened by "feeding the head" with cooked meat and blood from a sacrificial animal, and which is included as one part of the initiation of *organs* and *yaôs*. This ritual fortifies spirit and mind, enabling a person to confront life's difficulties, but its effects last for only a limited period, and even for initiated members must be renewed after several years. Another ceremony, meant to prevent misfortune, is "cleansing of the body." This is a simple rite consisting of a series of prayers uttered by the

Mãe-de-Santo while the supplicant performs predetermined gestures. Yet another prophylactic measure is bestowal of a necklace made in the *terreiro* with ritually prepared beads. While all *ogans* and *yaôs* receive a necklace of color and composition specific to their guardian *orixa* at their initiation, necklaces may be given to anyone in consultation, though they vary in color, size, and shape of beads. Other prescriptions made by Xango through medium of the *Mãe-de-Santo* include taking sacred herb baths, attending particular religious ceremonies, offering a sacrificial animal to an *orixa*, and offering a meal of a particular *orixa*'s favorite dish (*ebo* or *fazer um despacho*).

In a situation in which a woman is required to become a *yaô*, Dr. Rubim described the following process of initiation:

It is very different from the initiation of an *ogan*. Many years ago in Axé Opô Afonja the period of initiation extended to nine months of seclusion in the *peji* [initiation house]. This time has been greatly diminished, I suppose because the process is expensive, and that it does not allow the person to work for too long a time. But even now the process of initiating a *yaô* in Axé Opô Afonja is never shorter than three months. Inside the *peji* the environment is shadowy, semi-dark, quiet, and isolated. The *iaquerere* (*Mãe Pequeno*) enters daily and directs the works, and on certain occasions the *ialorixa* (*Mãe-de-Santo*) visits to supervise and give directions. It can be a group of initiates, but there are different rooms. Sometimes they are in different rooms performing different rituals, and sometimes the same ritual is performed simultaneously for more than one. A part of the formation is specific to each *orixa*. The initiates don't talk to one another; they talk to the *iaquerere* only for essential things. She is the one who coordinates the ambience of the place.

I judge the process of initiation to be mainly a process of conditioning, where the *Filha-de-Santo* is prepared to be a person who dances in a certain way, mimics certain characteristics of the *orixa*, and has certain ways of behaving socially. I imagine that during this process there can arise resistances or duplicities to the adoption of a kind of conduct, and that the process of conditioning makes it possible to overcome this and adopt the proper behavior. This raises the issue of the separation of pathological processes from possession in the religious context, in which latter case it is perfectly normal. The *Mãe-de Santo* used to tell me that it is possible before or during the initiation that more than one *orixa* would try to possess the same daughter. But if the process occurs correctly there is a definite link established between a *yaô* and only one *orixa*, and possession occurs only in religious situations. In a situation of conflict, I imagine that this could be comprehensible to us as personality traits that appear to be in disagreement. But I have the impression that the conflicts about which the *Mãe-de-Santo* talks do not concern situations of personality but moments of possession – the conflict between two *orixas* possessing the same body. I imagine that this is purely personal. I imagine that the conflict the *Mãe-de-Santo* talks about as possession by more than one *orixa* has a connection with what I would think to be resistance of the person to adopting that pattern of behavior which is being induced as the pattern of behavior of that particular *orixa*. But the *Mãe-de-Santo* says that when the work of initiation is done correctly, the identification of the *yaô* with the *orixa* is perfectly defined. (Csordas interview with Rubim de Pinho, 1979: 48–50)

In contrast to some possession cults, each participant in *candomblé* has only one guardian spirit. A person often resembles, or has certain personality traits in common with, the guardian *orixa:* it is common to say that a person is "for Oxala" or "for Oxun" in the same way that a North American might say that a person "takes after her grandmother." This suggests caution in concluding that spirit possession in *candomblé* is a cultivation of the multiple personality phenomenon, wherein repressed or unrecognized motives are acted out (Bourguignon 1983). Those who are initiated into the possession experience undergo a careful process of training over a period of several months, since they will be responsible for incarnating their deity in human form. During this period, initiates make the elaborate costume characteristic of their patron, and learn both the complex mythology associated with that divinity and its typical patterns of behavior and speech as manifested on ritual occasions. During initiation the novice *Filha-de-Santo* is secluded in darkness in a twilight state of semi-trance characterized as one of childlike suggestibility or regression, and referred to in Yoruba as *ere*. While totally absorbed in the sacred presence, the novice is sensitized to the drum rhythm sacred to her *orixa*, so that on ritual occasions her possession experience is intimately tied to a particular musical experience. Thus, there is no uniform susceptibility to sonic driving (Neher 1962) as a mechanism of trance induction, but rather a selective suggestibility based on cultivated sensitivity to the interweaving of musical themes in the ceremonies (compare Rouget 1980).

The effects of this training are seen not only in the carefully stylized behavior of the deities during ritual possessions, but in interactions among *orixas* that reflect their relations in myth. For example, Bastide (1958) recounts that one of Xango's wives, once tricked in myth by her co-wife, often flies into a rage during ceremonies, and must be restrained by assistants from beating her malefactress in revenge. Thus, instead of therapeutic acting out, spirit possession in *candomblé* can be seen as a pure form of ritual drama, where the parts of deities are not played by humans, but where the deities in effect play themselves. Also according to Bastide, the relation of the individual to her possessing *orixa* is essentially one of mystical communion. On an interpretive level, the mystical relation in this instance takes precedence over features of social pathology or marginality that are often invoked in the explanation of possession cults. In Bastide's words:

> (T)he social can only inscribe, in the domain of interpersonal relations, the laws of the mystical life. The degrees of participation in the group can only follow those of the identification of a person with the *orixa*. The variations of social solidarity are finally only the reflection, and the consequence, of the variations of solidarity established between the person and the world of the gods . . . It is not social morphology that commands religion or explains it, but on the contrary the mystical that commands the social. (Bastide 1958: 27, 28, my translation)

Case Vignettes

If illness is not the primary concern of *candomblé* participants, and the cult's existence is not adequately explained as a response to social marginality, it is still necessary in a balanced ethnopsychiatric approach to view it as a resource for the health and well-being of a community through the measures of ritual prophylaxis prescribed by the *Mãe-de-Santo* in consultation. Although on occasion people with various medical illnesses consult the *Mãe-de-Santo*, most consultees are people with psychosocial issues such as marital problems, financial difficulties, or problems with drugs and alcohol. The following is an example of such a situation, as recounted by Dr. Rubim:

> *Case 1*: It concerns a family that lives in the Amazon region. A lady, mother of one child, had a conflict with her daughter-in-law. The difficulties grew worse for the family, so the lady went to Bahia to have an appointment with the *Mãe-de-Santo*. In this case it was my *Mãe-de-Santo* in Axé Opô Afonja. I know this family very well, since they are from my home town: the lady wanted to go to a *Mãe-de Santo*, so she consulted me and I recommended this one for her. From what she told me, she gave very little information to the *Mãe-de-Santo*, and the *Mãe-de-Santo* completed her description of the family situation with absolute fidelity.

The initial conflict was between daughter-in-law and mother-in-law but the older woman's husband took a position of solidarity with his wife against their daughter-in-law. This in turn had repercussions for their son, who was their only child. All four live in the same city, but not in the same house; they share a lot. Now this mother always had great affection for her only son, who does not have any children himself. The marriage was well accepted, but the daughter-in-law began to think that the mother-in-law was overprotective of her son. So the daughter-in-law tried to avoid seeing the older woman too much – but she still wanted to profit materially and financially from her in-laws. The situation became very difficult, to the point that they did not see each other unless the daughter-in-law would go to ask for something. The situation would be tense, and the young woman would be demanding. She tried to ask for jewelry, and once she demanded a car. The mother-in-law gave her the car, and soon after they sold it to get cash.

In this case, the orientation given by the *Mãe-de-Santo* was for the lady to use, in perpetuity, a necklace prepared and made sacred by the *Mãe-de-Santo*. Another necklace was prescribed for the lady's husband. Even though the husband is a lawyer he agreed to wear it, saying that it didn't matter because if it does not do any good, it will not do any bad. I do not want to judge the consequences of all this as it evolves, because this happened only a few months ago and many factors can influence the situation. However, as of now, the situation seems to have become better. The lady believes that the relationship is much better. I think that the consultation had been made with many doubts, even though the woman had traveled a long way to do it. But it seems that she acquired a lot of trust – after all, she had confidence in the *Mãe-de-Santo* and the necklace. What seems curious to me in this case is not the situation's development, because although my information is that the ambience improved quite a lot, it is still too early to judge. But the mother-in-law's confidence in the *Mãe-de-Santo* improved because the *Mãe-de-Santo* described the facts as they happened, having heard very little of the story. She did the diagnosis, made some recommendations, and decided upon the use of the necklace for the lady and a smaller necklace for her husband. (Csordas interview with Rubim de Pinho, 1979: 73–5)

If this case is an example of religious mediation of interpersonal conflict, the following is one where religious participation itself is an issue in the conflict between spouses. Note also Dr. Rubim's role as a psychiatrist in this instance, which appears typical of his self-described openness to religious treatment as long as it is compatible with therapeutic goals, as well as his tendency not to consult directly with his religious counterpart.

Case 2: This was a very curious case that concerned a lady who was not a participant in the cult of *candomblé*. She was a white woman about thirty years of age. She was from Ceara State in the north of Brazil, though her family moved to Bahia when she was an adult. She had gone to Europe when very young, and spent six years there pursuing her education. On returning she became a Professor of Literature at a university. Then she got married. In this case a conflict arose within her marriage because she wanted to participate in the Afro-Brazilian cults, and her husband did not let her. Her orientation towards this had come through contact with a house of Umbanda in Rio. The conflict grew worse and became aggravated. Her husband suggested that they go on vacation to take her away from her anxiety. So the couple spent several weeks at the beach of Espirito Santo in Guarapari. One morning the husband woke up and did not see her – she had disappeared. The police were alerted, and they found her in Minas Gerais, in the city of Manana, in an Afro-Brazilian *terreiro* – another place, another state, completely different. She was having a possession. She would agree to leave only if she could go to Bahia to consult another house of religion, the address of which she had obtained in Minas. She had simply fled from the hotel room in Guarapari and gone to Minas.

She did have relatives in Bahia; someone in Minas gave her the address of the *terreiro* there, saying it was a very good one. In Bahia I was called to help this lady, who, besides having lived in Europe and being a professor at the university, had for more than two years submitted herself to psychoanalysis. I found her in a very agitated and anxious state. After two consultations with her, I decided that a psychotic condition did not exist. It was a neurotic state, aggravated by her reaction to the situation – the condition was psychogenic, as we say in psychiatry. But she refused psychiatric treatment. She did not accept me. I tried to get another psychiatrist, but the problem was not with me – she wanted a religious solution. In trying to get her to accept me, I told her about my contacts with *candomblé*. I just used my position as *ogan* in order to be well accepted. She continued to refuse me, saying that when intellectuals go to *candomblé* it's out of curiosity, and not because they believe. Then I surprised the family. I advised them to take her to the cult whose address she had brought back from Minas.

After two weeks of frequenting the house and fulfilling religious obligations, her anxiety disappeared. She went to the *Mãe-de-Santo* daily, talking with her and participating in the cult. She received the indoctrination and fulfilled obligations, but I do not know which ones. The anxiety disappeared. A prayer was given to her and she was told to continue to use it. But it was indicated to her that she should not become a *yaô*. I do not know if this indication was proper through religious means or because it coincided with the wish of her husband.

The evolution of the situation was quite normal. But it seems to me that this was funny behavior on the part of the *Mãe-de-Santo*: she gave religious orientation and obligations, but she advised that on returning to Rio de Janeiro, the woman should not frequent the cults. That was the major conflict with her husband. But what was said was that there had been an orientation from a superior entity. From the description, I understood that it was not a traditional *terreiro*, but one characterized by a syncretism of *candomblé* and the beliefs of Kardecist spiritism. The spirits who advised through the medium was not an *orixa*. I remember this because, although the ceremonials described were of *candomblé* type, the woman told me it was Irmão Basa – Spirit of the Brother Basa ("Irmão" is the Kardecist term for "spirit").

Very simply, I think she was neurotic. I have reason to think this because she submitted herself to psychiatric treatment for two years, a treatment which she interrupted. So there must already have been some reasons to motivate the consultation and treatment. In Rio, after she interrupted her psychoanalytic treatment, she had consulted an Umbanda house. There she was advised to have initiation. It would have been that she sensed a problem intuitively in Rio, and felt the incapacity of psychoanalysis to understand the problem. Religion was an alternative solution. I have heard that everything is now going well in this case. As a psychiatric instrument I would not have been able to resolve it, because it was not a psychiatric problem.   (Csordas interview with Rubim de Pinho, 1979: 75–9)

Two points must be made in commentary on this case. First, Dr. Rubim's simultaneous ability to diagnose a neurosis and his willingness to declare the problem not a psychiatric one is directly related to his own conception of psychiatry's proper boundary. He is critical of the trend in American psychiatry, since Adolph Meyer, toward increasing medicalization of human life to the point of presumed omniscience for psychiatry. Thus, for him, the area of "neuroses" is no more the privileged domain of psychiatry than it is of religion. His willingness to acknowledge "informal psychiatry" is tied to a critique of the lack of limits between pathological and normal socially conditioned phenomena in North American psychiatry; to a conception of Latin American psychiatry as limiting its scope to "psychiatric phenomena in the strict sense"; and to a view that those who are waiting for a solution through programs of mental health to societal problems of poverty, unemployment, and communality will ultimately be frustrated. Second, in this instance the prescribed level of religious participation goes well beyond that observed in the first case, but it stops short of full initiation as a cult devotee. The treatment approach of both Dr. Rubim and the *Mãe-de-Santo* – between whom there was apparently no direct contact – appears to have been aimed at compromise between the woman's perceived spiritual needs and her husband's adamant opposition to her cult participation. In the third case, which follows, the degree of ritual participation is greater still, actually reaching the initial stages of initiation, and the relation between medical and sacred realities becomes critical.

Case 3: Let me tell you about a case in which I was involved that illustrates the capacity of the *Mãe-de-Santo* to separate what comes from the religious side and what comes from the medical side. It concerns a recently graduated medical student, who had been an excellent student. After her graduation she went to New York for a time. According to what she told me later, she experienced certain perturbing reactions while she was in New York. She consulted a religious cult, and was told that her problem was a religious one; I have the impression that the cult had to do with black magic, demonology. When she was back in Bahia she decided, on the indication of a *Mãe-de-Santo.* to submit herself to the process of initiation and become a *Filha-de-Santo*. In this case, it was an Angolan *candomblé*.

She initiated the process, and stayed in the *camaria* (the room where the *Mãe-de-Santo* stays) for two months. So there she was, despite the fact that we knew that the process of becoming a *Filha-de-Santo* included modification of one's level of consciousness. The *Mãe-de-Santa* observed that there was a different disturbance that aggravated her to such an extent that one day she burned certain sacred objects. In the *peji* there were some days when she submitted herself in a disciplined way to the determinations of the *Mãe-de-Santo* and fulfilled her rituals, but there were some days when she interrupted the rituals with her behavior. This behavior would cause disturbances in the environment, and the *Mãe-de-Santo* identified it as not being proper within possession. She would be very talkative, talking too much during times when she should not have been speaking. She would have episodes of agitation and accentuated insomnia. In one of the nights when she could not sleep, in the middle of an agitation, she burned sacred objects. Later on, she told me she was having fun, playing – but that is proper to these manic syndromes. It is common that an ecstasy of happiness is associated with an activity that does not correspond to, or is inappropriate to, the feeling, and that the action is done without any reflection or inhibition.

Although the family of the girl was opposed to her initiation, the *Mãe-de-Santo* asked her relatives to come, and told them that she suspected that there was a medical problem in addition to the religious one. The *Mãe-de-Santo* felt uneasy, because according to the rule of *candomblé* she could not call a stranger or uninitiated person – a doctor

– to help her in the private area of the house. By coincidence, an *ogan* of this *candomblé* had been an attendant in a psychiatric hospital, and he knew me because of this. He knew that I was an *ogan* of another *candomblé*. He informed the *Mãe-de-Santo* about this, and she accepted. So I was called to give my opinion, and diagnosed that the young woman was in a psychotic episode. It was a manic-depressive psychosis. I explained this diagnosis to the *Mãe-de-Santo*, and we were in total agreement. The *Mãe-de-Santo* concluded that while she was ill, conditions were not right to proceed with the initiation. Later on, this girl was cured, but she then had other episodes. She continued to attend the house, but the *Mãe-de-Santo* did not accept her for initiation again, because she thought that the existence of a medical problem made a contrary indication.

What I find curious about this is that the *Mãe-de-Santo* did not attribute the agitation to religious causes, and thought it necessary, even in that moment, to obtain medical intervention. My contact with the *Mãe-de-Santo* wasn't good enough to know why she thought as she did, but she told me that there were situations of mental illness that were considered to be natural illnesses, and that in such cases Xango did not think that initiation was convenient. I don't know if in the past this would have been regarded as the correct procedure for a *Mãe-de-Santo* – it may be a consequence of some awareness of psychiatric subjects on the part of contemporary *Mães-de-Santo*. Nevertheless, although this *Mãe-de-Santo* looked like a very intelligent woman, she was very primitive in her knowledge; she didn't have the higher level such as does the *Mãe-de-Santo* in Axé Opô Afonja. The present *Mãe-de-Santo* in my *terreiro* was a public functionary who left that work when she was chosen as *Mãe-de-Santo*. This *Mãe-de-Santo* with whom I have been associated knows how to differentiate trance by possession of an *orixa*, hysterical crisis, and simulated trance – something we psychiatrists do not know. When she decides it is a hysterical crisis she does not use that term, of course. She simply decides it is a case for the psychiatrist by excluding possession by an *orixa* and simulation. I don't know how she can do it: but I have seen my *Mãe-de-Santo* observe trances even in the initiated *yaôs* of her *terreiro*, and tell them to see a doctor. Her evidence is that the Santo does not know what she is doing; the saint does not manifest itself in that way.

It is also curious in this case that the *Mãe-de-Santo* knew how to separate the infantile behavior of *ere* [preparatory trance: see above] from the euphoric behavior of mental disease. And there was another episode in which the young woman was hospitalized and it was necessary to use electrical shock treatment – a treatment done in few cases, but which in certain ones can be necessary, though it must be used with care. In that case it was administered under anaesthesia. The family was informed and authorized the treatment, but the patient didn't know about it;

even now she does not know that she underwent electroshock treatment. She passed through a period of several days during which she had a problem with fixation of memory, which is common among people who receive electric shock. When she commented to me about this period, she said she had the impression of having passed through several days which she remembered only as if it were a dream, and which she interpreted as a supernatural situation. She confused the effect of electroshock with a possession. But she herself told me that the *Mãe-de-Santo* listened to the narration of this period and did not confirm the possession. The *Mãe-de-Santo* does not know what happened, but told her that what she described was not a possession. She knows how to make the differential diagnosis. (Csordas interview with Rubim de Pinho, 1979: 82–90)

In this account of direct collaboration between psychiatrist and religious specialist, the medical expert is impressed by his counterpart's intuitive and practical ability to distinguish pathological from sacred experience; Dr. Rubim notes that this conforms to an observation made decades earlier by Ribeiro (1959). These judgments by a *Mãe-de-Santo* are apparently based both on observation of more or less subtle behavioral cues and on evaluation of states of consciousness entered by devotees. Ecstasy as a category of cultural experience is elaborated to a degree alien to western science, such that there are definite, if implicit, distinctions between normal ecstasy and pathological ecstasy. Contrary to the common generalization that individuals are initiated into possession cults as a form of psychotherapy for mental illness, this is a case in which initiation was denied precisely because the novice was discerned to be mentally ill. Likewise in the previous case, a neurotic individual was deemed an inappropriate candidate for initiation; it is unlikely that the opposition of her husband was the only factor affecting the *Mãe-de-Santo's* decision to limit her participation. Finally, all three cases described by Dr. Rubim involved individuals who were marginal not to their society – all were professional-class women of European ancestry – but marginal to the religious milieu, and hence not considered as viable candidates for initiation. As Dr. Rubim noted, even initiated *yaôs* will be referred to a doctor if their possession behavior becomes inappropriate, indicating that the cult experience itself is not primarily a form of therapy. The ability to experience possession by an *orixa* is a highly valued religious skill and a serious ritual responsibility, entrusted only to those regarded as stable enough to function appropriately.

Conclusion

Using the example of African and Afro-American spirit possession, it has been argued here that certain religious or health-related phenomena can be adequately understood only by examining both their medical and sacred dimensions. To argue for the inclusion of the holy as a factor in the discourse of medical anthropology is not to advocate a return to older paradigms, or abandonment of the subdiscipline's important move toward clinical relevance. Indeed, the "new cross-cultural psychiatry" (Kleinman 1988) combines the sophistication of epidemiological method with the sensitivity or hermeneutic method. Kleinman and Good's (1985) recent outline of a research program for an anthropology of emotions specifies the need for detailed phenomenological description, analysis of relevant semantic domains, attention to local contexts of interpersonal power, and recognition of the basic somatic dimension of culturally conditioned activity. Specific issues that must be addressed in the study of possession trance include the degree to which existential problems are defined in religious or medical idioms; cultural definitions of which health resources are appropriate for which illnesses; diversity in types of trance behavior and experience available in adherents' behavioral environment; the different levels of participation and identification attained by individual supplicants; and variations of symbolic structure within the repertoire of possessing spirits. A situation in which a variety of modes of possession are possible may be significantly different from one in which only a single form is recognized; a context in which "possession" is a manner of speaking about an emotional attachment may not have much in common with one where "possession" implies mystical communion with a deity (Bastide 1958). Careful empirical study and ethnological comparison along these lines are essential for a balanced approach to the relation between ecstasy and illness.

Our conclusion, then, is that one cannot a priori deny the psychiatric aspects of *candomblé*, and that one is remiss in denying the religious aspects of the *zar* cult. The controversy between Leacock, on the one hand, and Crapanzano and Garrison, on the other, over the latter's edited volume on possession in the end came down to the relative emphasis given to medical and religious features in defining the nature of the phenomenon. Each side accused the other of being one-sided, and each claimed even-handedness (Leacock 1978). Would it not be wiser to pose the issue at the outset rather than to let it arise in a post facto polemic? What are the implications of observations that some people appear to make no distinction between the spiritual domain and the domain of health, while others, such as the *Mãe-de-Santo* described here, are able to make surprisingly subtle distinctions? How and under what circumstances are the boundaries drawn? Is spirit possession predominantly an idiom for illness, as evidenced by the frequent accounts of initiatory illness; or can illness in some cases be an idiom for a certain type of encounter with the sacred (compare Csordas 1985)? Is there a religious "side" and a medical "side" to the issue, or are they ultimately two discourses on precisely the same existential problems? Are these discourses translatable from one to the other? Or is it possible to construct a "meta-discourse" that does justice to both? The methodological status of our own ability – or necessity – to distinguish between medical and sacred must also be counted as a problem. This is evident not only in terms of the overlap of existential concerns (health and illness, life and death) between religion and medicine, but also in terms of the differing cultural assumptions about the proper boundaries of psychiatry in Latin and North America, as pointed out by Dr. Rubim. It is certainly spurious to resolve a dualism in our own thought by opting for one of its poles and claiming that all can be accounted for from that perspective. Confronting the issue is not to straddle the fence; it is to recognize that medical anthropology and ethnopsychiatry raise fundamental problems of meaning in human experience.

Acknowledgments

I am grateful to Dr. Enka Bourguignon for comments on an earlier version of this chapter. I am also grateful to Dr. Ann Dunbar of the University of North Carolina Program in African and Afro-American Studies for the opportunity to interview Dr. Alvaro Rubim de Pinho, to my co-interviewer Ms. Linda Guthne, to our thoughtful interpreter Mr. Antonio Simoes, and of course to Dr. Rubim himself. An earlier version of this chapter was completed during the tenure of an NIMH research training fellowship under the direction of Elliot Mishler, administered through the Laboratory of Social Psychiatry, Massachusetts Mental Hospital, and the Department of Psychiatry, Harvard Medical School.

References

Bascom, W. (1969) *Ifa Divination: Communication Between Gods and Men in West Africa*. Bloomington, IN: Indiana University Press.

Bastide, R. (1958) *Le Candomblé de Bahia* (Rite Nagô). The Hague: Mouton.

Bastide, R. (1972) *La Rêve, La Transe, et la Folie*. Paris: Flammarion.

Bastide, R. (1978) *African Religions of Brazil: Toward a Sociology of the Inter-penetration of Civilizations*. Baltimore, MD: Johns Hopkins University Press.

Bourguignon, E. (1976) "The Effectiveness of Religious Healing Movements: A Review of Recent Literature," *Transcultural Psychiatric Research Review* 13: 5–21.

Bourguignon, E. (1983) "Multiple Personality, Possession Trance, and the Psychic Unity of Mankind," in E. Duerr (ed.), *Die Wilde Seele/The Savage Soul*. Frankfurt: Syndikat.

Carneiro, E. (1940) "The Structure of African Cults in Bahia," *Journal of American Folklore* 53: 271–8.

Carneiro, E. (1961) *Candomblés da Bahia*. Rio de Janeiro: Conquista.

Csordas, T.J. (1979) *Candomblé: Conversation with Dr. Alvaro Rubim de Pinho on Cultural and Psychiatric Aspects of Afro-Brazilian Religion*. University of North Carolina Program in African and Afro-American Studies, Chapel Hill.

Csordas, T.J. (1985) "Medical and Sacred Realities: Between Comparative Religion and Transcultural Psychiatry," *Cultural Medical Psychiatry* 9: 103–16.

Csordas, T.J. (1990) "The Psychotherapy Analogy and Charismatic Healing," *Psychotherapy* 27(1): 79–80.

Frank, J. and Frank, J.F. (1991) *Persuasion and Healing*. Baltimore, MD: Johns Hopkins University Press.

Guimares de Magalhaes, E. (1974) *Orixas de Bahia*. Salvador: S.A. Artes Grafias.

Kleinman, A. (1988) *Rethinking Psychiatry: From Cultural Category to Personal Experience*. New York: Free Press.

Kleinman, A. and Good, B. (1985) *Culture and Depression*. Berkeley, CA: University of California Press.

LaBarre, W. (1972) *The Ghost Dance: The Origins of Religion*. New York: Delta.

Leacock, S. (1972) *Spirits of the Deep*. New York: Doubleday.

Leacock, S. (1978) "Review of Crapanzano and Garrison: Case Studies in Spirit Possession," *Review of Anthropology* 5: 399–409 (reply by Crapanzano and Garrison, 420–25).

Lewis, I.M. (1969) "Spirit Possession in Northern Somaliland," in J. Beattie and J. Middleton (eds.), *Spirit Membership and Society in Africa*. New York: Africana.

Monfouga-Nicolas, J. (1972) *Ambivalence et Culte de Possession*. Paris: Anthropos.

Neher, A. (1962) "A Physiological Explanation of Unusual Behaviour in Ceremonies Involving Drums," *Human Biology* 34: 151–60.

O'Gorman, F. (1977) *Aluanda: A Look at Afro-Brazilian Cults*. Rio de Janeiro: Livraria Francisco Alves.

Pressel, E. (1973) "Umbanda in São Paolo: Religious Innovation in a Developing Society," in E. Bourguignon (ed.), *Religion, Altered States of Consciousness and Social Change*. Columbus, OH: Ohio State University Press, pp. 264–320.

Ramos, A. (1939) *The Negro in Brazil* (trans. R. Pattee). Washington, DC: Associated Publishers.

Ribeiro, R. (1952) *Cultos Afrobrasileiros de Recife: Um Estudo de Ajustámento Social*. Recife: Instituto Joaquim Nabuco.

Ribeiro, R. (1959) "Análises Socio-Psicológico de la Posesión en los Cultos Afro-brasileños", *Acta Neuropsiqologica*, Argentina 5: 249–62.

Rodriguez, N.R. (1935) *Animisma Fetichista dos Negros Bahianos*. Rio de Janeiro: Civilizacao Brasileiro.

Rouget, G. (1980) *La Musique et la Transe*. Paris: Gallimard.

Varella, J. (1972) *Cozhinha de Santo (Culinario de Umbanda e Candomblé)*. Rio de Janeiro: Editora Espiritualista.

Williams, P. (1979) *Primitive Religion and Healing: A Study of Folk Medicine in Northeast Brazil*. Cambridge: D. S. Brewer.

Young, A. (1975) "Why Amhara Get Kureyna: Sickness and Possession in an Ethiopian *Zar* Cult," *American Ethnologist* 2: 567–854.

Chapter 11

Here Comes the Sun: Shedding Light on the Cultural Body

Simon Carter and Mike Michael

Illuminating the Scene

This chapter comprises a tentative and partial step toward a "sociology of the sun." Though this might appear oxymoronic, with a little unpacking of both "sociology" and "sun," such a project will make sense not least in the context of a volume on "cultural bodies."

The "sociology" with which we align ourselves is a recent one that is undergoing a turn to materiality and the object (Haraway 1991; Latour 1993; Urry 2000). Within this overarching project, there is a developing view that the key concern is with heterogeneous relationalities out of which emerge such entities as the body, the sun, and technology. The upshot of this focus upon heterogeneity, relationality, and emergence is a happy indifference to traditional disciplinary and subdisciplinary boundaries. As we shall see below, even within the limited purview of this chapter, we must range across sociologies of the body, technology, medicine, environment, consumption, and culture, to list but the most obvious.

In focusing upon the sun, we are informed by Benjamin's injunction (Arendt 1992) to seek the character of an epoch in the smallest and least noticeable. Ironically, the sun is neither the smallest nor the least noticeable, but it is certainly, in one respect, amongst the most neglected. Although there are accounts of the symbolic role of the sun, there is little on the social and cultural mediation of the sun's multifarious impacts upon people's bodies. For those people living in temperate geographical zones and with western cultural backgrounds the sun is produced by and associated with many (apparently) contradictory practices, objects, and artifacts. We seek the sun out on our holidays and in our gardens yet we are told that skin cancer is reaching epidemic proportions. When we visit the supermarket or chemist we are confronted by an alarming array of creams and lotions, all offering differing degrees of sun protection, while also promising the "ultimate tan." We think and feel that "getting out in the sun" is something wholesome and good – yet we are told that 80 percent of one's exposure to dangerous ultraviolet rays happens before the age of 20. When we visit gyms or health clubs we notice the equipment for producing an "artificial" tan but we worry about our bodies and an "authentic" look. Even doing something as innocuous as buying a new fridge (and disposing of the old one) may be making the sun more dangerous and damaging to others' bodies.

This is all to say that the sun as material culture – or better still, culturalized materiality – remains strangely unexplored as an element in the (re)production of various sorts of heterogeneous networks out of which emerge various sorts of cultural bodies. Embroiled within such networks are not only a variety of cultural artifacts (discourses about the healthiness or glamour of the tan, or the different qualities of illumination in different parts of the world such as Provence, or the dangers posed by global warming, ozone depletion, and solar flares) but also technological artifacts (suntan lotions and creams, sunglasses and visors, supercomputers for global climate modeling, and telescopes). But of course, to begin with, a dichotomy between cultural and technological artifacts is highly problematic – these are inherently intertwined (e.g. Latour 1993). Better, then, to speak, for want of a better term, of "sociotechnical artifacts"; we follow Benjamin again and examine the neglected cultural role of these entities.

Now, in embarking upon mapping an exploratory sociology of the sun, we cannot hope to do justice to the range of concerns that will fall under this rubric. For example, we will resist the obvious temptation to review the multifarious symbolism associated with the sun. Such cultural analysis can miss out on the role of the technological and corporeal. What concerns us here is the symbolization and representation of the sun that are intimately tied to body techniques (Mauss 1985) and the corporeality of sociotechnical artifacts. In other words, it is this nexus of sun–body–sociotechnical artifact that we address here. In so doing, we move in two distinct directions.

First, we engage with the substantive: we consider how the material impact of the sun upon bodies is mediated by a series of sociotechnical artifacts – such as past medical therapies, suntanning lotions, and even architectural design. As such we trace some of the complex dynamics by which the nexus of sun–body–sociotechnical artifacts shift and change historically as the meanings and practices around sun, body, and technology develop in sometimes contradictory ways. Our aim here is to provide an initial foray into what it might mean to "do" a sociology of the sun. Secondly, as a reflexive twist, we consider the epistemological implications of this nexus by focusing especially on the materiality and corporeality of vision. Insofar as it is possible to warrant (a version) of the visual as the guiding "epistemological sense," we ask: What epistemological lessons can we learn by paying attention to the body techniques of vision, especially the wearing of sunglasses? Our answer will dwell on the situated aestheticization of knower and known.

Sun, Sunshine and Heavenly Bodies

The idea of intentionally darkening the skin by exposing one's body to the sun is a relatively recent phenomenon. In order to unravel the complex dynamics linking the sun, the body, and the sociotechnical it will be useful to consider this brief history. As we shall see, the various associations between the sun and the body, mediated by the socio-technical, have been, and still are, in a constant state of flux and debate.

At the end of the nineteenth century there is little doubt that the suntan was still commonly regarded as dangerous and a marker of low social status, especially for women. Thus, self-help guides and women's magazines (such as *Vogue*) from this period stress the dangers of the sun's rays and the unattractive appearance that a suntan may cause (Corson 1972). Thus the sociotechnical interface between the body and its environment followed the axiom of bodily isolation from the sun, especially for women.

Yet while sun avoidance was being promoted there was already, in the later half of the nineteenth century, a differing relationship emerging between the sun and the body. One example of this can be found in the writings and diaries of early British travelers, who engaged in a form of "cultural tourism" in which the remaining artifacts of the ancient civilizations of Greece, Egypt, and Rome were visually consumed. But as well as visiting the historic ruins, these visitors also noticed the locals who lived in these regions – who were often viewed as living "classical" exhibits. "Taught to see life in Greek statues, British travelers looked for Greek statues in life" (Pemble 1987: 118). This was reflected in references made to the perfection and beauty of the brown body. George Frederic Watts, on traveling up the Nile in 1887, commented on the body of a young workman who was "[a] very distinctly Greek type . . . every movement of his limbs . . . magnificent" (Watts, quoted in Pemble 1987: 119). Watts also lamented the negative effects that modern habits had on the body. Writing after a return from Italy, Watts observed that:

> The limbs, deprived by the fashion of modern clothing of freedom, and shut off from the action of sun, and air, never acquire their natural development, texture or color.   (Watts, quoted in Pemble 1987: 119)

We can here see how the tanned skin, via references to ancient civilizations, was beginning to denote a fantasy escape from bourgeois propriety into a more sensuous, sexual, and direct physicality. The suntan was becoming a material and corporeal link to the ancients who were so highly valued. Yet these writings were still largely based on the observations of others' bodies. However, by the start of the twentieth century, the suntan was beginning to emerge as a material indication of bodily health and psychogenic strength for North Europeans themselves.

Camping and Campers

Throughout the nineteenth century concerns about health were often linked to fears about the growth of urban cities and the "problem of population" – the possible drift by the urban working classes into physical or moral degeneracy (Mort 1987; Weeks 1981). A particular concern was young men and one solution was thought to be the pursuit of "muscular Christianity": the idea, established in British public schools, that healthy "manliness" could be obtained through disciplined and codified physical activity. Two social movements of this period sought to introduce these practices to less privileged young males: the Boys' Brigade (established in 1872) and the Scouts, with Baden-Powell publishing *Scouting for Boys* in 1908 (Baden-Powell 1997). Both these movements put a great stress on the health benefits to be gained from physical training conducted in open-air camps away from the negative influence of the city. Baden-Powell believed that an outdoor life of physical activity would promote not only a healthy body but also a "moral" mind (Warren 1987). Thus Baden-Powell makes the following observation about an early member of the Scout movement:

> In addition to his load he carries a more important thing . . . a happy smile on his weather-tanned face . . . Altogether a healthy, cheery young backwoodsman. Yet this chap is a "Townie", but one who has made himself a Man.   (Warren 1987: 204)

The suntan is here seen as healthy because it describes a visible connection between the body and nature – it was a corporeal sign that the wearer of the tan has been engaged in "worthy" outdoor activities. This, no doubt, also contributed to the emergence of camping as a leisure pastime – an activity previously associated with the military. There already was an established industry specializing in the manufacture of camping technology, due to the needs of the military (see Ward and Hardy 1986). In 1906 the National Camping Club was founded and soon after T.H. Holding wrote *The Camper's Handbook*. Holding, in his description of coming across a family camping, refers to both the suntan and the positive effects of a temporary return to nature:

> Here the family and their servants were spending a "savage" holiday . . . The brown limbs of the children, the bronzed faces of the parents . . . At the end of the month they were not tired, but were counting with regret the remaining days in camp.   (Ward and Hardy 1986: 3)

Garden Cities of Tomorrow

Both the Scouting movement and leisure camping were connected to wider ideals of pastoralism – the "image of lost rural bliss and to an affinity with Nature" (Hardy and Ward 1984: 9). The reaction against the perceived distortion caused by modern urban life was expressed by contemporary writers such as William Morris (Morris 1880, 1881; see also Williams 1989) and Edward Carpenter (Carpenter 1914). Raymond Williams (1973), in his study of the country and the city, traced the rural/urban dichotomy that, since early industrialization, has divided localities between ideals of peace, innocence, and virtue versus worldliness, noise, and ambition. The rural has been associated with a unity between humans and nature and as the true site of meaningful community. This tradition has also penetrated the socio-technical boundary between body and sun. Nowhere was this more apparent, particularly in its more utopian guises, than with town planning and the built landscape. The desire to build a better environment for the urban masses and offer an alternative to the perceived deprivations of the industrial towns was one that informed the influential Garden City movement led by the campaigner Ebenezer Howard. The best of the rural and the urban were to be combined into hybrid "garden cities." These were to be decentralized urban clusters encircling existing cities and separated by green belts. The model for these urban clusters was to be the English village, in which self-contained cottages, with gardens, would be served by local services and employers. The importance of direct sunlight was seen as one of the principal considerations in these utopian town plans. Thus Howard, in 1902, describes his project as allowing that "as it grows, the free gifts of Nature – fresh air, sunlight, breathing room and playing room – shall be still retained in all needed abundance" (Howard 1965: 113). The architect for Letchworth Garden City, Raymond Unwin, proposed that "every house should . . . be so placed and planned that all its rooms should be flooded with light and sunshine"(Unwin 1909). Only a small proportion of the envisaged Garden Cities were built as originally intended (e.g. Letchworth and Welwyn Garden Cities), with the characteristic for "suburb spreading beyond suburb" dominating. Yet corrupted semblances of places like Letchworth can be found in any suburb where the "cottage vernacular" style, with "sunny aspects," has become the architectural model for suburban development.[1]

It would seem that the sociotechnical solutions suggested by both the camp advocates (either the Scouting movement or the new leisure activity of camping) and the proponents of new urban designs shared a pastoralist understanding of the benefits that material contacts with the rural would bring to urban dwellers, and here we can discern several related points. For the campers vitality of the mind and body was linked to a return to the "innocence" of nature. The suntan was the most prominent indicator that an individual had engaged in such a worthy activity and thus was merely a marker of a good health acquired by other means. On the other hand, within the Garden City movement we can detect, in their house designs and urban plans, a more direct connection between sunlight and health. Sunlight was here expressed as a material element, as important as fresh air, and to be integrated into the design of urban housing. Here sunlight was not the marker of some other aspect of health. Rather, sunlight was to be incorporated into dwellings because it had health-enhancing and tonic effects in its own right – in other words because it was *hygienic*.[2]

The Sun Cure

The Garden City movement was not a lone attempt to incorporate a healthy sunlight into a sociotechnical solution to a contemporary problem. In the period from the turn of the twentieth century there were widespread endeavors to enroll the medical establishment into a therapy based on sunlight to fight a range of pathologies – with the principal target being tuberculosis (TB). All forms of this disease had been in decline since the mid-nineteenth century. However, for the first half of the twentieth century it was still a major health problem (Smith 1987). Until the invention of streptomycin in 1943, a common therapy was for the affluent TB sufferer was to retreat to a sanatorium. The sanatorium was a descendant of the health spas found in Europe since the eighteenth century, and the underlying therapeutic principle was that the frenetic pace of modern life may "exacerbate consumption and that removal to a salubrious environment could cure or arrest the disease" (Smith 1987: 97).

A section of the sanatoria movement additionally saw exposure to sunlight as in itself a curative agent with "hygienic" properties. The treatment of illness, with sunlight, was known as *heliotherapy* and throughout the 1920s and 1930s mainstream medical journals frequently discussed the issue. Several themes can be found in these discussions but two in particular stand out. First, there was an ongoing struggle to make heliotherapy durable as a therapeutic practice – one that was distinct from allopathic medicine. Second, while it was believed that sun exposure was beneficial and healthy, it was still thought to be a hazardous activity in which caution, care, and medical supervision were needed to prevent injury. Therefore, many of the discussions in this period concerned themselves with the development of a technique that would reduce the perceived hazards of sun exposure.

The aspiration to use the effects of the sun's rays for a curative aim also represented a move toward a more "natural" or "organic" form of healing. The body could be changed without the intervention of drugs or surgery that, at the time, had little effect on TB. As Proctor has pointed out, this interest in naturalistic healing, at the beginning of the century, marked not only a desire for a return to a preindustrial society but also a general belief "that something was wrong with the way medicine was heading" (1988: 226).

The struggle to make heliotherapy durable rested in part on convincing a skeptical medical profession of its benefits. Thus a copy of *The Lancet* in 1900 reported on a paper given to the Tenth International Congress of Hygiene and Demography by Monsieur Emile Trélat, a distinguished French sanitary reformer and "a well known authority on hygiene." Monsieur Trélat claimed that the health-giving properties of light were now established and "insisted on the action of the direct rays of sunlight in preserving the health of urban populations" (*The Lancet* 1900: 818). In a 1915 edition of the *British Medical Journal* (BMJ), reference was made directly to the suntan, and hygiene, in an article entitled "The Healing Powers of Sunlight":

> To return from a holiday with a well-tanned skin, whether it be from seaside or mountain tops, has always been regarded as the outward and visible sign of sound health. Sunlight in each case, together with wind, has been the agency by which such hygienic perfection has been brought about.   (*BMJ* 1915: 936)

As we have seen, part of the attempt to establish heliotherapy as a durable therapy relied on its articulation to naturalistic practices. There were also frequent references made to the origins of sun healing in the "classical" period of antiquity. Thus Henry Gauvain, in the 1933 Hastings Popular Lecture to the British Medical Association, stressed the continuity between the modern practice of sun exposure and the sun baths taken by the ancient Egyptians, Greeks, and Romans: "for ages physicians have recommended the value of sunny climates, and have recommended sunny districts to their patients" (Cawadias 1936; Gauvain 1933: 1483).

The second common area of discussion around heliotherapy was the urge for caution and the need for strict medical supervision. In establishing heliotherapy as a durable medical practice its advocates have to take care not to undermine their own status – after all, the sun is freely available to medic and lay person alike. Thus an article in a 1915 copy of the *Journal of the American Medical Association* compares sunlight to the medical use of other types of radiation: "sun rays, like x-rays and radium, possess the property of doing harm, instead of the good which is desired of them. . . . The universally tanned skin takes many weeks to attain" (Rosslyn Earp 1929: 475). Much of the information about an appropriate regime for sun exposure follows this example in urging gradual exposure and avoidance of the midday sun. Indeed much of this advice would be recognizable today, in the health education advice given to travelers and tourists. Thus in 1909 one medical author comments on the observed hazards of certain continental practices:

> A number of persons who have suffered from the damaging effects of prolonged exposure to sunlight. . . . In these cases the persons bath first, then lie for a time on sandy banks of the river or lake, then go into the water again, and so on for many hours.   (*BMJ* 1909: 1300)

Ultimately the advocates of heliotherapy failed in their attempts to make the therapy a mainstream medical practice (although it still enjoys a minor role as therapy). Resistance came from microbes (heliotherapy was only effective against a limited range of TB infections), from patients (who were less than patient about the time and expense needed for sunlight treatment), and from the medical profession (who were successfully enrolled by allopathic medicine's new antibiotics, as sponsored by the UK's Medical Research Council). Yet the medical interest in sunbathing established the association between health and a suntan (especially in the context of a possible cure for a widely feared illness) and importantly established a set of practices whereby one could acquire a tan with a minimum of discomfort.

Hence by the 1930s articles in medical journals, about sun exposure, were talking less about disease and more about the general health enhancement that tanning might bring. As Urquart wrote, in a 1933 copy of the *BMJ*, suntanning is a "fashionable habit . . . which when properly used, cannot fail to be of benefit to all" (Urquart 1933: 150). Gauvain went further than this and claimed that the sun did not only benefit the physique but also improved mental health. "The sun bather who is benefiting from insolation is always cheerful and happy. None are brighter in spirits than those who are sun-worshippers . . ." (Gauvain 1930: 475).

The promotion of suntanning as a worthwhile activity in its own right was tacitly acknowledged in medical texts with the appearance of papers providing advice for the would-be sun lover without necessarily assuming that they were suffering from any illness. One such example is provided in a 1933 paper from the *Journal de Médecine de Paris*, entitled "L'A. B. C. de l'ensoleillement," which provides advice about how best to enjoy the benefit of sunlight while avoiding potential problems. This paper begins with common themes – namely hygiene and the classical origins of suntanning. "Light hygiene is the most precious form of hygiene available to man. Its origin goes back to ancient history" (Fougerat 1933: 667). The essay then goes on to stress the need for careful preparation before any attempt at tanning is undertaken:

> One must prepare oneself, by preparing the skin for direct contact with the surrounding air: 1. Every morning, perform one's ablutions NAKED; 2. Every day do at least 5 minutes of exercises NAKED; 3. Sleep NAKED, like our forefathers, which is, very often, at one and the same time, the best of remedies for insomnia. All this should be done, as much as possible in open air. (Fougerat 1933: 667)

The stated goal of this "sun initiation" was to obtain a "pigmentation of the skin while avoiding l'érythème [abnormal redness] of the skin which is always painful and sometimes dangerous" (Fougerat 1933: 667). Other practical advice which was offered included: avoiding going to the beach straight after getting off the train; and rejecting any type of sun cream, because they might cause permanent scars.

However, not all medical opinion believed the use of sun creams to be dangerous. Indeed, the 1930s were marked by the appearance of a number of articles speculating about the ideal formula for a tanning cream (e.g., Sharlit 1935). For example, another French journal, *La Presse Médicale*, carried a short note entitled "quelques formules de produits pour brunir" (Juster 1934: 1331).[3] This document also talks of particular formulas for browning oils that "have the advantage of being easily absorbed without giving the skin an oily look" (Juster 1934: 1331) – a claim that still features in advertisements for suntanning creams. In 1935 the sun cream *Ambre Solaire* was launched in France, an event that coincided with the first paid vacations for French workers.

The appearance of medical articles that begin to deal with tanning as not directly related to a "cure" shows that the acquisition of the suntan, at least among certain sections of society, was already desirable. In addition the change toward a more positive view of the suntan was to articulate well with other social changes taking place, particularly as related to travel, in the early twentieth century. The idea of health travel was well established, with many invalids seeking the sun cure in sanatoria. However, the wealthy invalid was able to travel further – to locations where they could be assured of receiving sunlight, such as the Swiss Alps or the Mediterranean. These wealthy visitors tended to reproduce elements of British fashionable society life in the locations they made their temporary habitats (Shields 1990). This was especially true of the south of France, where the British had had an established presence since the nineteenth century (see Blume 1992; Howarth 1977; Pemble 1987). A 1920s edition of *Cook's Traveller's Gazette* made the following observation:

> The Riviera has again become the gathering place of all nationalities anxious to bask in the warm sun which never seems to desert this favoured region – the goal of those who seek pleasure and health amid surroundings realizing every desire. (*Cook's Traveller's Gazette* 1920: 8)

The pleasure seekers and those seeking a "cure" did not always coexist so easily. As early as 1902, letters can be found in *The Lancet* lamenting the fact that Riveria hotels were boycotting consumptives. This was seen as an "unjustifiably harsh measure" (Reynolds-Ball 1902: 56) inasmuch as the invalids were being displaced in favor of casino clients. By the 1920s, within the Mediterranean region, the replacement of the sick by the affluent, seeking enjoyment, was fully underway. This coincided with a transition from using the Riviera for the winter season, to its increasing use for the summer season (see Howarth 1977). This was partly helped by other sociotechnical developments such as the use of air-conditioning and the elimination of the mosquito pest. But this transformation was also aided by the marketing of the region as an exclusive playground for the rich and famous. To do this the earlier established idea of the sun as a signifier of sensuality and health was drawn upon. The medical use of heliotherapy had partly legitimated the public exposure of the unclothed body. For instance, guide books and medical journals in the 1920s carried advertisements for clinics at health spas with photographs of the unclothed bodies of invalids sunning themselves on terraces and balconies. These show a surprising resemblance to the photographs of modern tourists used in holiday brochures.

There can be little doubt that the nexus around the body, sunlight, and the sociotechnical artifacts discussed here (such as heliotherapy, the sanatoria movement, and the new sun creams) helped establish the idea of the "sun resort" and the suntan. As the use of these resorts began to change toward a more exclusive focus on enjoyment, then in turn the suntan became more of a material mark of leisure and affluence, while still retaining its healthy associations. For the desire to acquire a suntan to become a truly mass phenomenon depended

on a range of other sociotechnical developments. These would include: mundane, but nevertheless complex, changes in patterns of sea
bathing, such as a move from medical therapy to leisure pursuit and
the growth of mixed gender bathing (see Walton 1983); the evolution
and aestheticization of modern bathing costume technologies (see
Stafford and Yates 1985); the aestheticization of the suntanned bodies
of celebrities and film stars (see Dyer 1979); and the development and
organization of technologies of mass tourism (see Lash and Urry 1994).
However, despite the recent mass growth of both sun seeking and the
desire for a tanned body, many of our contemporary practices and
sociotechnical artifacts linking bodies and sunlight can be traced to
the period discussed here.

Shades of Knowing: Epistemology, Aestheticization and Sunglasses

In this second case study, we consider another technology in relation
to our advocacy of a sociology of the sun – sunglasses. However, while
we will certainly touch upon the relation of sunglasses to the cultural
body, our main purpose here is to explore the ways in which sunglasses
can serve as a figure by which to grasp the process of knowing. As
such, we are concerned to engage with the materiality and corporeality
of vision. In particular, we want to investigate the epistemological
implications of a close attention to the body techniques of vision,
especially the wearing of sunglasses. Our grander purpose is to take
sunglasses as technologies which, in their disparate cultural-material
functions, can model a "heterogeneous knowing" which makes any
"sociology of the sun" less a "sociology" and more a "hybridology."

Body, Vision, and Knowledge

Vision, it has frequently been noted, is the preeminent western sense
(e.g. Urry 2000). As a mode of apprehending the world it has dominated western thought. As a modality it has underpinned a relationality
between observer and observed that is distanced, disembodied, and,
some would say, diseased. As Jay (1993) has argued, in his majesterial
critique of the critique of vision (or rather ocularcentrism) in French
philosophy, vision has been traduced as the criminal sense that has
been instrumental in western thought's worst cultural, social, and
political injustices.

This criminality has been extended and enhanced through the use of technologies which enable ever more intense scrutiny of the social and natural worlds. Thus, we are witness to the seemingly limitless visual surveillance of persons – CCTV (closed-circuit television) is becoming iconic in this respect. Thus we are collectively informed by innumerable techniques for imaging nature, ranging from the microscopic (e.g. electron microscopy and liquid xenon bubble chambers) to the global and cosmic (e.g. satellite photography and radiotelescopy).

These "exotic" forms of visuality serve in the representation of knowledge as disinterested and disembodied; of course, they are nothing of the sort. Such technologies entail in their very design assumptions about the world, not least in partly predetermining what can count as "data" and what as "noise". More relevantly, these technologies are deeply and multifariously corporeal. On one level, such elaborate visualizing technologies are made workable by virtue of the co-presence of the most mundane technologies and techniques that are pivotal to the everyday animation of human bodies. Without light bulbs and chairs which allow scientists to see and sit, we could "see" neither speeding galaxies nor speeding violations. On another level, we need skilled human bodies simply to get these exotic technologies to work – embodied skills are crucial in any laboratory simply in getting them to do what they are supposed to do. As complex assemblages these machines are always liable to go wrong – it is embodied human skill that keeps these observing machines functional (Collins 1985; Pickering 1995).

The upshot is that vision is deeply corporeal, even when the knowledge that supposedly "flows" from that sense is putatively of the most rarified and disembodied sort. This process of disembodiment can be approached in a number of ways (c.f. Burkitt 1999). In the present case, we draw on the work of Ingold (1992), not least because of his concern with the corporeality of visual perception in the context of local practices.

Accordingly, our understandings – that is, cultural constructions – of the environment are the result of "a contemplative disengagement from the world" (ibid.: 52). However, even this process of contemplation must take place within a context of engagement with the world. Elaborating on Gibson's (1979) concept of "affordance," Ingold captures the fact that the surfaces and structures that make up an animal's environment specify a range of possible actions for that organism. These surfaces and structures are visually available by virtue of the ambient light which they reflect. Crucially, possible actions afforded by these surfaces are related to the capacities and limits of the animal's body. An area of flat ground thus "affords" a variety of actions – lying, sitting, standing, crawling, hopping, jumping – that mirror the animal's corporeal capabilities. The sort of setting in which one can engage with disengagement thus reflects the peculiarities of the engaging body.

The environment, as a set of surfaces, does not determine an animal's doings. Rather, it "suggests" the array of possible doings to an active organism that explores its environment, actively seeking (picking up) information. In other words, "to have seen something is to have sought out information that enables one to know it . . . the knowledge gained through such perception is essentially practical . . . Depending upon the kind of activity in which we are engaged, we will be attuned to picking up a particular kind of information, leading to the perception of a particular affordance" (Ingold 1992: 46). On the basis of this ontology, and in his attempt to theorize the sociality of the environment, Ingold (1993) portrays landscape as "dwelling" which incorporates both nature and culture. Landscape is constitutively tied up with those who dwell and do there. It is what he calls a "taskscape," which is characterized by collective practices which inscribe the landscape with certain features (fields, walls, paths) which work back to render certain affordances to the people who dwell there.

Affordance, then, encompasses both other humans and their everyday technologies which shape the world. In other words, affordances relate to complex combinations of settings, humans, and technologies. Michael (2000) has explored these relations in terms of "cascades of affordance." Thus, the affordances of snow (walking or skiing) are enabled by technologies such as sunglasses (or in the case of some far northern peoples, wooden eyeglasses with narrow slits which protect against glare from snow and ice). The making of these technologies is enabled by the affordances of certain tools. Unsurprisingly, in more globalized societies, these cascades of affordance are extremely complex.

Now, MacNaghten and Urry (1998) have attempted to extend the meaning of "taskscape" to accommodate the recent processes of globalization. For example, they suggest that the dwelling of moderns is constituted by new media of communication and diverse new spatial practices (including mass travel, tourism, photography) which involve both somewhat different trajectories through the landscape and a reshaping of our apprehension of nature. Our late modern taskscape is one of transit and it is in this context of movement and dynamism that we wish to situate sunglasses as a material-semiotic means of engaging with the world.

Sunglasses have, obviously enough, the effect of screening out light (including ultraviolet wavelengths). They make it possible for one to see for longer in bright sunshine, with fewer supplementary movements (such as shielding the eyes with hands or adjusting a hat brim or staying in the shadows). They enable the brightly sunlit world to afford more. Of course, that is not all they do. They also aestheticize the world. Culturally specific aesthetic schemas through which we regard, for example, the landscape have always been fundamentally shaped by technologies, such as, latterly, the camera and the train, which have both served in the "framing" of landscape. With sunglasses, we have the world's light filtered – some colors are screened out, others emphasized. The limited palette of colors that, with sunglasses, characterize the world at once allow us to see more and see less. Insofar as individuals make choices about what color lens they find most "suitable," they are exercising aesthetic judgment. But such judgment extends beyond the lenses to the frame. In other words, to state the obvious, sunglasses also aestheticize the seer as well as the seen: in their material and semiotic specificity, sunglasses allow a range of function-expressions (that is, simultaneously and irreducibly sunglasses enable both certain practical doings such as the protection of the eyes and certain performances of distinction such as the signification of class or subculture – see Michael 2000). At the most obvious level, sunglasses aestheticize because of the brand or the style or their placement in a clothing ensemble. For example, Rayban "Aviators" signify a particular sort of militarized masculinity.

More interestingly, sunglasses are also actively used to perform particular sorts of gaze, some of which concern, in one way or another, "reverse screening": just as limited light can get in, so limited light can get out. The eyes are obscured and the mode of obscuration signifies a variety of things. Here is a selection of examples:

- In countless TV cop shows and cop movies, police officers and secret service personnel have routinely worn sunglasses in their dealings with both the innocent and the not so innocent public. The glasses totally obscure the eyes, making the face inscrutable and sinister, not least when these are mirror glasses. With an impassive face, there is no indication of how the officer will act and react. These sunglasses remove all predictability in a social exchange in which the micro-relations of power turn on not only the authority of the police, but also the dangerousness of the individual officer. Another way of putting this is that the sunglasses partially reflect a key aspect of Foucault's panopticon, namely the unobservability of the putative observer. Ironically, this unobservability is made highly observable. We might call this the *unhidden hidden gaze*.

- In countless rock bands (archetypally, *The Velvet Underground*, *The Ramones*, and *The Blues Brothers*) sunglasses have been a standard accoutrement. In contrast to the police officer, the rock star's inscrutability derives from a seeming indifference to the world. They can see the fan, but have neither interest in the fan, nor interest in the fan's interest in them. It is as if the blasé attitude is grounded in self-absorption, where that self almost seems reflected back from the inner surface of the sunglasses. We might call this the *anti-gaze*.

- On the poster of Kubrick's *Lolita*, Lolita looks over her heart-shaped sunglasses while sucking a lollipop. The partial sighting of the eyes signifies a glimpse of the secrets behind the barrier of the dark glass; they seem to invite the viewer onto the other mysterious side. The highly problematic sexual politics entailed in this image does not directly concern us here. Rather, we wish to point to the partiality of the gaze that is always threatening to disappear behind the sunglasses. This is a complex corporeal performance to pull off: the movement between showing and hiding the eyes needs to be subtly managed or else it all too readily becomes parodic. We might call this the *fleeting partial gaze*.

- In *Close Encounters of the Third Kind*, as the alien mother ship descends closer toward the human welcome party, a large group of scientific and administrative personnel all, more or less simultaneously, put on sunglasses. This is parodied in *A Grand Day Out*, when the rats in Wallace's cellar all, more or less simultaneously, put on sunglasses as Wallace and Gromit's spaceship blasts off toward the presumed cheese of the moon. In the *Close Encounters* case, the mass act of putting on sunglasses serves to evoke the common humanity of the wearers in the face of the alien spaceship and the appearance of the aliens themselves. The humor and sentiment that attached to this episode partly derive from the way this collective putting on of sunglasses is orchestrated – these characters are de-individualized in the process of engaging in a mass activity, and in the process a moment of communitas is evoked. In the case of the rats in Wallace's cellar, the joke rests on both the parody of *Close Encounters* and on the unexpected way in which the rodents become purposeful observers of what is in actuality an irrelevance to them, or rather, "merely" a spectacle. If *Close Encounters* uses sunglasses to evoke some "basic" concern with the "profundity beyond" that somehow (even corporeally) binds humankind together, *A Grand Day Out* parodies this by tacitly pointing to the binding of a collective through its fascination with spectacle. We might call this the *communitas gaze*.

- A comedy character (in cinema or in situation comedy) is rendered instantly recognizable as such by wearing clip-on sunglasses turned up at the hinge so that the colored lenses stand upright above the corrective lenses of the spectacles. The "joke" operates partly on the basis of the positional contrast between (and surfeit of) different lenses. Clip-ons can also function comedically in another way: they are on one level a low-tech solution but are seen to be enacted as a high-tech object. This ironic interplay of dual meanings makes them "funny" (Mulkay 1988). But perhaps the key dimension to the humor attached to this eyewear is that the seer, who has raised their clip-ons in order to see better, sees less insofar as they are oblivious to the ridiculous impression they give. We might call this the *unreflective gaze*.

Now all these gazes need to be actively enacted. As such the body must be deployed in the appropriate way – from the stillness of the face to the coordination of one's own bodily action with that of numerous others. It is the performance with a material-semiotic prop – the sunglasses – that allows for a particular gaze to be accomplished. In "seeing" the world, one is also "making it" by virtue of the performative impact on those whom one is seeing. That is to say, the performance of the gaze imparts a certain subject position to those who are the objects of that gaze: the observed are "invited" (interpellated) to react in a certain way. But further, the gazing individual is also signifying laterally, so to speak (Carter and Michael 2002), to observers of the performance. The gazer's performance of the gaze thus impacts "sideways" on observers who are not objects of the gaze. For example, the rock star's anti-gaze might signify indifference to the object of that gaze, but "coolness" to the observer. The process of seeing is thus a means of acting both directly and indirectly upon the world. When we look at and through sunglasses, we find that not only is what is seen aestheticized, not only are the instruments of seeing aestheticized, but so too is the enactment of the gaze for subject, object, and observer of that gaze.

What are the epistemological lessons that might be learned from this all too superficial analysis? Donna Haraway (1991) used the metaphor of diffraction to re-found a role for vision in the production of (situated) knowledge. We have, by comparison, stressed the processes of performance in the semiotic-material management of (the sun's) brightness. If sunglasses deal with over-illumination, the body enacts illumination to both object and observer. When it comes to a sociology of the sun, our exploration of sun–body–sociotechnical artifact nexus suggests that instead of asking the question, "What can this show us?," we ask "How is the illumination afforded by the sociological gaze enacted?"

However, in one crucial regard, this latter question misses the mark, for it overhumanizes both the sociological gaze and the various other gazes listed above. As Latour (1999) has argued, in the interaction between human and nonhuman both have changed, there is an exchange of properties, and a new entity is born – it is this that can be said to act. What is enacting the gaze, then, is not a human with a material-semiotic prop, but a combination of human and nonhuman. There are various generic names available for this combination: hybrid, monster, cyborg, co(a)gent. However, it is in their specificity that the particular hybrid nexus of sun–body–sociotechnical artifact needs to be analyzed: it is these particular heterogeneous combinations that should become the objects of the (hybrid) sociological gaze.

Concluding Remarks

In this chapter, we have attempted to sketch tentatively what it might mean to practice a "sociology of the sun." In the present context, we have pursued this with special reference to the cultural body. Thus, in the first case study of suntanning, we traced the historical shifts in the meaning of the tan, and the ways that such meanings were associated with modifications in the meanings of the body, health, propriety, leisure, civilization, and so on. As we also showed, these changes were partly mediated by innovations in a number of technologies such as suntan lotions and heliotherapy. As such, this first analysis drew out some of the ways in which a study of the material and semiotic role of the sun could illuminate a number of key social and cultural historical trajectories. Several themes can usefully be identified. First, the suntan has, despite many recent warnings about the dangers of tanning, now emerged as and remains a referent of health and beauty (Carter 1997). As such, the suntan has become an element in a narcissistic identity performance based on self-surveillance and the consumption of sociotechnical artifacts (Featherstone 1982; Lasch 1976). Second, part of this consumption involves travel and tourism. Urry (1990) has discussed the centrality of visual consumption to the tourist experience, with the modern tourist resort being organized around the idea of a collective gaze. However, an important part of this visual consumption involves the suntanned body itself becoming an object of gaze. The suntan is a visual symbol for the consumption of others and is acquired within the gaze of others – originally the gaze was that of the approving medical professional but now this medical gaze has been replaced by the self-reflexive tourist's own gaze. Finally we wish to make a comment about sunlight, the suntan, health, and failed technologies. Taking a symmetrical approach, we should be interested in the specificities of both durable and failed technologies. In many ways both heliotherapy and the Garden Cities could be regarded as failed sociotechnical artifacts. Yet both have helped established a durable, albeit unintended, connection between bodies and the sun – sunlight is something we welcome in our homes and sunshine is something we now routinely associate with good health, even when told otherwise by current medical opinion.

The second case study – of sunglasses – likewise illustrated how an analysis of the role of the visual screening of sunlight could throw into relief a series of issues about identity, consumption, material culture, corporeality, and so on. However, the main purpose of this section was to inquire into some of the epistemological implications of corporealizing the visual modality. This was explored by using sunglasses to show how the gaze is variously enacted, and how such a corporealized gaze is performative in a number of ways. The upshot for sociological practice was the suggestion that a revisioning of the units of sociological analysis was needed, units which could encompass the materialized cultural body distributed across heterogeneous nexus.

In both sections, we followed a particular methodological tack: from "obvious" and "neglected" entities like the sun, and from "small" technologies such as heliotherapy, houses, and sunglasses, we attempted to unravel a whole series of cross-disciplinary issues that span environment, medicine, epistemology, consumption, and so on. Of course, we can make no claims to being comprehensive and the historical examination of the suntan largely refers to the United Kingdom. Other localities may have slightly different accounts associated with sun exposure. But it is likely that elements of this history will find a resonance in other regions. As stated in the opening sections to this chapter, we can hope to address but a minute portion of the potential domain of the sociology of the sun.

Having noted this, it is still nevertheless possible to describe some other additional avenues by which a sociology of the sun could shed light on cultural bodies. Most obviously, there are many further technologies that can be explored, especially in relation to the construction of local and world risks. In the context of such emergent risks, there will be, we suspect, many new modes of comporting cultural bodies, that is, many new nexus of sun–body–sociotechnical artifacts. These will need some urgent analytical attention. Less obviously, there are supplementary projects concerned with the variants of a sociology of the sun. Why not a sociology of artificial light, or a sociology of the night or dark? We do not want to treat these possible projects ironically – in all seriousness, they hold out the promise of further insights into the cultural body.

Notes

1 While the Garden Cities were a "planned" utopian solution to urban problems, there was also a more anarchic access to rural areas by the urban working classes in the first half of the twentieth century. This was the "plotland" developments that emerged alongside the coasts, rivers, and in the countryside of the UK – a patchwork world of hastily constructed huts and shanties or converted bus or railway carriages on plots of varying size, cheaply purchased from advertisements in papers (see Hardy and Ward 1984). Anti-urbanism and a desire for a communion with fresh air and sunlight contributed to this ad hoc sociotechnical development in the first half of the twentieth century.

2 It should be noted that hygiene was associated with a wider set of practices than today. Rather than simply referring to the exclusion of microbes, hygiene meant any measure that might help resist weakness. Thus hygiene could equally be applied to ideas of morality, or even "racial" purity, as to the elimination of bacilli.

3 Although articles such as these implicitly assume that a tan was worth achieving, it is significant that the modern language of the tan had not yet emerged. This paper uses the verb "brunir," which literally means "to brown" (and can be applied to anything – skin, hair, food, etc.). Nowadays "bronzer" would be used in the context of getting a tan ("to bronze oneself"), rather than "brunir."

References

Arendt, H. (1992) "Introduction", in W. Benjamin, *Illuminations*. London: Fontana Press.

Baden-Powell, R. (1997) *Scouting for Boys: A Handbook for Instruction in Good Citizenship* (35th edn.). London: Scouting Association.

Blume, M. (1992) *Cote d'Azure: Inventing the French Riviera*. London: Thames and Hudson.

British Medical Journal (1909) "The Action of Sun Baths," *British Medical Journal* October 30, 2548: 1300.

British Medical Journal (1915) "The Healing Powers of Sunlight," *British Medical Journal* May 29, 2839: 936.

Burkitt, I. (1999) *Bodies of Thought: Embodiment, Identity and Modernity*. London: Sage.

Carpenter, E. (1914) *Intermediate Types Among Primitive Folk: A Study in Social Evolution*. London: G. Allen.

Carter, S. (1997) "Who Wants to be 'Peelie Wally'? Glaswegian Tourists' Attitudes to Sun Tans and Sun Exposure," in S. Clift and P. Grabowski (eds.), *Tourism and Health: Risks, Responses and Research*. London: Pinter.

Carter, S. and Michael, M. (2002) "Signifying Across Time and Space: A Case Study of Biomedical Educational Texts," unpublished manuscript.

Cawadias, A.P. (1936) "Heliotherapy and Actinotherapy," *British Journal of Physical Medicine* 10: 211–14.

Collins, H.M. (1985) *Changing Order*. London: Sage.

Cook's Traveller's Gazette (1920) *Spring on the French Riviera: Cook's Traveller's Gazette* LXX: 8.

Corson, R. (1972) *Fashions in Makeup: From Ancient to Modern Times*. London: Peter Owen.

Dyer, R. (1979) *Stars*. London: British Film Institute.

Featherstone, M. (1982) "The Body in Consumer Culture," *Theory, Culture & Society*, 2: 18–33.

Fougerat (1933) "L'A. B. C. de L'Ensoleillement," *Journal de Médecine de Paris* 31: 667–9.

Gauvain, H. (1930) "Sun Treatment in England," *Journal of State Medicine* 38: 468–75.

Gauvain, H. (1933) "Hastings Popular Lecture on Sun, Air, and Sea Bathing in Health and Disease," *British Medical Journal* 92 (Suppl.), February 25: 57–61.

Gibson, J.J. (1979) *The Ecological Approach to Visual Perception*. Boston, MA: Houghton Mifflin.

Haraway, D. (1991) *Simians, Cyborgs and Nature*. London: Free Association Books.

Hardy, D. and Ward, C. (1984) *Arcadia for All: The Legacy of a Makeshift Landscape*. London: Mansell.

Howard, E. (1965) *Garden Cities of Tomorrow*. London: Faber and Faber.

Howarth, P. (1977) *When the Riviera was Ours*. London: Routledge & Kegan Paul.

Ingold, T. (1992) "Culture and the Perception of the Environment," in E. Croll and D. Parkin (eds.), *Bush Base: Forest Farm – Culture, Environment and Development*. London: Routledge.

Ingold, T. (1993) "The Temporality of the Landscape," *World Archeology* 25, 152–174.

Jay, M. (1993) *Downcast Eyes: The Denigration of Vision in Twentieth-Century French Thought*, Berkeley, CA: University of California Press.

Juster, E. (1934) "Quelques Formules de Produits pour Brunir," *La Presse Médicale* 42: 1331.

Lasch, C. (1976) *The Culture of Narcissism*. New York: W. W. Norton.

Lash, S. and Urry, J. (1994) *Economies of Signs and Space*. London: Sage.

Latour, B. (1993) *We Have Never Been Modern*. Hemel Hempstead: Harvester Wheatsheaf.

Latour, B. (1999) *Pandora's Hope: Essays on the Reality of Science Studies*. Cambridge, MA: Harvard University Press.

MacNaghten, P. and Urry, J. (1998) *Contested Nature*. London: Sage.

Mauss, M. (1985) "A Category of the Person: The Notion of Person; The Notion of Self," in M. Carrithers, S. Collins, and S. Lukes (eds.), *The Category of the Person*. Cambridge: Cambridge University Press.

Michael, M. (2000) *Reconnecting Culture, Technology and Nature: From Society to Heterogeneity*. London: Routledge.

Morris, W. (1880) "The Beauty of Life," in Morris, M. (ed.), *The Collected Works of William Morris*. London: Routledge, vol. XXII, p. 61.

Morris, W. (1881) "Art and the Beauty of the Earth," in Morris, M. (ed.), *The Collected Works of William Morris*. London: Routledge, vol. XXII, p. 166.

Mort, F. (1987) *Dangerous Sexualities: Medico-moral Politics in England Since 1830*. London: Routledge & Kegan Paul.

Mulkay, M. (1988) *On Humour*. Cambridge: Polity Press.

Pemble, J. (1987) *The Mediterranean Passion: Victorians and Edwardians in the South*. Oxford: Clarendon Press.

Pickering, A. (1995) *The Mangle of Practice: Time, Agency and Science*. Chicago and London: University of Chicago Press.

Proctor, R. (1988) *Racial Hygiene: Medicine under the Nazis*. Cambridge, MA: Harvard University Press.

Reynolds-Ball, E.A. (1902) "The Boycott of Consumptives at Menton," *The Lancet* January 4, 1902: 56.

Rosslyn Earp, J. (1929) "Dosage in Heliotherapy," *Journal of the American Medical Association* 92: 312.

Sharlit, H (1935) "Ointment for Preventing Sunburn," *Archives of Dermatology and Syphilogy* August, 32: 291.

Shields, R. (1990) "The 'System of Pleasure': Liminality and the Carnivalesque at Brighton," *Theory, Culture & Society* 7, 39–72.

Smith, F.B. (1987) *The Retreat of Tuberculosis, 1850–1950*. London: Croom Helm.

Stafford, F. and Yates, N. (1985) *The Later Kentish Seaside, 1840–1974: Selected Documents*. Stroud: Alan Sutton Publishing.

The Lancet (1900) "The Window, the Room, and the Sun," *The Lancet* 818–819.

Unwin, R. (1909) *Town Planning in Practice: An Introduction to the Art of Designing Cities and Suburbs*. London: Bern.

Urquart, D.A. (1933) "Sequel to a Sun-Bath," *British Medical Journal* 2: 150.

Urry, J. (1990) *The Tourist Gaze*. London: Sage.

Urry, J. (2000) *Sociology Beyond Societies*. London: Routledge.

Walton, J.K. (1983) *The English Seaside Resort: A Social History, 1750–1914*. Leicester: Leicester University Press.

Ward, C. and Hardy, D. (1986) *Goodnight Campers! The History of the British Holiday Camp*. London: Mansell.

Warren, A. (1987) "Popular Manliness: Baden-Powell, Scouting and the Development of Manly Character," in J.A. Mangan and J. Walvin (eds.), *Manliness and Morality: Middle-class Masculinity in Britain and America, 1800–1940*. Manchester: Manchester University Press.

Weeks, J. (1981) *Sex, Politics and Society: The Regulation of Sexuality Since 1800*. London: Longman.

Williams, R. (1973) *The Country and the City*. London: Chatto and Windus.

Williams, R. (1989) "Socialism and Ecology," in R. Gable (ed.), *Resources of Hope: Culture, Democracy and Socialism*. London: Verso.

Chapter 12

**Reaching the Body:
Future Directions**[1]

Jamilah Ahmed

Introduction

The papers in this volume represent a diverse and detailed collection of approaches and uses of ethnography. This concluding chapter draws upon the theories and practices previously discussed in order to consider how *Cultural Bodies: Ethnography and Theory* might be used to inform and generate further cultural research. While each of the papers has its own remit, when taken as a whole they constitute a richly layered discourse on how ethnography and contemporary cultural theory can enable research on the body. This chapter develops the volume's key concern with the embodied self and explores how we speak, read, and write about how our selves are embodied. A large discourse exists that details how the body is disciplined, controlled, and presented, but there has been far less written about the body that "speaks," moves, and interacts. The papers collected in this volume speak to and across each other, traveling across geographical and disciplinary boundaries, but always communicating their relation to the body and ethnography. This conclusion to the volume reflects on the merits of ethnography as a methodology that is not just about being "in the field," but is also about refiguring the dynamics that frame social research.

The Body as a Site of Contestation

The issue of the body has become increasingly manifest in academia and in popular culture. In the UK there have recently been a spate of documentaries that take a quasi-ethnographic approach toward their subject.[2] Contemporary journalism no longer simply investigates via interviews and distanced interpretation. Instead, interviewers and reporters pride themselves on prolonged and repeated contact between themselves, their crews, and their subjects as a means of generating better understanding and better communication. The teams involved in a "fly-on-the-wall" documentary now often engage in a version of participant observation and indeed encourage the observer/ viewer to become a participant. In documentaries which take the human body as their focus (a subject area which has also experienced a growth), the trend has been for the presenter's and/or interviewer's body to be integrated into the viewing product. For example, the popular and highly acclaimed series, "The Human Body," was presented by Robert Winston, a respected scientist and writer. However, in a radical departure from traditional science documentaries, the camera focuses not just on him, but inside him: computer graphics enable the viewer to enter "his" body, and see his digestive system in action.

Aside from the technological innovation at play here, there is also a clear progression from the traditional role of the presenter as an objective observer. This is a noticeable shift for a viewer who is used to listening to a disembodied voice narrating and interpreting the visual material. Such a change seems to proclaim to the viewer that the increased contact time delivers increased accuracy and "truth." Thus, even as the hierarchy between interviewer and interviewee is broken down in front of the viewer's eyes, the move away from the objective voice of authority, toward the more "human" interviewer who befriends and integrates into the subject's world, in fact invests the documentary with an even greater degree of "realism."

As Thrift discusses in his paper in this volume, "Bare Life," modern science and technology have made it possible for us to get into previously unseen, unknown subparts/spaces of the body. The body, Thrift suggests, may now be thought of as a series of "micro-geographies," which can be blown up, speeded up, slowed down, dissected, and refigured, so that "the simple, living body" can be "sensed" and "experienced" in a much more concentrated way than was previously possible. As the previously unseen and unseeable in-between fragments of time become visible, they become "available to be worked upon." As such, they also become more susceptible to manipulation within the dominant discourses.

This trend has parallels within sociology too, as the body has become a burgeoning focus of study and the cause of much debate. As Michael (2000) notes, we are all very aware of the "turn to the body," thanks to the advance guard of "the body party" represented by such stalwarts as Featherstone et al. (1991), Turner (1984, 1991), and O'Neill (1985). However, a concern with the *role* of the body in the social framework can ignore the more immediate issue of what it means to *have* and *be* a body (Turner 1984). While "the body" has gained a certain currency in sociology, it can also be used as an object or symbol for sociocultural constructs without a concern for the material realities of bodies. The relative lack of grounded, empirical data (in comparison to the reams of theorizing about the body) suggests there is a need not only to explore the embodied self, but also to ascertain and redress the reasons for this lack (Burkitt 1999). This would mean that the representation of the body – as a symbolic construct – might no longer be prioritized over the concept of the body as a lived reality.

Classical sociology (that which has its origins in the work of founding theorists such as Marx, Weber, and Durkheim) could be described as primarily concerned with the regulations and patterns of the public sphere (Turner 1991). The system of dualisms lingers in contemporary sociology that divides private from public, nature from culture, woman from man, and the body from the mind. Traditionally the body has been seen as a disruption of the self's rational agency (Colebrook 1997). The work of Csordas (1994), Young (1990), Braidotti (1994), and Smith (1989) suggests that the sociology of the body has still not managed to wrench itself away from the theory long enough to engage with the lived materiality of the body. We can almost picture the body being approached from one side by reporters of popular culture and from the other side by sociologists, cultural theorists, and anthropologists. However on neither side is the body actually met; instead both advance guards have chosen to keep their distance. The significance is pointed to by Thrift:

> Probably 95 percent of embodied thought is non-cognitive, yet probably 95 percent of academic thought has concentrated on the cognitive dimension of the conscious "I". (2000: 36)

However, to interrogate "the theoretical body" can be a means of articulating "the material body," and of redressing the elusive body that features in much debate (Shilling 1993; Ussher 1997). A methodology that informs such research needs an alternative to the sociological model of the self that is an amalgam of "the self" and "the body," and which suggests the two are exclusive or are stable units within themselves. This assumption has traditionally meant that the self and the body are talked about as separate parts of a whole. In order to theorize the relation between embodiment and the "the other" we must go beyond the Cartesian roots that have contrived to sustain "the body" and "the mind" as discrete and oppositional categories. The term "embodied self" at least suggests a greater synthesis, and avoids the connotations of traditional dualisms. Young offers another term:

> [T]he important thing to investigate is not the strictly physical phenomenon, but rather the manner in which each sex projects her or his Being-in-the-world through movement. (1990: 156)

In Simon Shepherd's chapter, "Lolo's Breasts, Cyborgism, and a Wooden Christ," we see how even dancers whose bodies are highly trained require help to access their "everyday" bodies. In everyday life, when we are walking along the road, for example, we do not usually think of the relation of our feet to the ground or to the space around us. By forcing performers to become aware of the physical relation of the body to the world they come in contact with, such as the floor or the surrounding space, the actors are able to make a different "sense" of their "existence on the stage." The body on the stage becomes part of the world, not separate from it, as it is in everyday life.

The question then, is to consider how to develop methodological frameworks that do not measure or use the body as a social metaphor but instead begin to articulate the importance of the body on an experiential and subjective level of "the everyday." In order to be able to enunciate the embodied self, the self's place in space and time must be engaged with, and the relationship between experience and research must be reassessed. To approach the body, the researcher must recognize the multiple subject positions that are evoked by the presence of their own body and the materiality of their fieldwork. In this way, ethnography can represent an opportunity to bring the body in from "the field" and thus enable researchers to more easily bring other people's bodies into their texts.

In her chapter, "Being a Body in a Cultural Way," Sally Ness argues that the shifting positions of ethnographers may be characterized as a shift from an "objective" observational model of study where the researcher is "outside" of the research frame, to a "participatory" model involving an "embodied" methodology, which includes the participation of the researcher as well as the researched. Proponents of the embodied approach justify it through the assertion that it will reveal new knowledge.

Young (1990) suggests that there is always an endemic tension in the female subject between transcendence and immanence, between subjectivity and being an object. Thomas has further pointed to how difficult it can be to bring feelings about the physical self and activity "into the domain of verbal language" (1993: 78). The dominant discourse places "the body" and "language" at different ends of the spectrum. For Csordas (1994) the difference between "representation" and "being-in-the-world" is a crucial one. Csordas has identified two distinctive approaches to the body within the social sciences. The first he describes as a textual standpoint that is concerned with the semiotic representation of the body. The second approach is grounded in a phenomenological concern to understand embodiment: the body as "being-in-the-world."[3] He argues that the aim should be to integrate the two, and not overemphasize one to the detriment of the other. The former representationalist focus understands culture as an objectified abstraction and has developed a concern with semiotics: thus language is said to equal experience. However, the latter more phenomenological approach recognizes the existential immediacy of culture and the limitations of language.

In general a preoccupation with semiotics has shaped sociological theory and thus:

> [t]he polarization of language and experience is itself a function of a predominantly representationalist theory of language. (Csordas 1994: 11)

The term "transcendence," as used by both Csordas (1994) and Young (1991), suggests a subject who is not determined by the traditions of the dominant discourse. The term is a means of challenging the tension that is inherent in discussions of "the body" and "the mind." Splitting the subject in two requires one half to be dominant. Thus if the mind is rational and the site of agency and transcendence, then the body must be irrational and the site of passivity and immanence.

However, the concept of "the embodied self" overcomes the body–mind binary. The notion of transcendence enables the "livedness" of the body to have meaning for the social world and vice versa. The notion of transcending the dominant discursive representations enables the embodied subject to escape the traditional immanence. In this way, embodiment can be understood in relation to a concept of agency. Transcendence comes from a reworking of cultural and textual objects and is a result of a reflexive process of an embodied self.

For Csordas it is important to distinguish "genuine, transcendental expression from reiteration" (1993: 152). He argues that acts of expression do not constitute transcendence if they replicate the existing framework. In this way, Csordas conceives of the embodied subject as having the potential of transcendence:

> Although the habitus bears some of the schematism of a fixed text, it can be transcended in embodied existence.   (ibid.)

The habitus, as first identified by Bourdieu, refers to the bodily dispositions that constitute an individual's identity and engagement in social and cultural practices (1977). For Bourdieu, the habitus could not be easily recognized or changed by the individual. Csordas, on the other hand, suggests that there is more potential for the individual to recognize and therefore react to their habitus and its relation to the objective structures of the social and cultural world.

The capacity for this is best seen in Suki Ali's chapter on children's perceptions of "race" or "otherness." The children do not always replicate the labels that the dominant discourse seeks to impose on racial categories. Instead, they negotiate new categories, and also new subject positions both for themselves and for their companions.

When researching the attitudes and perceptions of schoolchildren toward race and raciality, Ali took care not to impose her sense of meaning on the children. Rather, she used the image of bodies in popular culture, particularly "star images," to establish some common meanings between her and the children regarding problematic terms such as "race," "ethnicity," and "mixed race." Although the children in the study were learning to "read" race inside and outside of the school environment, Ali found that the educators had little knowledge of the children's perceptions of racial matters. Her research revealed that the children's understandings of race and racism were influenced by their location, and thus "locatedness" became a key focus of attention. Drawing on Butler's (1993) insights, Ali shows that the children did not necessarily "fix" people racially in terms of skin color and often needed to have additional biographical details to make sense of "race." As with the other chapters, Ali's research questions and casts doubt on the dominant narratives associated with "otherness," that is, with the topics of "the body" and "race."

The project of thinking about the body of "the other" (as marked by gender/race/age/class) becomes a project that forces a reassessment of the binaries that characterize sociological discourses, as well as the methodologies used in research. This change in the agenda has in part been influenced by feminist and postmodernist criticisms of the power relations that uphold such inequalities (Frank 1991; Turner 1991). However, much sociology has continued to frame both "the body" (Elias 1978) and "the female" as other in dominant discourses. Simone de Beauvoir analyzed the female body as a restrictive, passive site in her powerful text, *The Second Sex* (1949), in which "Woman" was elaborated as a signifier of "the other." The female body has remained heavily encoded as a symbolic figure in dominant discourses (De Lauretis 1986).

The task of articulating the body ("the other" and/or "the female") requires an interrogation of how the concept is framed within the language of sociology. A consideration of textual strategies enables a more embodied concept of the self to develop, and therefore challenges the assumption that a body marked by "otherness" must necessarily occupy a position of weakness. Bodily markers of difference, and signifiers of "otherness" (the body, the female, race, and difference), can instead offer a means of reaching new epistemological possibilities for an embodied self: the body can be explored as a platform for one's "being-in-the-world." In order to articulate the concept of embodied agency, the challenge is to avoid using the body as a vehicle for explanations and reflections of the social structure.

Csordas suggests that far from supplanting the semiotic, the relationship between textuality and embodiment can be very fruitfully explored:

> The point of elaborating a paradigm of embodiment is then not to supplant textuality but to offer it a dialectical partner. (1994: 120)

Csordas points out that to address either the social or biology is a mistake:

> The errors are symmetrical: in one instance biology is treated as objective . . . in the other the social is treated as objective . . . and in

both instances the body is diminished and the preobjective bodily synthesis is missed.   (ibid.: 287)

The papers in this collection exemplify this approach. Martin's chapter demonstrates that within contemporary medical frameworks, the causes of depression can be explained in terms of a chemical malfunctioning of the brain, as opposed to biographical or environmental conditions. The aim would then be to treat the brain and not the "person," although in the end, as Martin argues, neuropsychiatrists still have to ask their patients questions in order to make sense of their mental state. Csordas's chapter in this volume combines the social and biological and also examines contemporary medical frameworks. As a result, his piece offers a methodological route for interdisciplinary dialog via the usually discrete discourses of medical anthropology and the comparative study of religions. In their chapter about the dancers in the Royal Ballet, Wainwright and Turner choose as the focus of their research the faltering, aging dancer, and point to a very often invisible "other": that of the aging body. This is made all the more striking because we are used to only seeing dancers in their prime, as healthy, extraordinarily able bodies. They offer a reminder that we need to learn to recognize "the other" and to look in often unexpected social and cultural contexts.

In all the chapters, research on the body is enriched by integrating the textual with the physical, the everyday with the unusual, and the obvious with the unspoken.

"The Other" in Ethnography

As the canon of sociology has been forced by postmodern and postcolonial agendas to address its Cartesian heritage, so too has the discipline of anthropology had to confront its Eurocentric foundations. Clifford's chapter in the *Writing Culture* collection (Clifford and Marcus 1986) sought to reassess the writing of cultural analysis and to de-center his own voice, in favor of a more inclusive text that allows others' voices to speak in his text. He proposes that the writer's voice should be used to situate the analysis, rather than be the sole presenter of an account. For Clifford the anthropological and representational practice of ethnography should acknowledge a multilayered process. He terms this process "ethnographic allegory" and argues that more of the symbolic meaning of an encounter can be shown by "bringing culture into writing" (1986: 103). Clifford argues that recognizing the potential for this kind of allegory enables the researcher to raise questions about the ethical and political dimensions of their work.

Writing Culture sought to stimulate the discipline of anthropology by interrogating key epistemological issues, and it provoked much discussion and debate. Most notably, it has been criticized for failing to include any feminist perspectives, as discussed by many feminists, including Stacey (1988), Abu-Lughod (1990), Mascia-Lees et al. (1989). This omission is not, however, what I will discuss here, since the volume nevertheless represented a highly significant turning point relating to questions of writing and representation in ethnographic research.

More relevant here is that while the volume marked a new critical assessment of ethnography and method, it was nevertheless also criticized for overemphasizing textual practice. It was argued that this emphasis could detract from the key issue – which is the fieldwork itself, not the consequent representation of that fieldwork (Atkinson and Silverman 1997; Wolf 1992). Wolf argues that a polyvocal text, and careful attention to form, does not necessarily save the researcher from colonial inclinations and biases (ibid.). Abu-Lughod (1990) points to a further problem raised by the notion of experimental writing which involves a move toward disciplines more elitist in nature than anthropology, namely philosophy and literary studies. She suggests that this:

> is a hyper-professionalism that is more exclusive than that of ordinary anthropology. (1990: 19)

In this way, "new ethnographies" could potentially replace one form of colonial hierarchy with another, perhaps more problematic, paradigm that may serve to distance women and symbolic "others" even further. While these warnings point to the dangers that can be implicit within new forms of writing, these obstacles can be overcome. The textual strategies suggested are a means of confronting layers of meaning inherent in the process of representation.

How we tell the ethnographic tale determines the devices we use to convince the reader of the tale's validity. The very traditional, objective voice has been challenged but so too have the more "open," personal accounts been critiqued. The conventions of scientific writing can create the illusion of an absence of style, and thus also contrive to hide the author of the tale (Sparkes 1995). Sparkes argues that the author of a text needs to be written into a text, not written out of it, and that the narrative form in which he or she situates themselves should not necessarily be rendered "scientific." The conventional scientific form is not always the most suited to "telling the tale," particularly in fields that deal with communicating aspects of the physical being.

Back's chapter, "Inscriptions of Love," seeks to address those whose voices are not usually heard in academic study – the nameless, the lost, or ignored – and to raise these to a level of visibility, in order that the often silent stories of these "others" might be told and celebrated. Back recognizes that there are more ways to tell a story than through words and, in any case, he argues, "others" do not necessarily or often articulate themselves through words. The photographs do not simply illustrate the discussion, but actually foreground the analysis; the ethnographic photograph is a key methodological device.

Freeman and Murdock identify the crux of the ongoing discussion, stating that the issue:

> involves the power of insider/outsider relationships and the mode in which these relationships and the broader body of knowledge acquired in the field are represented in the form of ethnographic text. (2001: 432)

A fundamental step in this process involves acknowledging the limits of a language that emphasizes the discursive and representationalist elements over the material experiences. This is not to suggest that all sciences should be written in literary or creative styles, but rather that attention must be paid to the effect the style has on the meanings that infuse a text.

The methodological stance that Entwistle adopts seems more like the "distant"/"objective" approach to her interviewees, in "From Catwalk to Catalog: Male Fashion Models, Masculinity, and Identity." The interviews and indeed the encounters between models, bookers, and clients in the agency are treated as "interactions," which show how models perform or "do masculinity" through their contextually negotiated understandings of whether they are engaging with heterosexually or homosexually orientated individuals. Citing the interview talk, Entwistle notes how, while in conversation with her, the fashion models at once played up their heterosexuality and "their laddishness" and downplayed the association with the feminization of their job. Entwistle's explicit owning of her place in the research enriches the conclusions she is able to draw. Thus she demonstrates that even though she has retained certain traditional oppositions (the interviewer who arrives and observes from "the outside"), she is able to open up her analysis of the dynamics by acknowledging her own impact on the encounter.

Entwistle's examination of the modeling industry inverts the usual "gender agenda" evident in most research in this area and perhaps, to a degree, this contrast highlights the role her own gender plays. However, the contrast may be less noticeable and the boundaries more blurred in other research situations. Cole (1991) asks how we might begin to negotiate the shifting locations which lead to the paradox of an author who is simultaneously a dispassionate observer who was there, saw, and knows, and yet is asserting a "contradictory, disembodied, objective presence" and "experiential authority" (1991: 39).

Braidotti (1994) has suggested that the figure of the "nomadic subject" can enable an alternative, embodied framework to develop:

> though the image of "nomadic subjects" is inspired by the experience of peoples or cultures that are literally nomadic, the nomadism in question here refers to the kind of critical consciousness that resists settling into socially coded modes of thought and behaviour . . . It is the subversion of conventions that define the nomadic state, not the literal act of travelling.   (ibid.: 5)

I would suggest that the construct of the nomadic subject – the self that moves beyond boundaries – offers an ethnographic means of escaping the fixed positions and epistemologies that can sometimes prevent research from reaching the body. Braidotti makes explicit her own position as a multilinguist who has lived in and identifies with many countries. In this her identity is "different" in its challenge to stability and community. Instead of the fixed, stable notion of the self, she posits a concept of "nomadic consciousness" as:

> a form of resisting assimilation . . . into dominant ways of representing the self . . . Feminists – or other critical intellectuals as nomadic subject . . . enact a rebellion of subjugated knowledges. The nomadic . . . is active, continuous . . .   (1994: 25)

Her writing endorses a transdisciplinary approach and multiple speakers, and suggests the deliberate use of a variety of citations, in a deliberate effort to dethrone the unified authority of the "I," and the accompanying social and cultural assumptions usually carried therein. Like the contributors to the Clifford and Marcus volume, she argues that to let other voices speak in her text is a technique that breaks down the authoritative voice of the author, the "philosophising I" (1994: 38). For Braidotti, collapsing distinctions and combining genres disrupts the mode of academia that has tried to confine "Woman," and is a means of producing "unexpected, destabilising effects" (ibid.: 207). Braidotti explains that she does not use the term "polyglot" only to refer to individuals who speak more than one language, but also those who can "move" within one language (1994: 15).

The ethnographic ground covered by many papers in this volume also disputes the more traditional frameworks that contain theories of "the body." In their chapter, "Here Comes the Sun: Shedding Light on the Cultural Body," Carter and Michael's examination of the "taken-for-granted" cultural role of the sun engages with the everyday accompanying cultural artifacts. In doing so, they direct the underlying assumptions that, arguably, have "shaded" the dynamics at play between the social, cultural, and physical worlds. Their paper profoundly challenges the reader to re-view their natural and manmade surroundings, and the way in which their embodied selves are interacting with the environment. In this way, traditional distinctions such as the mind/body and the public/private are dissolved and new relations have to take their place.

It is this type of inquiry in which spaces can become deterritorialized. St. Pierre argues that nomadic inquiry can mean:

> that traditional methodology and the knowledge it produces have been held together mostly by words, words propped by desire and power, and not by "Truth," as we have been led to believe. (1997: 413)

Significantly, she points out that this form of inquiry, which integrates writing with thinking and with being, means that "once a shift in subjectivity occurs, the rest of the world shifts as well, and it is impossible to go back" (1997: 410). Braidotti's construct of the nomadic subject offers possibilities for the ethnographer who chooses to recognize, and make explicit, the various subject positions they occupy throughout the course of their fieldwork.

Elspeth Probyn's paper, "Eating for a Living: A Rhizo-ethology of Bodies," demonstrates how this can work on a number of levels. The ethnographic data she draws on is from her own set of experiences, and encompasses a range of places and moments in time. However, her analysis begins to build a momentum that enables the reader to gather these strands together, and when, in the concluding part of her paper, she weaves them all together, the ethnographic journey has been shared. Probyn uses the personal together with strangers' accounts of occupying similar spaces.

In her work on *Strange Encounters*, Sara Ahmed (2000) writes that bodies and selves are constituted against "the other." That is, although the self is to a considerable extent already inscribed, she argues that it is in the moment of the encounter that it is also partly constituted. She identifies the ethnographer as occupying a privileged position in most encounters since it involves:

> the transformation of the stranger from an ontological lack to an epistemic privilege. (ibid.: 60)

This is perhaps the key to the potential – negative and positive – that ethnographic research can offer: it facilitates fluid subject/ object locations for the researcher and the researched. In a very formal interview, for example, such locations are static: the inter- viewer controls the proceedings and occupies a position of rational scientist/agent, and the interviewee must respond to their line of questioning and is therefore the passive other. By contrast, in an ethnographic fieldwork situation, the "location" of the interviewer/ researcher shifts: they negotiate access to their chosen environment as "a scientist" but, once involved, the boundaries become blurred as they try to learn, understand, and sometimes "live" in a new environ- ment which has rules and boundaries of its own. The members of the environment under study actively allow the researcher in, and offer their knowledge to the new member in their midst, thus creating a temporary location for the interviewer as at once part of their dynamic, but always about to leave. I would argue that it is worth exploring this ontological instability and the epistemological frame- works that accompany it in order to resolve the ethical "truth" issues that can cloud readings of ethnographic accounts. Ahmed goes on to warn against the trap that can lead ethnographers to become "implicated in the postmodern fantasy that it is the 'I' of the ethno- grapher who can undo the power relations that allowed the 'I' to appear" (2000: 64).

The fantasy is to assume that the benevolent ethnographer who renders different "I's" audible is any less a manipulator of their fieldwork than the researcher who maintains the dominance of the authorial "I." Ahmed suggests that ethnography must be a balance between being taught by interviewees and teaching the reader what has been learned about the interviewees. She argues that a good ethnographer must be skilled enough to relate to interviewees and elicit information, while recognizing the barriers that manifest between all those involved in this complex research process.

However, it is easy to imagine that the "I" can be chosen at will, rather than recognizing it as relating to a specific moment of research – what Ahmed refers to as an "encounter in time." Ethnography has come under fire as being a practice that can hide and distort the means and relations involved in producing the "cultural facts" that constitute a research report. Lather writes that:

> In contemporary regimes of disciplinary truth telling, the concept of voice is at the heart of claims to the "real" in ethnography. (2001: 206)

The long-overdue impact of postcolonial discourse has indeed done much to push many previously silenced voices to the fore. Moreover, if the researcher's own body is positioned in the research, then the interaction can be made more explicit and the "facts" enriched by being set in a more detailed context.

There is a further dimension to the particular nature of ethnographic research that should be highlighted. Perhaps a way to both resolve the ethical tension and further enrich the research process is to recognize the body as the constant and as the facilitator of this process. Perhaps there is no need to try to "fix" the subject positions. Rather, it is by interrogating how such fluidity occurs that we can understand how different versions of truths are arrived at, and at what moments they are most valid. Indeed, it may be the unraveling of these ontological shifts that enables and articulates a more sophisticated understanding of the embodied self.

The task is for the researcher to travel with all parts of the self to the ethnographic setting, to leave the secure ontological "home" and integrate into someone else's home, before leaving again. Ahmed writes that "the ethnographer turns strangerness into a profession, into a technique for the accumulation of knowledge" (2000: 60). In this way, ethnography can be a means of transcending the singular location of researcher, and enabling the self to travel into new spaces.

Conclusions

In this reflection on all the papers collected here, and their different uses of ethnography as a methodology, a discussion of both the theory and materiality of the body has been generated. The body-self/the embodied subject is hard to articulate because it is a shifting paradox, a continual navigation that takes place simultaneously on the place of the private/public, personal/political, and interior/exterior. I have argued that this elusive slipping is not to be pinned down, but to be used as a resource, both for the self and for the researcher who seeks to understand that which constitutes the members of our society – the cultural body.

As a means of moving out of this stalemate, the ethnographic approach holds great potential for the study of the embodied self. This rests largely on the inherent challenge to the traditional hierarchical relations between the researcher and the researched. However, ethnography is not without its traps, and I raised the figure of the nomadic self to make manifest the many selves that people the ethnographic encounter. If we choose to operate within a methodological framework that questions hierarchies, and within an epistemological framework that questions the "fixedness" of the self, then perhaps we may begin to reach the ever-elusive body, that is, after all, always being reconstituted in each moment of engagement. "The body" is heavily embedded in a history of symbolic representation in which it was traditionally defined as a site of immanence. The ways in which we are embodied are difficult to articulate, and to consider the significance of this bodily mode of being presents many difficulties. It is the taken-for-grantedness, ironically combined with a mysticism that accompanies discussions of real bodies, that this paper has addressed. An element of this mysticism is involved in many academic and textual discussions of the body, and there is perhaps an element of complicity, too, in keeping a distance from the body by hiding the personal behind the scientific. However, the papers in this volume have presented a dynamic and cohesive means of using ethnography to penetrate a range of social and cultural discourses, and in doing so, these papers offer innovative methodologies for exploring the body.

An ethnographic approach may enable us to move beyond a social science that forces "categories which make sense only in the universe of science" (Merleau-Ponty 1962: 11) and instead toward a recognition:

that the perceived, by its nature, admits of the ambiguous, the shifting, and is shaped by its context. (ibid.)

Notes

1 I am indebted to Helen Thomas for incorporating her interpretations of the papers in this volume.
2 Examples include "Doing Time" and "Diary of a Marriage."
3 Turner (1991) also makes a similar distinction between the foundationalist approach – a concern with what the body is – and the anti-foundationalist approach, which is concerned with how the body is represented.

References

Abu-Lughod. L. (1990) "Can There be a Feminist Ethnography?" *Women and Performance* 5: 7–27.

Ahmed, S. (2000) *Strange Encounters: Embodied Others in Post-Coloniality*. London: Routledge.

Atkinson, P. and Silverman, D. (1997) "Kundera's Immortality: The Interview Society and the Invention of the Self," *Qualitative Inquiry* 3: 304–25.

de Beauvoir, S. (1949) *The Second Sex*. Harmondsworth: Penguin.

Berger, J. (1972) *Ways of Seeing*. Harmondsworth: Penguin.

Bourdieu, P. (1977) *Outline of a Theory of Practice*. Cambridge: Cambridge University Press.

Braidotti, R. (1994) *Nomadic Subjects: Embodiment and Sexual Difference in Contemporary Feminist Theory*. New York: Columbia University Press.

Brownmiller, S. (1986) *Femininity*. London: Paladin.

Burkitt, I. (1999) *Bodies of Thought: Embodiment, Identity & Modernity*. London: Sage.

Butler, J. (1993) *Bodies That Matter: On the Discursive Limits of "Sex."* London: Routledge.

Clifford, J. and Marcus, G.E. (eds.) (1986) *Writing Culture: The Poetics and Politics of Ethnography*. Berkeley and Los Angeles: University of California Press.

Cole, C. (1991) "The Politics of Cultural Representation: Visions of Fields/ Fields of Vision," *International Review for the Sociology of Sport* 26: 36–49.

Colebrook, C. (1997) "Feminism and Autonomy: The Crisis of the Self-Authoring Subject," *Body and Society* 3 (2): 21–41.

Csordas, T. (1993) "Somatic Modes of Attention," *Cultural Anthropology* 8: 135–56.

Csordas, T. (1994) *Embodiment and Experience*. Cambridge: Cambridge University Press.

De Lauretis, T. (1986) *Technologies of Gender: Essays on Theory, Film and Fiction*. Basingstoke: Macmillan.

Elias, N. (1978) *The Civilizing Process*: vol. 1, *The History of Manners*. Oxford: Basil Blackwell.

Featherstone, M. (1991) "The Body in Consumer Culture," in M. Featherstone, M. Hepworth, and B. Turner (eds.), *The Body*. London: Sage, pp. 170–96.

Frank, A.W. (1991) "For a Sociology of the Body: An Analytical Review," in M. Featherstone, M. Hepworth, and B. Turner (eds.), *The Body*. London: Sage, pp. 36–102.

Freeman, C. and Murdock, D.F. (2001) "Enduring Traditions and New Directions in Feminist Ethnography in the Caribbean and Latin America," *Feminist Studies* 27 (2): 423–58.

Greer, G. (1973) *The Female Eunuch*. London: Granada Publishing.

Haug, F. (1987) *Female Sexualism*. London: Verso.

Lather, P. (2001) "Postbook: Working the Ruins of Feminist Ethnography," *Signs: The Journal of Women in Culture and Society* 27 (1): 199–227.

Mascia-Lees, F.E., Sharpe, P., and Ballerino Cohen, C. (1989) "The Postmodernist Turn in Anthropology: Cautions from a Feminist Perspective," *Signs: The Journal of Women in Culture and Society* 15: 7–33.

Merleau-Ponty, M. (1962) *The Phenomenology of Perception*. London: Routledge.

Michael, M. (2000) "These Boots are Made for Walking . . . : Mundane Technology, the Body and Human–Environment Relations," *Body and Society* 6, 3–4: 107–26.

O'Neill, J. (1985) *Five Bodies: The Human Shape of Modern Society*. Ithaca, NY: Cornell University Press.

St. Pierre, E.A. (1997) "Circling the Text: Nomadic Writing Practices," *Qualitative Inquiry* 3: 403–17.

Shilling, C. (1993) *The Body and Social Theory*. London: Sage.

Smith, D.E. (1987) *The Everyday World as Problematic: A Feminist Sociology*. Boston, MA: Northeastern University Press.

Smith, D.E. (1989) "Sociological Theory: Methods of Writing Patriarchy," in R.A. Wallace (ed.), *Feminism and Sociological Theory*. London: Sage.

Sparkes, A.C. (1995) "Writing People: Reflections on the Dual Crises of Representation and Legitimation in Qualitative Inquiry," *Quest* 47: 158–95.

Stacey, J. (1988) "Can There be a Feminist Ethnography?" *Women's Studies International Forum* 11: 21–7.

Thomas, H. (1993) "An-Other Voice: Young Women Dancing and Talking," in H. Thomas (ed.), *Dance, Gender and Culture*. Basingstoke: Macmillan, pp. 69–93.

Thrift, N. (2000) "Still Life in Nearly Present Time: The Object of Nature," *Body and Society* 6 (3–4): 34–57.

Turner, B.S. (1984) *The Body & Society*. Oxford: Blackwell.

Turner, B.S. (1991) "Recent Developments in the Theory of the Body," in M. Featherstone, M. Hepworth, and B. Turner (eds.), *The Body*. London: Sage, pp. 1–35.

Ussher, J. (1997) *Body Talk*. London: Routledge.

Wolf, M. (1992) *A Thrice-Told Tale: Feminism, Postmodernism and Ethnographic Responsibility*. Stanford, CA: Stanford University Press.

Young, I.M. (1990) *Throwing Like a Girl and Other Essays*. Bloomington and Indianapolis: Indiana University Press.

Young, I.M. (1998) "Reconsidering Throwing Like a Girl," in D. Welton (ed.), *The Body: Classic and Contemporary Readings*. Malden, MA: Blackwell.

Young, K. (1991) "Perspectives on Embodiment: The Uses of Narrativity in Ethnographic Writing," *Journal of Narrative and Life History* 1: 213–43.

Subject Index

Labanotation   150
language
  and articulation   289
  and culture   196, 203, 224
  and embodiment   49
  and feelings   287
  and history   196
  physical   170
  and psychoanalysis   48
  and rationality   194
  and society   196
  use   33
leisure
  and camping   264–5
linguistics   196, 204

Mãe Pequeno   244
Mãe-de-Santo (*ialorixa*)   244–55,
  257
masculinity   8, 9, 56–8, 63, 66–70,
  72–3, 173–4, 263, 292
mass consumerism   161–2
mass culture   2
material culture   20–2, 261–2, 278
meaning   194, 200, 203–5
media
  and advertising agencies   155
  age of   149
  graphic   156
  and identity   174
  mass   154
  and soft porn   173
medical   20, 193
men
  bisexual   9, 67
  black   57, 73
  gay   9, 57, 68, 70, 72–3
  heterosexual   57
  new   56–7
  and representation   57
  and retail markets   56–7
  white   57, 73
mental illness   20, 190, 193, 205–7,
  241–2, 246, 249, 255–6, 259

methodology   3, 6, 17, 22, 58, 236,
  241, 257, 278, 283, 286–7, 289,
  293–4, 297
mimesis   206–7, 209
mind   16–17, 191
model
  agency   9, 56, 73
  American   61–2
  and bookers   58, 63, 67
  British   61–2, 73
  as commodity   58, 65–7
  female   63
  male fashion   9–11, 58–9, 73
  male lifestyle   73
  as object of display   56, 57
modeling
  and aesthetic reinvention   64–5
  and age   60, 74
  and body investment   58, 67
  and body management/
    maintenance   58, 61–3
  and expansion   56
  and fashion industry   60, 69
  and masculinity   55–7
  as occupation   55–6, 63, 65–6,
    69, 73–4
  and personality   65
  and posing   63, 68
moral panic   2
multiculturalism   81
myth   242, 248

narrative   69–72, 117
nature   199–200
neo-Darwinist   3
neuro-physiology   201
neuro-reductionism   16–17, 190,
  199, 201, 203, 207
neuroscience   16, 192, 199
neurosis   242, 252, 255
noh   170–2

oba   245
objectivism   6

observation 59, 284
ogan 245–7, 251, 254
orixa 243–9, 252, 254–5
Other 5, 81, 89, 219, 221, 236, 286, 289, 290, 293, 295
Oxala 245–6, 248

Pai-de-Santo (*babalorixa*) 244
participant observation 9, 11, 13, 284
pastoralism 264–5
pathology 241, 247, 266
perception 150–1, 157, 160–1, 164, 196, 223
performance
  art 176–7
  and audience 177
  corporeal 275
  experiment 15–16, 177, 179
  history of 184
  and power 207
  practice 12, 14–16, 170–1, 173–4, 176–7, 182, 186
  ritual 218
performing art 14–15
pharmaceutics
  and business 202
  industry 202
  psychotropic drugs 191, 205
phenomenology 12–13, 19, 124–5, 133, 138–42, 177, 183–4, 207, 256, 287
philosophy 12, 123–4, 131, 138, 140–2, 163–4, 171, 191, 271, 291
photography 9, 33, 149, 273, 292
politics 14, 227
popular culture 5, 16
possession trance 19, 242, 245–6, 254, 256
postcolonialism 1, 6
postmodern approach 12
postmodernism 1, 5–6, 289
postmodernity 175, 179

poststructuralism 1, 5–6, 94
power/knowledge 6, 76, 94
proxemics 150
psychiatry 17, 192, 252, 259
psychiatric treatment 242, 244, 250, 251, 252
psychoanalysis 251–2
psychology 16, 200–1
public institution 5
puppetry 16
purity 172

qualitative research 6, 8, 99

race 215, 288
  and body 76
  and children 10, 288–9
  and everyday lived experience 76
  and ideology 76
  and mixed race 10
  and ontology 93
  reading 10, 77–8, 87
  and skin 76, 81–3, 85, 93
  as topic 1, 5, 8
racialization
  and class 79, 87
  and culture 77, 79, 81, 83
  and ethnicity 77, 79, 81, 83
  and everydayness 81, 84, 87
  and gender 79, 87
  and locatedness 10, 81, 85, 90
  and media consumption 81
  and nationality 77, 81, 84–6
  and normalizing discourses 77
  and popular culture 77–8, 81, 84, 89–92
racism 10, 32, 76, 78–9, 81, 83
radical social constructionism 11, 107, 109, 117
reason
  abstract 195
  evolutionary 202

Name Index